Winner of the Jules and Frances Landry Award for 2019

THREE HUNDRED YEARS of DECADENCE

New Orleans Literature and
the Transatlantic World

ROBERT AZZARELLO

LOUISIANA STATE UNIVERSITY PRESS   BATON ROUGE

Published by Louisiana State University Press
Copyright © 2019 by Louisiana State University Press
All rights reserved
Manufactured in the United States of America
First printing

Designer: Barbara Neely Bourgoyne
Typefaces: Whitman, text; Requiem, display
Printer and binder: Sheridan Books

Library of Congress Cataloging-in-Publication Data
Names: Azzarello, Robert, author.
Title: Three hundred years of decadence : New Orleans literature and the transatlantic
    world / Robert Azzarello.
Description: Baton Rouge : Louisiana State University Press, [2019] | Includes
    bibliographical references and index.
Identifiers: LCCN 2018036781 | ISBN 978-0-8071-7045-8 (cloth : alk. paper) |
    ISBN 978-0-8071-7087-8 (pdf) | ISBN 978-0-8071-7088-5 (epub)
Subjects: LCSH: American literature—Louisiana—New Orleans—History and criticism. |
    Literature and society—Louisiana—New Orleans. | Decadence in literature. | New
    Orleans (La.)—In literature. | New Orleans (La.)—Intellectual life.
Classification: LCC PS267.N49 A98 2019 | DDC 810.9/976335—dc23
LC record available at https://lccn.loc.gov/2018036781

The paper in this book meets the guidelines for permanence and durability of the Committee
on Production Guidelines for Book Longevity of the Council on Library Resources. ∞

CONTENTS

ACKNOWLEDGMENTS

Many people offered help during the years this book was taking shape, and it is a pleasure to give thanks. For pointing me to unknown authors and texts, for help with the preparation of the manuscript, and for opportunities to publish and present pieces of this book, I thank George Amedee, Jean Belkhir, Keith Cartwright, Jerry Giddens, Erich Nunn, Ruth Salvaggio, Caroline Stas, Joe Stern, and Zackary Vernon. The support of James Long at LSU Press, the expert copyediting of Todd Manza, and the extensive comments from the anonymous reviewer were especially invaluable. In addition to these friends and colleagues, I also wholeheartedly thank my students at Southern University at New Orleans for their crucial input and inspiration.

This book project benefited from a Faculty Communities of Teaching Scholars (FaCTS) Mellon Fellowship at Xavier University of Louisiana, in 2012. I thank Elizabeth Yost Hammer for her support and inspiration during that time. The project also benefited from an NEH Award to Faculty at HBCUs, in 2015. I thank William Belisle for his help with the preparation of my application, the generosity of the Endowment, as well as the anonymous reviewers who selected my project for funding. Per NEH policy, I must note the following: "Any views, findings, conclusions, or recommendations expressed in this publication do not necessarily reflect those of the National Endowment for the Humanities." I also thank the Board of Regents for an Award to Louisiana Artists and Scholars (ATLAS), in 2017.

Some parts of chapter 1 and chapter 3 were previously published as "The Withered Toe of Louisiana: Transatlantic Decadence in the Big Uneasy," in *Southern Literary Journal* (2014). Some parts of chapter 7 appeared as "Ecopoetics of the Storm," in *Race, Gender & Class* (2015), and a version of chapter 8 will appear as "New Orleans in the Twenty-Second Century," in *Ecocriticism and the Future of Southern Studies* (forthcoming).

I dedicate this book to my two grandmothers—Carmel Azzarello and Lois Leblanc—whose uniquely New Orleanian sense of comedy and tragedy punctuates many of my sentences.

Portions of the following works are reprinted herein with permission:

Robert Azzarello, "The Withered Toe of Louisiana: Transatlantic Decadence in the Big Uneasy," *Southern Literary Journal* 46. Copyright © 2014 by the Department of English and Comparative Literature of the University of North Carolina at Chapel Hill. Published by the University of North Carolina Press. Used by permission of the publisher. https://www.uncpress.org.

Sheryl St. Germain, "Getting Rid of the Accent," from *Let it Be a Dark Roux: New and Selected Poems*. Copyright © 2007 by Sheryl St. Germain. Reprinted with permission of The Permissions Company, Inc., on behalf of Autumn House Press, Pittsburgh, PA, www.autumnhouse.org.

Katie Ford, "Earth," from *Colosseum*. Copyright © 2008 by Katie Ford. Reprinted with the permission of The Permissions Company, Inc., on behalf of Graywolf Press, Minneapolis, MN, www.graywolfpress.org.

THREE
HUNDRED
YEARS *of*
DECADENCE

I

NEW ORLEANS DECADENCE
IN THEORY

The summer of 2013 was a particularly uneasy one in South Louisiana. The upcoming hurricane season was predicted to be especially active, the so-called dead zone was expanding to record circumference along the Gulf Coast, and fertilizer plants seemed to be literally exploding all over the place. "Nitrogen anxiety" entered the language with little regard for the proper procedure of the *DSM*, and the integrity of the vast levee system that purportedly held back potential surge was again cast into doubt. The summer of 2013 came eight years after Hurricane Katrina, and three years after the British Petroleum disaster, but South Louisiana was still on edge. Amid all this unease, a journalist for the *New Orleans Advocate* articulated yet another level of anxiousness. The source of *this* anxiousness was always there; it did not arrive seasonally with the heat of summer.

"We also look with concern," Dennis Persica writes, "if not outright fear, at the satellite images of Louisiana. The toe of Louisiana dipping into the Gulf of Mexico now looks like the skeleton of a toe, most of its flesh having withered away, leaving only a frail bone there."[1] The image of a human toe losing flesh, desiccating in the salty waters of the Gulf, is striking. It sounds like the world of pure imagination, the sheer fancy of a decadent mind, but the journalist assures us that the satellite image is there for confirmation. The southernmost tip of Louisiana running along the Mississippi River does indeed look like a withered toe, a dying and expendable part of the body. The end point of the toe is skinny, and it is jointed, and it seems to reach into the Gulf as if to test the waters.

In a compact and potent essay flatly called "The Big Toe" (1929), the French philosopher Georges Bataille argues that the image of the human toe elicits a fundamental uneasiness in the species. There is a "secret horror" of the toes, Bataille claims, because these parts of the body cast doubt on the human's positive image of itself as a species of nobility and elevation, as a species progressively evolving from one generation to the next and thus on its way to ultimate perfection. "Man willingly imagines himself to be like the god Neptune, stilling his own waves, with majesty," Bataille writes (22). But there is a problem for Bataille. Human beings cannot maintain this positive image of themselves as exerting Neptunian dominion over water and land. The ideal of godlike control over the human and other-than-human world, willingly cultivated in the imagination, is unsustainable. It simply must fall apart at some point over the course of a lifetime, a year, or even a day.

With his characteristically dramatic flair, Bataille tells the story of what might happen to someone:

> Blind, but tranquil and strangely despising his obscure baseness, a given person, ready to call to mind the grandeurs of human history, as when his glance ascends a monument testifying to the grandeur of his nation, is stopped in mid-flight by an atrocious pain in his big toe because, though the most noble of animals, he nevertheless has corns on his feet; in other words, he has feet, and these feet independently lead an ignoble life. (22)

For the philosopher sketching this stirring scene, our male antihero is struck by the commonness of his species-being, the vulgarity of human ontological reality, especially in the moments of his old age. His mind then looks up, despite the blindness of his own eyes, to the national monument, in the hope of finding hard and irrefutable evidence of the perfectibility of his own kin and kind. But the big toe, formerly an instrument of balance and locomotion, brings this confident flight of fancy quickly back down to earth. There is a pain there. Now long despised, the toe constantly prompts the human mind to think about the body's intimate and inescapable grounding in the muck and grime of the world. The toe serves as a relic, as the remnant and remains, of the inescapable ignobility of the species and of the individual self. Having to acknowledge the existence of the toe in general, the abject hinterland of the body, is bad enough. But what is worse, in the context of Louisiana, is having to acknowledge that the silhouette of that appendage is one's life-world, one's habitat, one's *home*, and it is withering away.

If the journalist was unhopeful about the satellite image of Louisiana, and the philosopher links such an image to existential crisis, the representatives of industry said little and did less to quell the fear during the uneasy summer of 2013. In fact, at the company's annual meeting in May of that year, Rex Tillerson, then CEO of Exxon, exacerbated the unease by asking his employees and investors a surprisingly direct question: "What good is it to save the planet if humanity suffers?"[2]

In theory, these few words could have formed an excellent question about the nature of good and bad, suffering and enjoyment, who and what matters. But Tillerson, of course, wanted no answer to his question. He did not want his audience to wax philosophical about the Anthropocene. He did not want stockholders to dwell on the interdependency of planet and humanity or to think about the fundamentals of ethics. He wanted instead to perform two tasks: first, to cast "saving the planet" as antithetical to human happiness; and second, to conjure an image of the *equitable* distribution of human suffering all across the twenty-first-century earth, as if we who comprise humanity are all on the same footing. We do not expect Exxon's CEO to be extensively trained in environmental studies, but this question would probably trouble even the most conservative, anti-EPA bayou folk.

How do these three concerns—the journalist's, the philosopher's, and the CEO's—relate to the concept of decadence? The most basic answer, of course, is "uneasily"; these three concerns have an uneasy relation to the concept of decadence. I would like to take a step back, then, and claim, first, that the concept of decadence is itself not easy to define, and therein lies one of the primary difficulties in tracing this network of relations.

At first glance, decadence seems easy to spot in a place like New Orleans. It shows up all over the city's spectacles of physical decay: brick buildings crumbling into red dust, houses half eaten by termites and cat's claw, water rising from the ground, wooden frames rotting from the inside out, mold growing and paint chipping away. Sections of town look as if they could be featured on an episode of the History Channel's *Life After People*. The built environment, always in a state of unbuilding, is constantly gnawed down by the elements in a discernibly more intense way than in other American cities. Then there is also the litany of vices: prostitution and miscegenation, homosexuality and gender deviance, and more than one of the seven deadly sins. Add to this list the city's stubborn Francophilia, its Afro-Caribbean connection, its Catholicism, its air of mystery and detection, its preoccupations with the dead and the undead, its seemingly perpetual state of human violence, and a strange pattern starts to emerge.

Observers of all sorts—natives and newcomers, scholars and the general public alike—have long noted this type of decadence in the city and its vicinity. The historian Alecia P. Long, for example, begins a book called *The Great Southern Babylon: Sex, Race, and Respectability in New Orleans, 1865–1920* (2004) in the following way:

> People believe two things about New Orleans. The first is that it is dif-
> ferent from the rest of the United States. [. . .] The second, related
> belief is that the city is decadent, and that its cultural distinctiveness is
> related to its reputation for tolerating, even encouraging, indulgence of
> all varieties. There is ample historical evidence to support both of these
> popular beliefs. (1)

For Long, perceptions of the city's exceptionality and its decadence go hand in hand.[3] Her valuable historical work on the postbellum period offers many important insights that I will build upon in the later chapters of this book. But the historian does not go below the surface to explore the complexity of what—and how—decadence means in New Orleans. Like many other writers, Long takes the word for granted. Part of my aim in *Three Hundred Years of Decadence* is to peel back the layers of signification in the word, to follow the linguistic leads, to reanimate the lingering traces of "decadence." My overarching argument here is that decadence reveals something more culturally and politically significant than polymorphous indulgence in so-called vice. That significance, like the meaning of the word itself, however, remains always elusive, never quite what it seems, just as the small barrier islands off the Gulf Coast tend to appear and disappear, depending upon the tidal currents.

DECADENT DIFFICULTY

The concept of decadence is medieval in etymological nature. Coming from the Latin word *decadentia*, a combination of the prefix *de-* (down, apart) and the root verb *cadere* (to fall), it signals a falling down or a falling apart. Its cognates range across many words including *decay*, *decline*, *degeneration*, and others that employ the same *de-* prefix. At least because of its etymological constitution, then, it necessarily must refer to something other than itself, some prior state of affairs, from which it has materialized through its fall.

So there is that difficulty: the word and its referent are always temporally out of joint. It never names a thing, an object, but a change between one thing and another. The more troubling thing about the term, however, as critics such as Matei Calinescu and Richard Gilman show, is that it contains multiple meanings and slippery connotations that are fundamentally paradoxical.[4] Decadence does not mean decay, it does not mean decline, and it does not mean degeneration or anything else precisely.

Decadence seems to name a problem—that is, it seems to name a temptation into which one ought not cave—but it also seems to be a problem itself in naming. It can be a trap, as Gilman cautions, bogging itself down in its own semantic gumbo, seducing users of language into language games where the house always wins. Part of the reason why this is so is because *decadence* is a word that is as fundamentally axiological as it is ontological. It is a word, in other words, that evaluates as much as it describes, and what it ostensibly describes changes from one evaluator to the next. This problem, of course, is true of many words and things, but decadence complicates the picture even further because it is so caught up in matters of history and temporality. Decadence is a word *with* history *about* history. It is a word weighted down by the heavy burden of historical change, even as it essentially refers to and attempts to judge historical change.

Thinking about the concept of decadence awakens a vast archive of imagery: the fall of empires, late-night cigarettes and Pernod, dark chocolate, the color purple, Caligula's leather boot, a heavily punctuated sentence. It would be difficult, if not impossible, to trace a single thread that runs through all these disparate images. There is a certain sensuality in some of them, but not exactly in others. Some images point to opulence and pure pleasure; others do not. Some suggest liking something that one ought not like; others do not suggest forbidden fruit at all. In a provocative statement on the enigmatic nature of decadence, Gilman writes the following crystalline sentence: "Its origins buried under successive drifts of culture, its resonances somehow greatly out of keeping with its putative formal tasks, it recommends itself to us now, or forces itself upon our attention, like some old and intricately specialized object of vaguely exotic use" (24). Despite its referential unpredictability, its uncanny ability to be both known and unknown, decadence still conjures a wide variety of figures that reverberate powerfully in the human imagination.

Since it is difficult to define exactly what decadence *is*, another way to approach the question might be to identify what it is *not*. The opposite of decadence, at least ostensibly, is progress. If decadence is supposed to indicate a fall from a former state of glory, then its opposite should indicate something like a strengthening, a bettering, or at least a sustaining of that glory. As such, one way to think about the opposite of decadence is to think about psychosocial health ensured, and often literally insured, by the positive values of business, industry, and technological advance. These are the values that are supposed to keep up the golden age and stave off the decadence.

But looking at decadence's antitheses still cannot provide a stable definition. The idea of progress in terms of business, industry, and technological advance may also signal decadence in another form. In fact, the twinning of progress with decadence has played a central role in Marxist thought for at least a century and a half. Decadence in this form can mean individual excess or corporate greed, an utter disregard for other people and the environment. The contemporary French philosopher Bernard Stiegler echoes the progress-decadence connection and puts it this way in a representative book called *Decadence of Industrial Democracies* (2004): "We live in decadent times for democracy, a decadence entailed by the becoming-consumerist of industrial societies" (36). For Stiegler and his fellow Marxists—as well as for the billions of other people who have experienced the negative results of industrialization firsthand—progress and decadence do not mean two antithetical things. Decadence, understood in this way, fits squarely within the all-too-visible operations of so-called progress in the modern world, with all its excesses of production and consumption, extraction and exploitation, waste and inevitable fallout in the pursuit of profit.

So, if we are tempted to oppose progress with decadence, we should follow Calinescu's warning: "Progress *is* decadence and decadence *is* progress" (156). As the twenty-first century advances further and further into the future, this paradox seems only to become more pronounced and dramatic, but where does the progress-decadence paradox originate? While there are linguistic reasons why binary oppositions are not really oppositions because each component term relies on its other to signify, let me focus instead on the historical background of the terminology. While it is difficult to trace the "strange life of an epithet," as Gilman puts it, back to a single source, literary scholars such as Gilman and Calinescu do date the paradox of decadence as emerging in the afterglow of romanticism. There were images of physical and moral decay, opulence and pure pleasure, throughout history, of course, that critics can retroactively identify as decadent. Such imagery, in fact, plays a central role in most of the world's religious and philosophical traditions from Buddha and Plato to Christ and beyond. But a fully self-conscious movement did not emerge until the last quarter of the nineteenth century.

Paris in the 1880s, especially, stands out as the fertile climax in the history of decadence, with J. K. Huysmans's *À rebours* (1884) being the pivotal text. It was during this time that decadence was figured not as something to be avoided or secretly admired from afar but as something—as some thing, body, or mind—that has immense value. Decadence, during this time, was cast as a kind of hope, a kind of antidote to the modern world's obsession with efficiency and organization, industrial capitalism and profit. In its careful lethargy, in its embrace of antisociality and ontological negativity, decadence characterized itself as circumventing the robotic imperatives of the modern world, as escaping the mind- and body-numbing habits of the bourgeoisie, and thus as paradoxically heralding the true signs of life and vitality. It is for this reason that Calinescu identifies decadence as one of the key "faces" of modernity; it names a Nietzschean transvaluation of values, or an axiological situation in which the supposed good and the supposed bad cannot maintain their stability and end up morphing into one another.

"The first entirely approbative and widely influential view of decadence as a *style*," Calinescu writes, "occurs in the preface that Théophile Gautier wrote in 1868 for Baudelaire's *Fleurs du mal*" (164). That view of decadence, Gautier's important statement, ought to be quoted in full once again. But notice that even Gautier's view, the one that is supposed to be "entirely approbative," begins with an admission of its own inadequacy:

> The style inadequately called of decadence is nothing but art arrived at the point of extreme maturity yielded by the slanting suns of aged civilizations: an ingenuous, complicated style, full of shades and of research, constantly pushing back the boundaries of speech, borrowing from all technical vocabularies, taking color from all palettes and notes from all keyboards, struggling to render what is most inexpressible in thought, what is vague and most elusive in the outlines of form, listening to trans-

8

late the subtle confidences of neurosis, the dying confessions of passion
grown depraved, and the strange hallucinations of the obsession which
is turning to madness. (Calinescu 164)

With all his vivid illustration and painstaking nonchalance, Gautier
in 1868 laid the foundation for Huysmans and the other Parisian decadents of the 1880s. Readers of that body of work will encounter the
following, at the very least: a symbolic overload designed to express the
inexpressible; a fulsome if not excessive use of detail, including lists
rendered with complicated syntax and heavy punctuation; a reveling in
inadequacy, debility, failure, and weakness; a desire to bend the laws of
nature to conform with this perverse human will; a bipolar if not schizoid relation to modernity; an obsession with artistic refinement at the
expense of rational judgment; a seemingly careless indifference toward
the world that is in fact carefully scripted and consciously performed;
a fixation on artificiality and ornamentation over substance; a tonality
of danger and urgency that brings about a general or specifically directed anxiousness; a pleasure in this danger; and a foregrounding of
the seductive nature of decadence itself, as if the decadent style had
an uncanny and contagious ability to infect others despite their better
reasoning and best efforts to escape.

The picture of decadence in human form is the picture of a man or
a woman who has had too much—too much nicotine or caffeine, too
much liquor or morphine, too much literature or philosophy or art—
and is thus reduced to a state of being that seems to oscillate between
comatose and enlightened. He or she sits with more or less patience,
more or less consciousness, on the very borderlands of health and life
itself, in a strange euphoria, a kind of undead. William S. Burroughs,
whom Jack Kerouac visits in the New Orleans section of *On the Road*
(1957), needs no introduction as America's twentieth-century avatar of
this persona. Indeed, the Beat aesthetic in general may be understood
as an Americanized version of a Parisian decadence developed seventy
or eighty years before. In New Orleans even today, images of this decadent type abound in the Charles Bukowskis and Tennessee Williamses

9

and Truman Capotes and Everette Madoxes of the world, who still seem to walk impossibly among us.[5]

The embrace of decadence during the 1880s, of course, was not shared across the board. Even among some of the first proponents and practitioners in Paris, decadence would be rejected outright or it would more subtly morph into other literary styles. Despite these changes, however, decadence would have a lasting effect on the literary scene both within and outside of France—for Friedrich Nietzsche in Germany, for Gabriele D'Annunzio in Italy, as well as for many other writers in New Orleans—and it would cause profound uneasiness as critics and detractors began to think through the implications of the movement. This uneasiness can be seen especially vividly in the larger, political backlash that occurred on an international scale in the wake of À rebours. Many European and American critical works—among them, Max Nordau's Degeneration (1892) in Germany and Eugene Talbot's Degeneracy (1898) in the United States—interpreted the ascendency of decadence as a full-fledged assault on the Protestant work ethic and the future health of the body politic.

These objections to the decadent aesthetic, coming as they did in the wake of Charles Darwin's Origin of Species (1859) and Descent of Man (1872), were often waged in evolutionary and devolutionary terms.[6] The movement's detractors understood decadence as an assault on fitness, working as it did against natural and sexual selection. It was a biocultural defect, a dangerous maladaptation, that could potentially come to inhabit individual human persons—their bodies and their minds—in deadly ways if it were not destroyed in its germinal stage. Moreover, because decadence was a communicable disease, it could potentially come to inhabit the species as a whole, taking up permanent residence without a cure, and could thus debilitate each generation more and more, until extinction was guaranteed. If such were the scenario, the contagion would spread concentrically from Paris, the origin of the disease, and would come to infect surrounding nations one by one. Transatlantic Europeans of the late nineteenth century thus thought they had good reason to be afraid and to take precautions against the enemy within.

With a tone and tenor that was decidedly apocalyptic, these objections made by the German Nordau, the American Talbot, and other vocal stewards of bourgeois family values on both sides of the Atlantic, of course, should not be surprising. Part of the aim of decadent writers, besides the lofty ideal of philosophical and literary innovation, was simply to scandalize. And if their detractors characterized decadence as a profound threat, and one with life-or-death urgency, that was at least partly because the founding architects of the movement characterized it that way themselves. Think again of the vivid imagery contained in Gautier's description of the decadent aesthetic sensibility: setting suns, decrepit civilizations, excessive color and sound, neurotic passion, and haunting hallucination. These are not exactly the ideal images of mental health and physical stability, nor do they pretend to suggest anything like moral rectitude or ethical integrity. But of course, as I have been trying to show, all of those things for the decadents were open to interpretation. "Southern Decadence," the annual LGBT festival held every Labor Day weekend in New Orleans, retains some aspect of this self-characterization and aim in its carefully orchestrated spectacle and in the predictable hysteria that results.

Despite its detractors, however, decadence as a desirable aesthetic emerged prominently in Paris during the 1880s in reaction to specific social changes happening both inside and outside of Europe. The year 1884 was significant not only for the publication of *À rebours*, the key decadent text in the French tradition, but also for the beginning of the Berlin Conference that lasted into the next year and would slice up the African continent in unprecedented ways, for European control. Understanding this historical moment helps us to frame and give meaning to Paul Verlaine's famous poem, also from 1884, called "Langueur," which begins with the astounding synecdochical assertion, "*Je suis l'empire à la fin de la décadence*" (Calinescu 162). Verlaine writes that he is "the empire at the final stage of the decadence," the climactic moment of imperial dissolution.

What is strikingly ironic in reading such a statement, today, is that Verlaine is identifying with the *end* of the empire at the exact moment

11

of its geopolitical beginning, its modern rebirth, at least in the form that it took in the period from the Berlin Conference of 1884–1885 to the liberation movements of the 1960s. While national leaders were meeting in Berlin to decide the fate of the African continent and Verlaine was languorously identifying with the end of empire in Paris, New Orleans in 1884 also saw a major event of transatlantic importance in the World's Industrial and Cotton Centennial Exposition and its accompanying Buffalo Bill's Wild West shows. Some scholars credit this event as a major impetus behind the development of the Mardi Gras Indians in the late nineteenth century, as well as the rise of "local color" fiction that would put the city on the literary map.[7] These events, all from 1884, indicate that decadence should be read not solely as an intra-European phenomenon but also as a revelatory movement intimately connected to transatlantic systems of culture and colonization, capital and industrialization.

With this complexity in mind, we can return to my introductory discussion of the journalist Persica, the philosopher Bataille, and Exxon CEO Tillerson. In figuring the southernmost tip of Louisiana as a withered toe, the journalist clearly appeals to a larger decadent tropology in the region. He takes as his primary subject the deteriorating effects of time on space, he elicits interested anxiousness, and he dramatizes if not also poeticizes the imagery and narrative of loss. The philosopher generalizes that decadent tropology as a psychosocial commonality among all *Homo sapiens* and not an exclusive predicament of southern Louisianians. So far so good.

But there is also something decadent in another register about Exxon's CEO, the epitome of industry, plotting ways to double his capital with no regard for the devastating consequences on the planet. Tillerson's utter disregard for the health and welfare of the other-than-human world is indeed not at all off the decadent mark, and once again the progress-decadence paradox is all too easy to understand. If progress is construed in terms of business, industry, and technological advance, then progress is indisputably caught up with decay, decline, and degeneration on both the human and environmental scales. Progress, furthermore, may be understood as both a *cause* and a *record* of that destruction. Indeed, what occasions the journalist's horror in viewing the withered toe of Louisiana is a *satellite* image of the state, an image made possible only through stunning breakthroughs in science and technology that were spurred historically to advance the Cold War.[8]

The satellite image of coastal Louisiana today, when compared to aerial images taken during the 1930s, cannot but shock. The Gulf water level on Grande Isle, the beach community made famous in Kate Chopin's *The Awakening* (1899), for example, rose a full two inches in just seven years as a result of local soil subsidence and global warming.[9] The imminent loss of this island, and indeed of the wetlands all across southern Louisiana, is real; it is scientifically verifiable as anthropogenic in nature despite the clamor of the naysayers, and it elicits an awkwardly twinned response of horror and wonder—a postmodern sublime?

But it also seems to be a thoroughly literary event, fitting squarely within the area's reputation for decadence and enacting the long story, ancient Greek in origin, of hubris and nemesis, of excessive pride and retribution. The concept of decadence in New Orleans reveals something more serious, and something more alarming, than simple indulgence in food or sex or alcohol. It points to the city's complex relation with its Dionysian elements, to be sure. The excessive, the degenerate, the unhealthy—all signs of ostensible decline—hold a peculiar attractiveness in the modern psyche of New Orleans and remain a seductive siren song, despite all the marks of danger. But decadence also points to the city's complex relation with its Apollonian elements: modernity, industrialization, and calculated risk.

The concept of decadence provides a unique avenue into complicated questions about the city of New Orleans and the larger transatlantic world. The French connection in New Orleans, both real and imagined, certainly helps us to understand the historical association of the city with decadence, an association effectively harnessed from the 1880s onward by Francophile writers such as Kate Chopin, Anne Rice, Sybil Kein, and Brenda Marie Osbey. But in the literary history of New Orleans, there are many examples of decadent themes that predate definitions of decadent style à la Gautier. The concept of decadence provides critical leverage into certain theoretical questions about human and environmental progress and the inherent complications therein, but it also provides a way to thicken the literary scholarship on New Orleans by breaking out of some past literary-critical molds.

NEW ORLEANS LITERARY SCHOLARSHIP

New Orleans literary scholarship has tended to confine itself in a number of ways. For one thing, critics have tended to focus on the period following the Civil War, and especially on the regionalists and local colorists like George Washington Cable, Lafcadio Hearn, and Kate Chopin, whose work brought the literature of New Orleans into the national imaginary. For another thing, students and scholars alike have tended to gravitate to the fictional genre, and especially to fictional representations of the city that are recognizable, "modern" in a certain sense, and thus more easily readable. And finally, critics have tended to study the English-language literature almost exclusively, at the expense of texts written in a variety of European languages (especially French, Spanish, and German) as well as orature and lyric spoken and sung in a variety of native and African languages (especially Choctaw, Chitimacha, Tunica, and Bambara).

There are good reasons to focus on the postbellum period, the fictional genre, and the English language, of course; they are an important part of the literary history of New Orleans.[10] But a more complete picture must more fully take into account other time periods, other genres, and other languages. Recent scholarship has revealed a vast and understudied archive of New Orleans literature that helps to illuminate the city's significance as a transatlantic contact zone. These are zones, according to Mary Louise Pratt in *Imperial Eyes: Travel Writing and Transculturation* (1992), that are "social spaces where disparate cultures meet, clash, and grapple with each other, often in highly asymmetrical relations of domination and subordination" (4). Within these contact zones, Pratt analyzes a process of transculturation, a term developed in ethnography to "describe how subordinated or marginalized groups select and invent from materials transmitted to them by a dominant or metropolitan culture" (6). Transculturation in the New Orleanian contact zone thus exemplifies this kind of dynamic, a twinned doubleness of subjectification and agency. "While subjugated peoples cannot readily control what emanates from the dominant culture," Pratt explains, "they do determine to varying extents what they absorb into their own, and what they use it for" (6).

Although much of the material that exemplifies this idea of contact zone and transculturation is extremely rare, much more has been preserved through transcription and translation, such as George Washington Cable's "Creole Slave Songs" (1886), Mary Haas's *Tunica Texts* (1950), and M. Lynn Weiss's dual-language anthology called *Creole Echoes: The Francophone Poetry of Nineteenth-Century Louisiana* (2004). These remarkable texts join other, more recent translations of some major documents, such as Ludwig von Reizenstein's important German-language novel called *The Mysteries of New Orleans* (1855) and the eighteenth-century French travel writing of Marc-Antoine Caillot and Dumont de Montigny. In addition to these translations, serious critical and theoretical work in literary studies by Joseph Roach, Ruth Salvaggio, Catharine Savage Brosman, Keith Cartwright, Rien Fertel, and John Wharton Lowe helps us to understand an American national culture beyond a strictly English, and even French, framework by exploring a range of texts traditionally considered to be outside the proper realm of the American literary canon.[11] My work builds on the increasing momentum of that scholarly effort.

The literary history I present in *Three Hundred Years of Decadence* traces the long story of four continents—Europe, Africa, and the two Americas—coming together under differentials of power and on uncertain terrain. While this book does not propose a full survey of this vast archive, it does propose the framework of decadence that can account for all of the literary texts, more or less.[12] My approach to this long story that cuts across time period, genre, and language, in other words, is through perceptions of decadence and the uneasy social relations that result. The concept of decadence, semantically engorged as the term is and despite its strange ability to penetrate and be penetrated by many modes of thinking, provides a distinct avenue into the story of New Orleans and the transatlantic world, and one that takes us from the city's very founding in 1718 to contemporary speculations about the city's future.

In the remainder of this chapter, I explore the concept of decadence within four different realms that will form the major linchpins around which my subsequent chapters will circulate. These four realms—bodies, languages, literatures, and environments—filter through and bleed into one another, and they are the sites in which the paradoxical nature of decadence is at its clearest.

BODIES

Bodies in forms both noble and grotesque, divine and beastly, elevated and degraded, triumphant and conquered, travel through each and every page of New Orleans literature. These bodies at times walk upright. At other times, they crawl on all fours or they pull themselves, legless, through the streets. These bodies—in motion and at rest, singular and collective—span the animal and vegetable kingdoms, the realms of the living and the dead, and the somewhere in between. They sink and bloat and they float again in chemical-laden, brackish waters. In the end, they may be buried six feet above.

One of the central questions that I seek to answer about the three-hundred-year literary history of New Orleans can be stated simply: How have bodies been figured as decadent over the course of three centuries, and what results from that figuration? What has been the ontological and axiological status of bodies, in other words, that do not seem to fit within the easy narratives and imagery of American fitness and progress? What effect have these bodies had on the local and national estimation of New Orleans, and how has that estimation influenced social and environmental deliberation on the local and national scales?

These uneasy questions about decadent bodies in New Orleans point to a larger problem in American literary history, about representations of human bodies in general—what they are (their ontological representation) and how they matter (their axiological representation). This larger problem has received substantial scholarly attention in literary studies, especially from queer and critical race perspectives. Siobhan B. Somerville, for example, develops an important argument that helps to guide my own thinking, in her groundbreaking *Queering the Color Line: Race and the Invention of Homosexuality in American Culture* (2000). In this book, Somerville looks at human bodies that "were culturally marked as nonnormative" in terms of race and sexuality, and the ways in which these bodies "lost their claim to the same rights as those whose racial or sexual reputation invested them with cultural legitimacy, or the property of a 'good name'" (9).

Why do supposedly "nonnormative" bodies lose social and political legitimacy? What underpins this political ideology that affords some human bodies different rights than others? Somerville claims that this political ideology is an effect of "a deeply held cultural fiction in the United States [that] the physical body offers transparent evidence of its history, identity, and behavior" (9). Because social and political agents are guided by a false premise—that physical bodies display their historical and behavioral nature, their capacities and their tendencies, without epistemological complication—human bodies that seem to diverge from the norm receive a different set of rights than others that do not. So if someone *looks like* something—black or white, homo or hetero, criminal or upstanding, poor or rich, and so on—one is assumed to *be* that thing. Somerville identifies the premise as false, but she does not claim that the body has no history, identity, and behavior. She does not claim that the body reveals nothing. Instead, she claims that it is false to believe that the link between the physical body and its identity is clear and transparent, especially in historical moments when scientific theories and legal realities were so indelibly marked by phobic ideologies of all sorts.

The problematic ideology that links three things—the physical body;

its supposedly obvious history, identity, and behavior; as well as its social legitimacy and legal rights—becomes all the more problematic as
it proceeds through real time, because the chain of linkage constantly
threatens to break down. *Looking like* and *being* very rarely align without flaw. In the field of race, especially, the sheer prevalence of creolized bodies that elude epistemological certainty always jeopardizes
the very foundations of this ideological system. But the ideological
system still somehow manages to survive despite the pressures of the
real world. In fact, it just seems to grow stronger.

In a book on the antebellum period called *Conjugal Union: The Body,
the House, and the Black American* (1999), Robert Reid-Pharr makes
a counterintuitive claim about transracial bodies that is essential to
bear in mind here. "The mulatto's body," he writes, "operates not as
the refutation of racial distinctiveness but as its proof. She was the
true hybrid, the third subject whose presence refracted the purity of
her antecedents, the black and the white" (41–42). For Reid-Pharr, the
epistemologically problematic body contains the paradoxical ability to
produce epistemological certainty. Because of—and not despite—its
uncertainty, in other words, the epistemologically problematic body
certifies the prior existence of racial dimorphism. If there weren't two
races before, the logic goes, how could they be mixed now? Out of the
confused jumble of bodies that resulted from transatlantic sex over
multiple generations came, paradoxically, a hardened and self-assured
color line.

To take one of the most famous cases of producing racial certainty
through uncertainty, as an example, think of Homer Plessy, who had to
announce his blackness on the train in New Orleans in order to be arrested and then set in motion the legal challenge to segregation. There
was nothing about Plessy's physical body that transparently showed his
history, identity, and behavior. There was nothing about his body that
confirmed or denied his social legitimacy and legal rights, despite the
anxious proclamations that said it must. Plessy lost his case in 1896,
of course, and the Supreme Court cemented the tortuous logic of the
physical body and its supposed transparency into constitutional law in

a way that would not be overturned until fifty-eight years later, with the court's 1954 decision in *Brown v. Board of Education*. My aim in *Three Hundred Years of Decadence* is to explore the essential questions that Somerville, Reid-Pharr, and others address about the body through the conceptual framework of decadence. How do the human bodies of New Orleans travel through the omnipresent paradox of progress and decline?

In a city like New Orleans, a city with a long history of sexual transgressions and creolization, the problem of bodies as they are considered signs of decadence remains dramatically apparent in both the social and literary history. Although the city has been hailed as a magical mixing of nations, for much of the city's history the legal reality of its inhabitants often shows something quite different. One of the many ironies of intense creolization—that is, situations in which human beings live in recognition of an abundance of transracial bodies—within a legally segregated contact zone is not democratic acceptance on egalitarian terms but instead anxious differentiation through paranoid means. One would hope that there would be too much difference to make a difference in the eyes of the law, but that is clearly not the case. In much the same way that the most homosocial spaces may also be at times the most homophobic (think of the military or the locker room), the most "mixed" may also be at times the most oppressive, with those in legal power always on the lookout to put Homer Plessy, his kin, and their kind in their place. Even if Plessy's body does not betray his identity and rights transparently, even if everyday life allows for a relaxation of custom and a generous commingling of types, the law will not be fooled.

The city of New Orleans is marked by a history of anxiety concerning the physical human body in its supposed manifestation of sexual transgression, but such an argument can be made about many, if not all, American cities. I am taking it a step further to argue that, in New Orleans, the history of anxiety concerning the physical body cannot be divorced from the city's entanglement with decadence, and especially decadence of a more or a less threatening nature, hovering between the good and the bad, the progressive and the regressive.

The creolization process of human bodies through transracial sex in the city has in fact been interpreted both negatively and positively. As a negative event, it is interpreted as a disruption of the purity of the races and thus as symptomatic of biocultural decline. Some of these bodies carry the mark of this transracial sex obviously on the surface of the skin. But this transracial sex also produces bodies such as Homer Plessy's, which threaten to travel undetected outside of their proper place in the psychosocial, economic, and legal system. On the other hand, the creolization process of bodies has also been interpreted as a positive event, as a progressive cultivation of strength and power. With precedents in the colonial French mind-set of the eighteenth century, this side of decadence sees the "blood" of four continents coming together as invigorating each. Often, in New Orleans, authors and their characters will hold these two interpretations of transracial sex simultaneously, or oscillate quickly from one to the other, and in doing so they shed additional light on the paradoxical nature of decadence itself as it operates in the city.

LANGUAGES

Bodies and the languages they use to express themselves go hand in hand. Like the body, its language is a site of intense psychosocial conflict that is often imagined through the paradoxes of decadence that I have been describing, that is, through an undecidable doubleness of progress and decline, of good and bad, of beauty and ugliness. One essential set of questions that I will consider in the coming chapters will be the following: How has the relationship between bodies and languages been figured during the past three centuries of New Orleans literature? How have languages, like the bodies they rely on, been figured as decadent during this time frame, and what results from that figuration? And finally, how have the two modes of language use—that is, orality and literacy, speaking and writing—factored into the long story of New Orleans decadence as well as into linguistic and bodily creolization more generally?

Historically speaking, the relationship between decadence and language is crucial to understand. The literary historian Linda Dowling goes so far as to claim that decadence as an entire literary movement in the nineteenth century was first and foremost a philosophical meditation on language. In *Language and Decadence in the Victorian Fin de Siècle* (1986), Dowling traces the way in which decadence emerged, in the 1880s, from a tension between two opposing views of language. On the one hand, there was the Victorian view that saw language as a positive and stable force in human history. Governed by certain rules and irrefutable regulations, language not only reflected the advance of civilization but also served as its motor by providing a kind of cognitive foundation for that advance. While they unfailingly used themselves as a model for this positive process, the Victorians championed not simply the English language as a generality but more specifically the high literary language of Shakespeare and the King James Bible. In their view, this English language was founded on sensible clarity and measured beauty. It was a controllable and controlling language, one that simultaneously expressed and strengthened—reflected and reinforced—the civilization's values.

On the other hand, though, there was the romantic view that saw language as a more unruly beast than the proper Victorians would have it. This view, made possible by philological research conducted primarily in Germany, saw language as an evolving network of sounds, words, and syntactical relations that changed not according to the dos and don'ts of the language police but independently and on its own terms. Languages evolve through the messy exigencies of everyday life and not through the self-conscious plans or aspirations—however intelligently designed—of the civilization. The romantic view, as Dowling puts it, "raised a specter of autonomous language—language as a system blindly obeying impersonal phonological rules in isolation from any world of human values and experience—that was to eat corrosively away at the hidden foundations of a high Victorian ideal of civilization" (xii).

What was more, and perhaps more threatening, was the related romantic view that saw the high literary language of Shakespeare and the King James Bible not as some universal model reflecting the ideal English but instead as a particular product of its time and place. It was one *dialect* among many others, and one that was becoming more and more of a kind of relic with each passing year. Because it was not keeping up with the evolution of actual speech, with the changes in oral usage (there was no way that it could), the English language of Shakespeare and the King James Bible was becoming more and more of a *written* language. It was becoming more and more ancient. It was becoming deader and deader.

Furthermore, the Victorians were caught in a catch-22 in terms of what they wanted with their language. In one moment, the Victorians saw their English as proof of their own perfectibility and therefore saw their burden as having to transmit that language (along with the rest of their cultural ways and means) all across the globe. But in another moment, the Victorians were also terrified of the potential for a kind of linguistic boomerang, a backlash in which the multiple languages of the empire would not stay put abroad but would instead come to inhabit their own English and cause its degeneration. The Victorians knew that, unlike their pet pigeons, pidgins were difficult to domesticate.

This tension came to head in the late 1880s with the publication of the Oxford English Dictionary. "When Volume I, comprising A–B, was finally published in 1888," Dowling writes, "Victorians were thus at once proud and dismayed. On the one hand, the volume was visible proof of the advance of Victorian civilization, yet on the other, even as it overwhelmed the mind with concrete linguistic detail, the dictionary suggested the darker possibility of cultural decline" (98–99). Try as they might to hold the English of Shakespeare and the King James Bible up as a model, the Victorians recognized that their language was changing on every level: phonologically (in the sounds contained in words), morphologically (in the words themselves), and syntactically (in the arrangement of words).

Unable to escape the tension between these two opposing views of language, the European decadent writers of the 1880s embraced it and developed a program—a paradoxical attempt, really—to show that language *can* be whipped into shape and also that it simply *cannot*. The prominent themes for which the movement is known—of death and decay, aestheticized and eroticized; of baroque excess caving in upon itself; of artistic refinement on the brink of madness—emerge from this uneasiness about language as such. Through formal or stylistic experiments that were often shocking at the time, decadent writers reveled in the fact that language always registers a human desire to control communication (literary or otherwise) but also always exceeds that desire.

For the decadents, moreover, there could be no final judgment that determines the progress or decline of a language; it eludes any attempt to nail it down axiologically. But, going one step further, the decadents employed a proto-Nietzschean strategy of transvaluating value and demonstrated again and again this fundamental point: what seems to be the corruption of the language may actually be the mark of its most beautiful or interesting expression. This is why the narrator of Huysmans's *À rebours*, Jean Des Esseintes, is so enamored not with the Latin language of the Golden Age—the language of Horace, Virgil, and Ovid—but with the Latin language of the Roman Empire's proverbial decadence, epitomized in Petronius.

Dowling develops the argument upon which I have been drawing in the context of European—and especially British—literature and philosophy, but her thesis is equally relevant for the United States in general and for New Orleans in particular. The profoundly multilingual nature of American life has elicited a powerful politics of language that has been charged, in turn, with celebrating or repressing, encouraging or controlling, that multilingualism, depending upon the evolving exigencies at hand.[13] In New Orleans, the inevitable transformations that occur within and among languages have often been figured through the paradox of decadence that I have been describing. While I do not want to claim that this figuration is exclusive to New Orleans, it does seem to be especially vivid in the city. It also seems to fit squarely within the city's other marks of decadence outside the field of language, that is, the fields of bodies, literatures, ecological realities, politics, and morals, among others. In *Three Hundred Years of Decadence*, therefore, I will be

23

interested in the evaluative judgments made about languages as they come into contact in the city, especially as those moments of contact have been figured in terms of either progress or decline, revitalization or decay, good or bad, beautiful or ugly, and the often dialectical quality of this either/or scenario.

LITERATURES

If the human bodies and their languages register uneasiness about potential decadence in the city, so does literature. In nineteenth-century Europe, in fact, literature and its interpretative apparatuses—literary criticism and historiography—were the principle fields through which the term *decadence* developed. At this time, the term was used to denote a specific literary period that followed in the wake of the so-called Golden Age of classical Latin poetry, especially the work of Horace, Virgil, and Ovid. The *Aeneid*, the national epic depicting the founding of Rome and written by Virgil in the twenties BCE, is perhaps the most famous of the individual texts, and it characterized all the tendencies of the Golden Age, revealing the health and vitality of the Roman body and body politic, the Latin language, and the beginnings of empire. This age was not to last, however, and the term *decadence* came to name that subsequent period of decline and fall from greatness as the empire became plagued by moral failure, excess and greed, corruption, and violence coming from all directions. In the time of the decadence, not only was the Roman empire falling apart but so was Roman literature and the Latin language in which it was written.

For the Parisian decadents of the 1880s, this disintegration—imperial, literary, and linguistic—was not something to lament. As I have noted, the character of Des Esseintes in Huysmans's *À rebours* is drawn not to the Golden Age but to the decadence, embodied most spectacularly in the figure of Petronius, the first century CE author of the *Satyricon*. In Petronius, Des Esseintes finds the kind of hero that can save us from Virgil's Aeneas and his muscular morality. In Petronius, in other words, Des Esseintes finds "an acute observer, a delicate analyst, a mar-

24

velous delineator [who] calmly, without prejudice, without animosity" recounted the everyday life of Rome, "its incidents, its bestialities, its sensualities" (28–29). Des Esseintes's rumination on the Roman author is worth considering in full.

> All this told with an extraordinary vigor and precision of coloring, in a style that borrows from every dialect, that cribs words from every language imported into Rome, that rejects all the limitations, breaks all the fetters of the so-called "Golden Age," that makes each man speak in his own peculiar idiom—freemen, without education, the vernacular Latin, the argot of the streets; foreigners, their barbarian lingo, saturated with African, Syrian, Greek expressions; idiotic pedants, like the Agamemnon of the *Satyricon*, a rhetoric of invented words. (29)

Huysmans here sounds like William Wordsworth on crack. He takes the Wordsworthian impulse to weave the vernacular into the poetic form, but he takes that impulse way past its ostensibly healthy limit. While there is much to explore in this passage in terms of intellectual history, a kind of manic middle ground hovering between romanticism and naturalism, I would like to highlight two essential components of the character's vision. First is the way that the literature—the *national* literature—is conceptualized as an animate object, a quasi-literal corpus or body, that is susceptible to progress and decline, evolution for the better and devolution for the worse. The literary corpus, in other words, is subject to life and death understood through a neat logic of biological stages: birth, growth, senescence, and expiration. This conceptualization resurfaces again and again in the modern world, such as in Max Nordau's *Degeneration* of the 1890s, for example, as well as in the so-called culture wars in the United States a century later. Second is the way in which this literary dynamic of life–death is cast as a result of transculturation in the contact zone. The national literary corpus can be improved or corrupted by associating with others.

In *Three Hundred Years of Decadence*, I will be interested in tracing the history of axiological adjudication of literary expression—efforts that relate to "taste" and canonization more generally—as a process of transatlantic exchange within the conceptual framework of decadence. How has New Orleans literary history been figured in terms of progress and deterioration during the past three hundred years, and what results from that figuration? How does the concept of decadence—the undecidable doubleness of progress and decline and the tempting spectacle of that undecidability—lend itself to literary historiography in the city of New Orleans? How have the golden ages and the not-so-golden ages of New Orleans literature been figured, for what reason, and with what effect?

This problem of evaluation is not something that contemporary literary critics are now superimposing onto a past corpus but is structural to the corpus itself. The writers themselves take it up—in speaking about themselves, in editing anthologies, and even in referencing the problem in their own creative work—often in the wake of uneasiness about the tenuous literariness of the city *vis-à-vis* a larger and more national corpus. The famous novelist Walker Percy writes in "New Orleans Mon Amour" (1968) about this tenuousness:

> The peculiar virtue of New Orleans, like St. Theresa, may be that of the Little Way, a talent for everyday life rather than the heroic deed. If in its two hundred and fifty years of history it has produced no giants, no Lincolns, no Lees, no Faulkners, no Thoreaus, it has nurtured a great many people who live tolerably, like to talk and eat, laugh a good deal, manage generally to be civil and at the same time mind their own business. (15)

In this way, the literature does not just "contain" decadence, either as a theme or as a style or as both. Authors who take up New Orleans as their subject ask readers to think of them metacritically within the long story of decadence.

Liliane Crété blames it on the weather. In her 1978 study of the early nineteenth century, called *Daily Life in Louisiana, 1815–1830*, she writes, "The climate of the region certainly seemed unhealthy for literature" (128). Registering a kind of anxiety of unexceptionality that pops up frequently in the city's literary historiography, Crété continues, "One might have expected the Creoles, as part of the effort to assert the validity of their culture, to have developed a strong native literature. Such, however, was not the case. Creole authors modeled themselves after contemporary French authors—the most popular rather than the best—and mimicked them so slavishly that their own work sometimes reads like parody" (127). For Crété, the white Francophone authors of New Orleans cannot invigorate the national corpuses of France and the United States; in fact, their literary output should be seen as a sign of decline in terms of literary history.

But there is an upshot for Crété, who then goes on to differentiate the literature of the ethnic French from that of the Africans in early New Orleans. She writes:

> The French-language literature of Louisiana, although popular in its own time, is bound to seem tedious to a modern reader. Noble and high-flown, it is also curiously thin and empty—scarcely a literature for the ages. The black cultural heritage, in contrast—the *gombo* songs, folktales, proverbs passed on from generation to generation and preserved by such writers as George Washington Cable, Lafcadio Hearn, and Alcée Fortier—retains much of its original vitality. (136)

For Crété, the axiological adjudication of literary expression turns on two axes: European and African, on the one hand, and literacy and orality, on the other. For her, it is not the white, highly literate Francophone New Orleanians writing in standard French who invigorate literary history but their black, orally based counterparts transcribed the creole language who do so.

What we see condensed in this passage is a major evaluative move that can best be described as a transvaluation of value in which the good and the bad transpose. What was traditionally deemed "vital" and what was traditionally deemed not switch places. Many other critics, for example Catharine Savage Brosman in *Louisiana Creole Literature: A Historical Study* (2013), seem to take a very different approach and assert instead the positive value of the highly literate French New Orleanians and their body of work.

The dynamic of literary progress and decline, poetic renovation and decay, lyrical evolution and devolution is structural to the literary history of New Orleans and makes its most recent appearance in the wake of Hurricane Katrina and the human migration that ensued. Tom Piazza, writing immediately after the storm, takes up this dynamic in his book *Why New Orleans Matters* (2005) and argues that New Orleans invigorates American culture despite the city's negative reputation. He goes so far as to claim, in fact, that American culture itself would be under threat with the loss of New Orleans. But the discourse of damage and decline, of loss, of the irrevocable shattering of something literary, has a long history in the city of New Orleans and resurfaces during every moment of perceived catastrophe: the French takeover of the natives, the Spanish takeover of the French, the American takeover of the Europeans, the breakdown of state relations that reached a crisis in the Civil War, the segregation and desegregation of the public sphere, to name some of the most dramatic, as well as the major hurricanes, fires, and epidemics that punctuate the city's history. *Three Hundred Years of Decadence* explores the ways in which decadence, in its paradoxical nature, may help literary critics understand those historical shifts as well as the transformations in mood, worldview, and literary sensibility that result.

ENVIRONMENTS

The paradoxical nature of decadence in New Orleans can be seen most clearly within the conceptual realms of bodies, languages, and literatures. What grounds each of these realms, however, is the physical environment of southern Louisiana. New Orleans is a city surrounded by brackish wetlands, morphed into unruly submission by anthropogenic means, seemingly always on the brink of disaster, and succumbing to a fate dictated by the unsteady hands of those who live far away. The late summer catastrophes of hurricanes Katrina and Rita in 2005, as well as their lingering diseases in the minds and bodies of all who were affected, continue to haunt, even as major new pockets of wealth and investment crop up, however temporarily, on the higher grounds of the cityscape. But these most recent catastrophes are only a part of the much longer story of New Orleans decadence.

In one of its prominent iterations, decadence means revelry in the supposedly unhealthy aspects of life: day drinking under the cool recesses of shade trees, indifference to the world with an occasional knocking of shame, a relatively easy carpe diem before an uneasy deluge. But what looks like decadence at first glance may be in fact the city's most expressive form of life and vitality. Industrial progress and technological advance, decadence's supposed opposites, may be in fact the real decadence, the true sign of decline, the actual harbinger of death.

This difficulty in making that judgment is why I believe the historian Lawrence Powell begins his recent history of colonial New Orleans, called *The Accidental City* (2012), with an epigraph from Nietzsche: "The secret for harvesting from existence the greatest fruitfulness and greatest enjoyment is—to live *dangerously*! Build your cities on the slopes of Vesuvius!" (vii). What Powell seems to find so apt in Nietzsche, what Nietzsche inherits from the Parisian decadents of the 1880s, what he develops into a fully articulated philosophical system, and what he prefigures so presciently in the context of New Orleans, is that what seems to be the good choice, the right choice, the healthy choice, may not be so after all.

Such a transvaluation of value, of course, is not without its dangers. The volcano may indeed erupt, the water may rise, the toe may wither away, and one may come to regret living so *dangerously*. Despite its dangers, however, decadence remains an important fixture in the literature of New Orleans and inhabits a range of texts from the most famous to the forgotten. As we move slowly but not so surely into the twenty-first century, as we reach the city's tricentennial being of two or more minds, how might the paradoxes of decadence help us to understand the paradoxes of New Orleans itself?

2

COLONIAL NEW ORLEANS,
BEGINNINGS TO 1803

In Europe, in America, what did it matter where I lived, so long as, living with my mistress, I was certain of being happy? Is not the whole universe home to two faithful lovers?

—ANTOINE-FRANÇOIS PRÉVOST, *Manon Lescaut* (1753), 130

When the first edition of Antoine-François Prévost's *Manon Lescaut* was published in 1733 in France, it was banned for its indecency. The novel tells the story of the Chevalier des Grieux, a promising young theologian and gentleman, who falls in love with the irresistibly beautiful Manon Lescaut, a prostitute, whose faithfulness and true motives remain in question throughout the course of their tumultuous relationship. In falling in love with Manon, in following her through the streets of Paris and ultimately to New Orleans, where she has been exiled for her illegal sex work and where she ultimately dies, Des Grieux betrays everything that he was bred dutifully to respect. He denounces his religion; he defies his father and brothers; he associates with some of seediest characters of the Parisian underworld; he gives Manon his fortune so that she will not be enticed by other men; he agonizes and he suffers and he seems, oddly enough, to like it.

The novel's threat, in the minds of the French censors, resided not so much in its portrayal of vice and criminality—of twisted desire and prostitution, of gambling, thievery, and murder—as in its insistence that an aristocrat had the capacity to descend into such depths of depravity. The fact that the oldest profession in the world existed in France's capital city was beyond dispute, but the possibility that an upper-class gentleman could be caught in such a web of desire was another thing entirely. Here was a story of a seventeen-year-old student who hails from one of the best families in France, who is held up as a model of studiousness and virtue, and who, over the period of five years, falls horribly from his proper place in society.

For the exact reason that the novel was censored in 1733, of course, *Manon Lescaut* found a titillated audience. The Marquis de Sade admired it as one of the best works in French literary history, and over the course of almost three hundred years it has been adapted into many artistic forms, including an opera by Puccini in 1893. Even if it is not named as such, its themes have found their way into countless other texts. It is one of the great Parisian novels and a classic of French literature, but it also extends itself from its European origin across the Atlantic and has come to occupy a unique place in another set of literary histories: American, Louisianian, and New Orleanian.

Prévost's use of New Orleans as a fictional device, a trope, cannot help but reflect the popular thinking of its time and place, but it also reinforces and propels this tropological trajectory of the city. Colonial New Orleans, for Prévost, is Manon's climax and denouement. It is the end of the road for the hustler, incorporating plots of desire and of death, and its symbolic trajectory can be traced for hundreds of years through the long story of New Orleans literature. The novel's impact, furthermore, is not only confined to the literary imagination; one historian, for example, finds in the character of Manon and her depraved sexuality a central historiographical principle in the early life of the city.[1]

When the novel was published in a second edition, in 1753, Prévost wrote an extensive preface designed to temper the threat of scandal and satisfy the censors. The preface works as a kind of pedagogical rationale in good eighteenth-century fashion, with a narrator named M. de Renoncour presenting the story to the public as "a terrible example of the power of the passions" (3). The narrator alludes to Horace, among others, and argues that artistic depictions of immorality will not serve, as Plato insists they do, as a catalyst for imitation in the real world. The novel is "a pleasure to read" as well as "an aid to moral instruction," Prévost claims (3). By retelling Des Grieux's story and casting it as a cautionary tale, the writer hopes—or says he hopes—that other young Frenchmen will not follow in his decadent footsteps.

Despite the novelist's didacticism, however, *Manon Lescaut* fails in its Enlightenment objective to be of "exceptional utility" in joining aesthetic pleasure with moral instruction (5). The novel cannot complete the Enlightenment project in which rationality is presented as the tool to overcome the passions. Well educated in theology and philosophy, the character of Des Grieux has the full range of European rationality at his disposal, and still he falls. Moreover, after he survives his fall in Louisiana, he returns to France to rejoin his aristocratic kin, carrying with him the memory of a five-year adventure, and becomes an impassioned, autobiographical storyteller who seems to revel in that odd conjunction of shame and pride.

In this way, *Manon Lescaut* ought to be read as part of the prehistory of decadence that emerged more fully articulated and practiced in the nineteenth century. It lays the groundwork for decadence, so to speak, despite its own claims against decadence. It ostensibly is told to prevent such a thing as decadence, but by doing so, by speaking the unspeakable, by providing a thrilling example of the lost soul unwilling or unable to follow duty and submit to decorum, it paves the way for a further descent into the world of vice, the intoxication of passion and pleasure.

Manon Lescaut is a fictional twice-told tale, initially narrated by Chevalier des Grieux to M. de Renoncour, *un homme de qualité,* and presented in its second iteration as the finale of his seven-part memoir. It relates the story of the young Des Grieux, whom Renoncour has met on two occasions. The first time is in Pacy, France, as Manon is imprisoned and escorted along with a group of other prostitutes from Paris to Le Havre, from which they set sail to New Orleans. During that meeting, Des Grieux has followed Manon's group of arrested prostitutes and their guards, and he says to Renoncour, "I cannot see the least ray of hope. I must submit to the full harshness of my destiny. I will go to America. At least there I will be free to be with the woman I love" (10). The second time is in Calais, two years later, after Des Grieux has returned to France from America. Interweaving these transatlantic geographies, the story Des Grieux tells to Renoncour begins when Des Grieux is seventeen years old, and it transpires over a period of five years, probably between the late 1710s and early 1720s. Although the exact years are never specified, Prévost's use of historical events, such as the forced exile of French prostitutes during the city's founding, points to this time frame. Manon is thus indeed more than a literary figure; she is a sign of the time.

When Des Grieux meets Manon in the first instance, he is immediately initiated into the world of sexual desire and becomes "inflamed all of a sudden to the point of rapture," and he loses control of himself despite the abiding pressure of his rational mind (14). Because Manon will soon be sent away by her parents to become a nun, the two make a plan to run away together. What follows is a detailed description of the couple's financial struggles, Manon's desire for the luxurious life, and her means of achieving that life through questionable transactions with wealthy men. Throughout their relationship in Paris, Des Grieux maniacally circles through intense attachment to Manon, fits of jealously, outbursts of rage, and histrionic renunciation of Manon, followed by guilt, thoughts of suicide, and reattachment to the Janus-faced lover. It is no wonder why the Marquis de Sade was so enamored with the novel, and why it was so ripe for operatic adaptation. The psychosexual drama is Sadean, if not purely sadistic.

After Manon is forced into exile in Louisiana and Des Grieux follows her there, the lovers gain some reprieve. "Anyone who wants to taste love in all its sweetness," Des Grieux says, "should come to New Orleans. For only here can one love and be loved without self-interest, jealousy, or inconstancy" (135). The two are welcomed into New Orleanian society and attempt to pass as a married couple. But when it is revealed that the two are not actually married, the governor threatens to give Manon to his nephew. With the two forced into exile once again, this time outside of New Orleans, the novel draws to an end. The two lovers lie down to sleep for the night, but when they awake the next morning, Des Grieux notices that Manon's hands are trembling and cold. Though there is not much medical explanation of her illness, she quickly dies right then and there. "I determined to bury her," Des Grieux says theatrically, "and await death lying on her grave," but he is found and becomes "resolved to return to my native land, and to rectify, by a wise and well-ordered life, the scandal of my past conduct" (142, 145).

The female Manon is dead at the end of the novel. Well suited, perhaps, as a hustler in her native habitat of the Parisian underworld, she is unable to survive in a foreign land, and her frail and decadent body is laid to rest in the soil of the American South. At the birthplace of the French colonial adventure in the Gulf South, Manon's body is dead and buried, decomposing in the withered toe of Louisiana. The more fortunate Des Grieux returns to France, but by the time he returns, his father is also dead. Des Grieux is therefore unable to make amends fully, but the character presumably takes the place of the father, acting as a surrogate in the next generation of the family's affairs. The overall story line of the novel may thus be stated simply: Des Grieux falls under the spell of Manon's decadence, he loses control of himself until that spell is broken with her death in the colony, he recovers as he makes his way eastward across the Atlantic, and he reestablishes himself as a proper and upstanding citizen of France.

Manon Lescaut occupies an important place within a number of interweaving literary traditions on various geographic scales: Parisian, French, European, transatlantic, American, Southern, Louisianian, and New Orleanian. As one of the first and famous depictions of New Orleans in literary form, and having a lasting effect on subsequent imaginations of the place, the novel ought to be considered within the context of the long story of New Orleans literature, a story that cuts across times and places, languages and cultures. But how did the story of Manon Lescaut and the Chevalier des Grieux come to be? What colonial pressure was put upon the author in devising the tale? What history occurred between Europe, Africa, and the two Americas, and what kinds of texts circulated that provided literary fodder for Prévost, a Frenchman who traveled extensively throughout Europe, who never crossed the Atlantic, but for whom America, and New Orleans in particular, exerted such a powerful force on the imagination?

COLONIAL WRITING

The earliest writings that exist about the area upon which New Orleans would eventually rise are travel narratives. In the sixteenth century, the Spanish explorer Álvar Núñez Cabeza de Vaca wrote of his famous journey from Cuba to Florida and along the Gulf Coast, passing by the lower Mississippi delta in the year 1528, then heading across the Southwest to the Pacific Ocean and into Central America. *La relación* would be published in Spain in 1542 and would become the first written account of the not-yet-withering toe of Louisiana, the landmass that would be the future home of New Orleans.[2] The region would also be explored by other Spanish conquistadors: Hernando de Soto, traveling up from Florida, who came across the Mississippi River near Memphis in 1541, and then Luis de Moscoso, who took over the expedition after de Soto's death. But unlike the British and the French in America, the Spanish in the sixteenth century were not seeking permanent colonies, only immediate riches. For this reason, there is a gap in the colonial presence and thus in colonial writing in the lower Mississippi delta during this period.[3]

The late seventeenth century is instead the real period during which European writers began to produce a steady stream of texts. In fact, the date can be specified as 9 April 1682, when René-Robert Cavelier, Sieur de La Salle reached the mouth of the Mississippi River after sailing down from the interior and laid claim to the entirety of its vast watershed through the power of speech and supplemented by the technology of writing. In one of the most far-reaching performative utterances of the transatlantic world, La Salle spoke possession over an expansive and peopled territory, giving exclusive sovereignty to King Louis XIV, paving the way for the building of New Orleans at the base of the river to protect the king's land and waters, prompting Prévost to invent Manon and Des Grieux, and inciting many other writers to write.[4]

In his official narrative of the expedition, Jacques de la Metairie writes of this major transatlantic utterance. According to the report, La Salle spoke in the French tongue the following verbose performative:

> In the name of the most high, mighty, invincible, and victorious Prince, Louis the Great, by the grace of God, King of France and Navarre, fourteenth of that name, this ninth day of April, one thousand, six hundred and eighty-two, I, in virtue of the commission of his Majesty [. . .] have taken and do now take in the name of his Majesty and of his successors to the crown, possession of this country of Louisiana, the seas, harbors, ports, bays, adjacent straits; and all the nations, people, provinces, cities, towns, villages, mines, minerals, fisheries, streams, and rivers comprised in the extent of Louisiana. (17)[5]

He continues in this long-winded and greedy vein for some time more, specifying what he considers a comprehensive list of Native American tribes, other peoples, places, and things. Afterwards, La Salle and his expedition set up a cross and a plaque that bore the French arms alongside a Latin inscription claiming possession of the territory by right of them thinking they were the "first on this river" (18).

Cabeza de Vaca, de Soto, La Salle, and many of the other earliest explorers—all of these figures, all of these *characters*—resound powerfully in the literary history of the city and give credence to Keith Cartwright's haunting claim that "New Orleans is a space imbued with multiple temporalities fueled by the fossil structures of its colonial past" (131).[6] Mark Twain, in *Life on the Mississippi* (1883), for example, writes in his singularly impressive style of that day in April 1682. La Salle, Twain writes, claimed the land "while the priest piously consecrated the robbery with a hymn," and during the theft, the thieves were standing protected "in the shadow of his confiscating cross" (20–21). In a more contemporary moment, Joy Harjo, a poet of Creek Indian heritage, leaves La Salle alone but instead takes up the figure of Hernando de Soto in a signal poem called "New Orleans" (1983), where she says bluntly, "He should have stayed home" (108). LeAnne Howe likewise includes Jean-Baptiste Le Moyne, Sieur de Bienville in her short story "The Chaos of Angels" (1994). "Bienville still roams the streets of New Orleans," Howe writes, "the city he platted out of swamp land in 1718" (109). She continues, "I saw him one night on D'Iberville street in the French Quarter. Ears back, eyes rolling in his head, he more resembled a tree frog hugging a lamppost than a jazzman fingering a saxophone. But it was him" (109). Even if critical readers of Howe may wonder about her supernatural sighting, there is no question that the Bienville type still exists and walks downtown even today.[7]

While the Spanish conquistadors and the French thieves are centrally important, the deep time involved in the formation of the New Orleanian literary canon stretches back millennia, well before the Europeans arrived on-site and the place saw writing, well before the place even saw people or heard human voices of any kind. The formation begins with the geologic processes that made land rise from the Gulf, that created ground where none had been, processes that would incite so many to discourse in so many languages, for so many reasons, and in so many generic registers. Those processes would enable life and cause death; they would spur centuries of environmental experimentation in order to prolong the former and delay the latter.

The literal ground on which the New Orleanian literary canon has evolved is relatively new compared to the more northern areas of the state. The landmass south of Baton Rouge took approximately 7,200 years to build itself slowly up as the Mississippi River flooded annually and deposited its rich sediment throughout its ever-moving delta, whereas the ground upon which the city of New Orleans now sits is even newer, starting to build itself up approximately 4,300 years ago. The city, as Richard Campanella writes in *Bienville's Dilemma: A Historical Geography of New Orleans* (2008), "stands not on the ancient, solid North American lithosphere, but on a thin, soft alluvial 'doormat' cast recently out upon the continent's margin" (78). This origin story helps to explain the environmental precariousness of the city and its region, especially today, as the vast levee system designed to protect its human inhabitants from the rising river also robs the delta of its land-building sediments.

Human perceptions and understandings of the uneasy nature of this ground—its thinness and fragility, its juvenescence and shiftiness—go as far back as the native presence and the earliest European travel writers. In a good expression of this uneasiness, Pierre François Xavier de Charlevoix writes, in 1722, of the ontological plane upon which the city of New Orleans sits:

> A little below New Orleans the soil begins to be very shallow on both sides of the Mississippi, and its depth continues to diminish all the way to the sea. This is a point of land which does not appear to be very ancient; for if it be ever so little dug up, water is sure to be found, and the great number of shoals and small islands, which within these twenty years have been formed at all the mouths of the river, leave no room to doubt that this neck of land has been formed in the same manner. It appears certain, that when M. de La Salle went down the Mississippi to the sea, the mouth of this river was quite different from what it is at present. (170–171)

This early prescience about the changing landscape prefigures centuries of uneasiness that comes in wave after wave, rising once again today in the state's master plan to open the river's levees, diverting the flow of water and sediment in the hope of building up land in some of the most critical areas south of the city. And yet the ease of creation also signals the nagging probability of destruction. The landscape itself, therefore, has been a ripe incubator for the city's decadent tropology, oscillating as it does between decay and possibility, death and desire.

Many of the writings from the earliest days of the city depict a world unfit for human inhabitation. Many other writings, often penned by the same authors, depict instead a world shimmering with optimism and possibilities. While the former sentiment undeniably stems from the sheer difficulty of bare human life struggling to survive against the swampy elements—a struggle against dense flora, dangerous fauna, swarms of disease-bearing insects, and unpredictable deluges—the latter mode often has political and economic motivations. Early depictions of New Orleans and southern Louisiana as an Edenic new world, in other words, stem primarily from the propagandistic function of the texts. Charlevoix admits as much in his own writing, stating bluntly that transatlantic writers and their readers are "not unacquainted with the reasons for publishing that Louisiana contained in its bosom immense treasures" (180).[8]

The aim of propagandistic travel writing, of course, is to convince people not only to invest their time and money in the colonial enterprise but also to risk their very lives in crossing the Atlantic and settling in a dangerous place. Nonetheless, much of the travel writing resists the purely propagandistic by combining the novel's narrative excitement and dialogic expression with the newspaper's timeliness and factual objectivity.[9] In this vein, for example, the memoirist André Pénicaut takes pains to describe the genuine caliber of his action-packed travel narrative: "I am not giving this work to the public as an invented fable but as a sincere and true account of that to which I have been an eyewitness during the twenty-two years I have lived in Louisiana" (xxxii).[10]

Despite their assurances, however, many travel writers cannot help but oscillate between realistic depictions of the newborn colony and narrative that sounds very much like "invented fable" and propaganda. Charlevoix, for one, writes in 1722 that he has no doubt that New Orleans will become the "future capital of an immense and beautiful country" (156). "Rome and Paris," he continues, "had not such considerable beginnings, were not built under such happy auspices, and their founders met not with those advantages on the Seine and the Tiber, which we have found on the Mississippi, in comparison of which, these two rivers are no more than brooks" (156). But then comes a very different sentiment. Charlevoix warns, "M. de Pauger, whom I still have the honor to accompany, has just shown me a plan of his own invention; but it will not be so easy to put it into execution, as it has been to draw it out upon paper" (172). Referring to Adrien de Pauger, the royal engineer who drafted the layout of the French Quarter, Charlevoix reminds his readers that the land and waterscape itself, the intermeshing of river, levee, and swamp, will always present a troubled counterpoint to the famous Enlightenment grid. Like other early travel writers, Charlevoix reveals a profound sense of impermanence and instability as he witnesses the imprecision of a wetlandscape in which an island—a glorified sandbar, to be more precise—could exist one day and be gone the next.

Perceptions and evaluations of this kind of *oikos*—these grounds of various viscosity, land in its making and unmaking—and its figuration in spoken and written language depended not only upon the author's motives but also upon his or her continental origin. It mattered whether the perceiver and evaluator set sail from Europe, was forced from Africa, or had native roots in America. For the native tribes who had lived for thousands of years in the region before the arrival of the Europeans and Africans, the swampy *oikos* provided a means for transportation; it provided nourishment, in terms of food and water, as well as cultural symbols of status and wealth—pearls, for example—and materials for religious expression and rituals. For the earliest African slaves who were taken from Senegambia, the swampy landscape of southeastern Louisiana likewise held both utilitarian and aesthetic value. It was beneficial for growing rice and other nutritious food, for hunting, and for fishing. They also saw the swamps as a means of escape from the brutalities of bondage. But such a positive estimation of the landscape, cultivated for generations before enslavement and their forced transatlantic migration, was often put in check by the reality of their new lives and deaths in southern Louisiana, especially the danger of drowning. Indeed, in some of the earliest writings—in Marc-Antoine Caillot's *Relation du voyage* (1731), for example—readers must confront many descriptions of African slaves dying or being put in extreme danger as the expedition makes its way slowly and unsurely up the powerful Mississippi River from La Balize to New Orleans.[11]

The Europeans—the Spanish and French, and later the British and Germans—would see something very different in the landscape. Unlike the Africans and natives, they would not see *oikos* but anti-*oikos*, not home but dangerous wasteland. The historical geographer Craig E. Colten writes, "Earliest assessments of New Orleans reflect Europeans' association of wetlands with insalubrious conditions and a degenerative influence" ("Meaning" 60). Without the medical knowledge we have today of diseases such as malaria and yellow fever, colonial Europeans attributed these deadly maladies to the landscape itself rather than to a specific insect—the mosquito—that evolved within the habitat. Colten writes:

> These threats were previously unknown to native peoples. Malaria was common in Europe and gave rise to the miasmatic theory of disease— which held that putrid emanations from stagnant water and decaying vegetation spawned disease. Wetlands such as swamps and marshes, in the view of Europeans, were the source of such miasmas. Thus waterlogged locations, which also served as habitat for disease-delivering mosquitoes, acquired an old-world reputation as unhealthful. (61)[12]

The political, economic, and military advantages for developing New Orleans where it developed, however, proved too tempting and trumped these health concerns about the swampy location. Nevertheless, the "old-world reputation" of the swamp persisted for hundreds of years and influenced the psychosocial oscillations between attraction and revulsion regarding this particular type of physical environment.

In his recently discovered memoir, the Frenchman Marc-Antoine Caillot details his travels to New Orleans from Paris in 1729. For the European traveler, there is very little to celebrate in the city and surrounding wetlandscape. Disembarking first at La Balize at the base of the river before traveling upriver to New Orleans, Caillot writes that the place "is a place swamped by the sea, so swamped that, when the sea is heavy, you are forced to walk on planks" (84). The journey upriver is even worse: "The eight days it took us for that bit of navigation tired us more than the whole crossing from France to this place" (68). For the European, the swampy anti-*oikos* of southeastern Louisiana at the deltaic base of the Mississippi River proves to be a difficult and degenerate place, always out to injure or kill its human arrivals.

For Caillot, moreover, the transatlantic journey itself, from France to New Orleans, involves a kind of degeneration. The climate, coupled with the social relations evolving under the aegis of slavery, created a particular and peculiar type of human. Before his arrival in Louisiana, Caillot travels through Saint-Domingue—present-day Haiti—where he found "very pretty Creole women" who wore clothes of "a dazzling white, whereas they are not, though they would seem to be. [. . .] These Creole women have many slaves," Caillot continues, "and this is the reason they are so lazy, even to the point that if they drop something on the ground, they have the patience to call a slave five or six times to come pick up what is just at their feet" (51, 53).

Despite the clear depravity of these women, Caillot is still drawn to them. Unlike the unlucky Des Grieux, however, Caillot does not fall prey to their temptations. He writes:

> If I had followed the inclination that drew me toward these Creoles, I would have been able to satisfy my desires, but the warnings I received—and also the predicament in which I would have found myself if I had the misfortune to be among the number of so many young men who were very afflicted because of the lack of help—stopped me and bridled my passion." (53)

In the end, the decadent spell cast on the toe of Louisiana does not sway the young company man Caillot. He knows too much and too well what lay in store for those guided only by sexual desire and romantic passion, with no regard for their deadly consequences. "I left New Orleans on April 1 in the year 1731," Caillot concludes his narrative, "as happy to the same degree as I had been sad upon arriving there" (156).

The European writings from the colonial period—from the earliest travel narratives to Prévost's *Manon Lescaut* and beyond—constitute a prehistory of decadence, an intellectual fertilizer that helped to spawn a more developed, consolidated, self-conscious, and recognized movement that exploded in Paris during the final quarter of the nineteenth century. But there is also a text—a double text, really—that comes at the very beginning of the nineteenth century and that registers a shift away from these eighteenth-century texts: François-René de Chateaubriand's *Atala* (1801) and its sequel *René* (1802). If the eighteenth-century texts display a decadence lodged in New Orleans, a decadence that may be overcome through rational regard, a Dionysian temptation conquered by Apollonian means, Chateaubriand tells a very different type of story.

FRANÇOIS-RENÉ DE CHATEAUBRIAND

Like Prévost's *Manon Lescaut,* and like many of the region's earliest travel narratives, Chateaubriand's novellas are rarely considered part of American literary history. From the perspective of the Anglophone United States, such texts are "losers of an imperial and linguistic competition," to quote literary critic Gordon Sayre (386).[13] But these loser texts ought to be factored more thoroughly into American literary history—and especially New Orleanian literary history—because they demonstrate the transatlantic nature of literary development. They also reflect and create many of the themes that abide in the city.

Although set in Louisiana, Chateaubriand's *Atala* and *René* expressed a profound uneasiness on both sides of the Atlantic when they appeared at the beginning of the nineteenth century. Published in postrevolutionary France, when the dreams of enlightened peace and justice built on *liberté, egalité,* and *fraternité* and achieved through objective logic and coolheaded rationality began to fall apart, the novellas exposed an increasing awareness of the darkness and violence that lurked below the surface of an ideal humanity. For at least this reason, the books found a special place in romanticism's philosophical, literary, and political quarrel with the Enlightenment, and they were quickly translated into English, German, Italian, and Spanish.

Atala consists of three main sections: a prologue, the tale itself, and an epilogue. The first and third of these sections are written, presumably from Chateaubriand's perspective, in the autobiographical mode. The second section, the tale itself, is written as a transcription of an oral story first told by Chactas, a seventy-three-year-old Natchez warrior, to René, a young Frenchman who comes to Louisiana "impelled by passion and sorrow" (20). Though this story is supposedly told in 1725, it is set many years before, around 1672. What further complicates the time line is that Chateaubriand claims that the tale was passed down from generation to generation and that he recorded it in writing during his travels to North America sometime between 1791 and 1792. "I," Chateaubriand writes, "a traveler in far-distant lands, have faithfully set down what I received from the Indians" (76). The temporal complication can be laid out as follows: 1672 (the setting of Chactas's story), 1725 (the year Chactas tells it to René), 1725–1791 (the many years it is retold orally), 1791–1792 (the time Chateaubriand hears it in America), and 1801 (the year it is published as a novella in Paris). The novella thus brings together a number of moments in the history of imperial France: the initial exploration of the Gulf Coast, the founding of New Orleans and the rise of the colony, the weakening of France's ability to control the region, the decline and fall of the empire in Louisiana and the loss of New Orleans, and the birth of the colony as a beautiful memory in the French collective imagination.

"In days gone by," Chateaubriand begins, presumably as himself, in the prologue, "France possessed a vast empire in North America, extending from Labrador to the Floridas and from the shores of the Atlantic to the most remote lakes of Upper Canada" (17). For a French audience reading the novella in 1801, such a sentence would immediately evoke a sentimental complexity, a mixture of joy and pride that comes with the glory of empire, as well as the sadness and regret that comes with the knowledge that those days have slipped and are slipping into an ever-receding past.

In addition to this kind of romantic nostalgia, Chateaubriand's romanticism animates his descriptions of the Louisiana landscape. The Mississippi River, for him, is a river that connects "a delightful country, which the inhabitants of the United States call New Eden, while the French have bequeathed to it the gentle name of Louisiana" (17). Images of fertility abound, and the land is everywhere on the rise. Of

the masses of silt and vegetation encountered on the Mississippi, Chateaubriand writes:

> The river takes hold of them and carries them down to the Mexican gulf,
> where it leaves them on the sandy banks, thus multiplying its mouths.
> At times it lifts its voice as it passes the hills, and pours its flood waters
> around the forest colonnades and the pyramids of the Indian tombs; it
> is the Nile of the wilderness. (17)

Chateaubriand continues, "A host of animals placed by the Creator's
hand in these retreats radiate gladness and life" (19). Unlike the texts
written in the early days of the colony, these descriptions, in 1801, no
longer need to serve a propagandistic function. They aim, then, only to
create a particular type of memory in the French mind, of something
beautiful that was once possessed but is now gone forever.

In reading these romantic descriptions, it is important to remember
that, unlike Prévost, Chateaubriand did indeed make the transatlantic
trip to America and spent five months on the continent, from 1791
to 1792. He was, however, probably confined to the mid-Atlantic region and did not set foot in Louisiana. Therefore, when Chateaubriand
presents his material as an eyewitness account of the landscape, he in
truth lacks such experience, and his descriptions are drawn from other
writers, especially Charlevoix and William Bartram. Chateaubriand's
texts thus fit within a kind of orientalism in his approach to the former
French colony. Indeed, his Louisiana, to borrow a diagnosis from Edward Said, "is less a place than a *topos,* a set of references, a congeries
of characteristics, that seems to have its origin in a quotation, or a
fragment of a text, or a citation from someone's work" (177).[14]

Through the allusive topology of Louisiana, Chateaubriand writes
his novella, a text which is essentially another's text, an extended quotation, since it supposedly does nothing more than retell the story
Chactas told to René almost seven decades before. Chactas's story is a
sad one. After an intertribal war in 1672 in which his father is killed,
Chactas flees to Saint Augustine, where he is adopted by a Spaniard
named Lopez and Lopez's sister. But, after some time, Chactas longs to

return to his native culture. Lopez is disappointed, but he cannot help but understand Chactas's desire: "'Go, son of nature!' he cried. 'Go back to man's freedom; I do not wish to rob you of it. If I were younger myself, I would accompany you into the wilderness" (23).

After leaving Saint Augustine, Chactas is caught by a rival Indian tribe and threatened with execution. In captivity, Chactas falls in love with Atala, the adopted daughter of tribe's chief, and with her help he manages to escape from his imprisonment and imminent execution. The two make their way into the freedom of the forest under cover of darkness. In vivid imagery, the two, barely clothed, find bliss and happiness in an Edenic state of nature free from want: "The black walnut, the maple, and the sumac supplied wine for our table. Sometimes I would go into the reeds and find a plant with a flower elongated in the form of a horn, containing a glass of the purest dew" (40). In this state of nature, their sexual desire for each other grows ever stronger, but Atala "had recourse to the God of the Christians," which helps her to maintain her virginity (31).

There is some trouble brewing in this Edenic world, however, for the young Chactas and his beautiful Atala. "The further we went," Chactas says, "the sadder she became" (40). He continues, "What especially frightened me was a certain secret, a thought hidden in the depths of her being, which I could just glimpse in her eyes. Repeatedly she attracted and repulsed me, raising and then crushing my hopes, so that every time I thought I had made some inroads into her heart, I found myself back where I had begun" (40).

This "certain secret" that Atala keeps from Chactas is finally revealed in the novella. Within Chactas's story, Atala tells her own. "My sad fate began," she says, "almost before I saw the light of day," having been conceived by a native mother and a Spanish father who turns out to be Lopez (58). Atala explains her situation: "My mother had conceived me in grief; I was a burden to her womb, and I came into the world sharply rending her body. My life was given up for lost, and to save me from death, my mother vowed to the Queen of Angels that, if I were spared, my virginity would be consecrated to her" (58). This vow made by the mother on behalf of the daughter's virginity prevents Atala from marrying Chactas, and she surrenders herself to her sad fate of torment. She gives up on life and love.

In a strange mixture of religious faith and legal theory, however, Father Aubrey, whom the two lovers have met in the woods, offers Atala a way out. He volunteers to "write to the Bishop of Quebec" because, as he tells Atala, "he has the power to absolve you of your vows which are not permanently binding, and you will end your days beside me with Chactas as your husband" (62). But Father Aubrey's news comes too late. She has poisoned herself just before discovering this possibility, and she calls out theatrically, "Must I die the very moment I learn I might have been happy?" (62). The answer, of course, is yes. That is exactly when she should die, according to the rules of high drama. "When you were kissing my trembling lips," she tells Chactas in a moment of pure morbidity, "you did not know that you were embracing death!" (62). She succumbs to her own poison, and Chactas is left with only inconsolable loss.

René's story, which the character tells to Chactas and Father Souël on the banks of the Mississippi River in the eponymously titled novella, published in 1802, is no happier. It traces the story not of events, and certainly not of important events, but of moods and states of mind. Chateaubriand writes, "He therefore set a day to tell them, not the adventures of his life, for he had never had any, but the innermost feelings of his soul" (85). He is full of shame and anxiety, desperate for his audience's pity though all the while passionately announcing he does not deserve it, and yet there is no clear source of these emotions. Speaking in the third person, he claims that he is "a young man with neither strength nor moral courage, who finds the source of his torments within himself, and can hardly lament any misfortunes save those he has brought on himself" (86).

He blames himself for his mother's death during childbirth, his father dies in his arms, and he is drawn only to his older sister, with whom he shares certain bipolar tendencies. "As I alternated turbulence and joy with silence and sadness," he says, "I would gather my young friends around me, then leave them suddenly and go off to sit by myself

47

watching the swift clouds or listening to the rain falling among the leaves" (87). His melancholic tendencies cause him to seek out poets and artists, who he believes have more intuitive knowledge of the inner workings of the soul, to admire the cultures of early centuries, and to visit the relics of past civilizations, "peoples who exist no more" (90). When not misanthropic, he also sublimates his suicidal tendencies into religious conviction and desire, transforming his will toward death into a longing to be in Europe's old cemeteries and the cloisters of the monastery. René, furthermore, is awed by the power of nature to consume the human; he is thrilled by the unrelenting assault of time on human creations: "I went and sat among the ruins of Rome and Greece, those countries of virile and brilliant memory, hidden beneath the brambles. O power of nature and weakness of man! A blade of grass will pierce through the hardest marble of these tombs, while their weight can never be lifted by all these mighty dead!" (90).

René begins one of the famous scenes of the novella thusly:

> One day, I amused myself by stripping the leaves from a willow branch, one by one, and throwing them into the stream, attaching a thought to each leaf as the current carried it off. A king in fear of losing his crown in a sudden revolution does not feel sharper pangs of anguish than did I, as I watched each peril threatening the remains of my bough. O frailty of mortal man! (96–97)

This unshakable obsession with the fleeting nature of the present, with death and decay, haunts him. René travels from Caledonia to Sicily, climbs Mount Etna, looks down into its fiery pit, and then moves on to Greece. But still he cannot find the relief he seeks. In his lengthy descriptions of his character's strenuous travels through the Western world, Chateaubriand underscores the fact that René's body must be healthy in order for him to be drawn to the spectacle of biological decay. It is not the old, the sick, the otherwise debilitated who long for the destructive agents of time, who revel in the wilted flower, the brush of gray around the temple, the ever-changing stream, the slow bell tolling of the funeral procession nearby. It is the young romantic who longs for such things *in aesthetic form.*

Because he cannot find a cure for his melancholic tendencies in his travels from Scotland to Greece, René hedges his bet on a transatlantic journey. In contrast to Europe, René imagines the Americas to be a place of juvenescence, innocence, peace, and uncomplicated happiness. He exclaims:

> Happy Indians, oh, why can I not enjoy the peace which always goes with you! While my fruitless wanderings led me through so many lands, you, sitting quietly under your oaks, let the days slip by without counting them. Your needs were your only guide, and, far better than I, you have reached wisdom's goal through your play and your sleep—like children. Your soul may sometimes have been touched by the melancholy of extreme happiness, but you emerged soon enough from this fleeting sadness, and your eyes rose toward heaven, tenderly seeking the mysterious presence which takes pity on the poor Indian. (93)

Despite the symbolic and material presence of the American Indian, René is not one of them, nor can he be. His depression only increases, and he begins to consider life itself as too great a burden to bear. He writes to his sister, "who was accustomed to reading into the recesses of my heart, and she guessed it at once" (99). He swears to his sister that he will not commit suicide, but she is overwhelmed by her own emotions and enters the convent. René is tormented by their separation and resolves to leave for Louisiana.

If the romantic melancholic suffers without enjoyment, by the end of the nineteenth century the decadent melancholic will find pleasure in the pain and will use it as a productive tool in the creation of life, literature, art, and philosophy. In this way, René's suffering is more romantic than decadent, but it provides the figurative grounds for the latter innovation. In 1802, when *René* appeared, furthermore, there was still the voice of reason echoing from the Enlightenment. After the tale is over, Father Souël responds to René:

Nothing in your story deserves the pity you are now being shown. I see a young man infatuated with illusions, satisfied with nothing, withdrawn from the burdens of society, and wrapped up in idle dreams. A man is not superior, sir, because he sees the world in a dismal light. Only those of limited vision can hate men and life. Look a little farther and you will soon be convinced that all those griefs about which you complain are absolutely nothing. (112–113)

The religious man and paternal figure tries to help the young René escape from his melancholia, but Father Souël's harsh and insulting words fall on deaf ears. René's griefs, his nagging tortures taking a thousand different forms, do not abate.

How do these two texts, set during the French colonization of Louisiana and published during its unraveling, fit into New Orleans literary history and transatlantic decadence? On the one hand, Chateaubriand's approach to Louisiana is part of the colonial effort to rationalize the conqueror's conquering as a benevolent gift to the conquered. "In spite of the many injustices which Chactas had suffered at the hands of the French," Chateaubriand insists, "he loved them" (20). It is also part of a larger and related project to defend the spread of Christianity across the Atlantic. When Chactas and Atala meet the old missionary Father Aubrey, who lives alone in the woods and ministers to the natives, the priest says, "I marveled at the triumph of Christianity over primitive culture. I could see the Indian growing civilized through the voice of religion" (55).

On the other hand, Chateaubriand's approach to Louisiana is part of colonial critique. The imperial ego comes to North America in the form of a gloomy and suicidal young man who fails to succeed by any measure—financially, socially, politically, emotionally, reproductively. He fails even biologically to simply survive. "René returned to his wife," Chateaubriand concludes his tale, "but still found no happiness. Soon afterwards, along with Chactas and Father Souël, he perished in the massacres of the French and Natchez in Louisiana" (114). If Des Grieux is able to shuck off his dangerous Manon and leave her dead body in Louisiana in 1731 before returning to his aristocratic position in France,

René cannot return to Europe. As symbol and myth, René must die, and the death of the Frenchman, a young man who realizes none of his potential, must happen in Louisiana.

After Chateaubriand publishes *Atala* and *René*, France's imperial ambition does not end with the forfeiture of Louisiana at the very dawn of the nineteenth century, of course. Its imperial gaze will move on, no longer looking westward to the American South but to the Caribbean, across the Mediterranean to Africa, and to the East. René's death does not signal the end of the French presence in New Orleans but, instead, the birth of its decline, its decadence, its withered fragility, which will always seem alive and well for at least the next two centuries.

3

AMERICAN NEW ORLEANS, 1803 TO 1865

I had brought to this country an extensive library. Being sent to Martinique, I could not, in wartime, take my library there. I wanted to keep
only a small part of it.

—PIERRE CLÉMENT DE LAUSSAT, *Memoirs of My Life* (1831), 98

On 31 March 1804, Pierre Clément de Laussat had an existential crisis of sorts. Appointed by Napoleon just two years before, in 1802, to
govern Louisiana, Laussat arrived in the colony in 1803 to oversee the
retrocession of Louisiana from Spain to France. He was then faced with
the surprise transfer of Louisiana from France to the United States, just
a few weeks later, which he would have to administer as well. After
these hurried tasks were complete—tasks which bounced a vast and
populated territory from one foreign power to another through the
commanding strokes of multilingual pens—his appointment ended,
and he was then sent to Martinique to administer the French colonial
empire there. At that time, war between the British and French was
being waged over the control of the island, and Laussat would have to
travel lightly and quickly.

In his *Memoirs of My Life* (1831), Laussat recounts the day in March
1804 when he had to plan for his quick move from New Orleans to
Martinique by giving away or selling large parts of his library. The details of that experience are worth quoting at length:

One after another, I sold several of the dearest and most faithful com-
panions of my life; it broke my heart to part with them. One lot deserted
me on March 31: Montaigne—the very copy I purchased when I was
nineteen and I have read and reread since; J.-J. Rousseau—a small eighteen volume set, which accompanied me on my promenades and in my
travels; Montesquieu—eight volumes of twelve, in which I read and
reread the *Décadence des Romains*, *L'Esprit de lois*, *Le Temple de Gnide*,
and *Le Dialogue de Scilla*; my Corneille and my Racine, which were daily
reading; and so on, and so on. They had been the witnesses and the
confidants of my early studies. I bought them myself. They had gone
to Béarn; Resposoir, rue Notre-Dame-des-Victoires, rue Caumartin,
rue de la Sourdiére, rue Daguesseau, and the rue Neuve-des-Capucins.
There was no memory, no joy, no sorrow in my life in which they had
not played some part. They had followed my fate, and one of its strange
aspects was that I had come to the banks of the Mississippi to separate
from them. It was done! I would never see them again. (98)

The specific names of the great French authors—Montaigne, Rousseau,
Montesquieu, Corneille, and Racine—the highest exemplars of French
literary culture, are attached for Laussat to the specific names of their
books. These book names are in turn attached to specific place names.
In the passage, names of authors become names of books which become
names of places. All these names are condensed and given another life
form—they are fetishized—in the physical books themselves in his
library, and they are now under threat.[1]

Amidst the violence of war and imperialism, the French bibliophile
mourns the loss of his books. Considering them friends, Laussat holds
his book objects near and dear with profound affective attachment,
but the objects themselves are also figured to be like himself, capable
of forming affective attachments all on their own. They are anthropo-
morphized, invested with a capability of witnessing and listening non-
judgmentally, of offering faithfulness and companionship, which pains
the author even more because of his own unfaithfulness towards them.
In the end, he betrays them, and he believes them to feel betrayed.

Although these book objects are considered friends capable of feeling betrayal, Laussat also considers them property, possessions to be bought and sold in the marketplace, first in France and then in New Orleans, probably at a higher rate, although Laussat dwells only on what he lost and not on what he gained in the transaction. The drama hovers between these two poles, between friend and property. In their denouement, the books end up being lost on the southernmost edge of the Mississippi River, abandoned in the wasteland of New Orleans.

Why does Laussat make such a fuss over these books, especially during a time of real danger, and what does it mean for the larger issue of decadence in the New Orleanian contact zone? Laussat's memory is significant for understanding decadence for at least two reasons. First, Laussat recounts here a drama of cultural capitalization and impoverishment in action. Not only has Laussat read the classic works of French literature but also he has read them in their proper place, their genetic home—a cultural capital twofer. The dead authors, channeled and given physical form in the book object, are connected for Laussat to specific place names, and he holds them in his possession. But this drama of cultural capitalization does not have a happy ending. In a moment of upheaval, of rushed transnational movement, Laussat's hold on the literary canon, imagined here as a fixed set of books condensed in the personal library, teeters on the edge of collapse. Once there is a break, Laussat imagines that he can never recover what he has lost.

There is an upshot, however, to this story of literary crisis. Ethnically and ethically marked as French, the man of high literary culture may resist the pull into the New Orleanian vortex by returning to the mother country. Like Des Grieux's adventure with Manon Lescaut in Louisiana, the decadent fall may only be a temporary setback. Even though Laussat sells and gives away most of his books in New Orleans, he does keep a "small part" of his library, a seed that he will later plant and nurture once again in France. This drama of cultural capitalization and impoverishment, furthermore, does not play out in him alone. Later in life, back safely in the home country, in an intergenerational teaching moment between father and son, Laussat does indeed reconstruct that lost set of books, the canon, at least virtually, through memory and writing. The scene in which he says he writes is the scene of a father telling the story of his life to his son, a memoir pedagogically birthed, to transfer the canon of French literature from one generation to the next.

Second, Laussat's sentiment may be read not simply as a personal reflection on a dark time but also as setting the stage for a poetic nostalgia about a withering French connection in New Orleans that extends throughout the nineteenth and twentieth centuries, and even now into the twenty-first. Although Laussat mourns the loss of his books as he is forced from New Orleans to Martinique, from the perspective of New Orleans itself, there is a benefit. Laussat keeps "only a small part" of his library to take with him, but the much larger part is left in the city. The greater part of the French literary canon has indeed been deposited on the lower banks of the river, but like the alluvial soil itself, it may become diffused, transformed, lost, perhaps mixed with others or simply sinking below the surface, into obscurity. The French connection, therefore, is thought to be fragile, always threatened in one way or another—by neglect and ignorance, by the outsider, by the uncultured and barbarian masses—and thus always requiring protection and proper nurturing. The decadent bibliophile paradoxically becomes the best hope for staving off the decay of the literary canon. Laussat's memory thus illustrates the axiological doubleness of progress and decline that comes with New Orleans's shift from being an eighteenth-century European colony to being a nineteenth-century American state.

In the eighteenth century, New Orleans was a small and dilapidated place. The colony, after all, began in the spirit of failure and disgrace, with the burst and sputter of capital in John Law's company. The best-laid plan of Adrien de Pauger's Vieux Carré, furthermore, designed so well on paper, could not realize the Enlightenment dream of order. Streets and buildings fell into immediate disrepair, public sanitation was shabby at best, and the city struggled to maintain the basic necessities of clean water and drainage. The beginning of the nineteenth century, however, signaled a period of intense change wrought by an influx of newcomers to the city. At the time of the Louisiana Purchase, in 1803, the population of New Orleans was 8,056. By 1850, however, the city's population had jumped to 119,460.[2] In his short story "'Tite Poulette" (1879), George Washington Cable captures this influx by describing one of his characters, the Dutchman Kristian Koppig, as "one of that army of gentlemen who, after the purchase of Louisiana, swarmed from all parts of the commercial world, over the mountains of Franco-Spanish exclusiveness, like the Goths over the Pyrenees, and settled down in New Orleans to pick up their fortunes, with the diligence of hungry pigeons" (213).

This demographic shift occurred in tandem with other major changes of a literary nature. After the Louisiana Purchase, and after Laussat moved on to Martinique to continue his colonial duties, New Orleans experienced a number of major changes involving population, capital, and printing technology that fundamentally transformed its literary culture. Although New Orleans was founded in 1718, the city did not see its first printing presses until almost half a century later, in 1764, and when they did arrive, these presses were not in the service of creative literary production. They were instead controlled by the government and used solely for colonial administration.

The literary culture of New Orleans began to change at the end of the eighteenth century with the launch of the city's first newspaper, the *Moniteur de la Louisiane,* in 1794. Printing presses became more prevalent, the population grew, economic activity increased, and the publishing industry expanded.[3] *The WPA Guide to New Orleans,* published in 1938 and composed by Lyle Saxon with the help of other New Orleanians, connects the nineteenth-century publishing industry with the rise of a literary corpus specific to the city: "The excellent French newspapers and revues published in New Orleans had a large share in the creation of this native literature, opening their pages generously to poems, short stories, and novels" (109).

Clint Bruce in "Caught Between Continents: The Local and the Transatlantic in the French-Language Serial Fiction of New Orleans's *Le Courrier de la Louisiane,* 1843–1845" (2012) offers a more nuanced interpretation of these Francophone periodicals. Many writers and editors before the Civil War—Bruce's main focus is on Jérôme Bayon, the editor of *Le Courrier*—juggled the desire for the French political philosophies of *liberté, egalité*, and *fraternité*, on the one hand, and the practical choice to continue the economically beneficial institutions of slavery, segregation, and white supremacy, on the other.

"Francophone writers of New Orleans used serial fiction," Bruce writes, "to explore issues of cultural solvency and political identity (inextricably bound up with racial anxiety) at a time when the Gallic element's assimilation to the American worldview, a decades-long process concomitant with that community's demographic and political marginalization, was well under way" (13–14). Bruce claims that the cultural situation of the Francophone writers in the city generates "certain paradoxes" (14). Their situation produces "a fragile aesthetic discourse in ephemeral format, wedged between the robust public sphere of the young New World republic and the universally revered belles lettres of the French homeland" (14).

Despite the unavoidable Americanization of French New Orleans after the Louisiana Purchase, and even despite the intense patriotism and affective unification with the rest of the nation that came in the wake of the Battle of New Orleans in 1815, many Anglophone travelers to the city were not convinced about the city's true assimilation into the American sphere.[4] In their preface to *Creole New Orleans: Race and Americanization* (1992), Arnold R. Hirsch and Joseph Logsdon claim that such travelers "recoiled when they encountered the prevailing French language of the city, its dominant Catholicism, its bawdy sensual delights, or its proud free black population—in short, its deeply rooted creole traditions" (xi). The stakes were high for the Americans as they struggled to strengthen and expand their nation; indeed, as Hirsch and Logsdon explain, the Americanization of New Orleans was "the infant republic's first attempt to impose its institutions on a foreign city" (xi).

One challenge in the Americanization process, which surfaces often in the primary texts, is the moral decadence that the Anglophone travelers perceive in the city. "As to the morals of this city," Arthur Singleton writes in 1824, "the word is obsolete" (De Caro and Jordan 80).[5] Many travelers to New Orleans felt this decadence even before they arrived in the city. The British writer Frances Trollope, in *Domestic Manners of the Americans* (1832), describes her ascent upriver from the mouth of the Mississippi River to New Orleans:

> I never beheld a scene so utterly desolate as this entrance of the Mississippi. Had Dante seen it, he might have drawn images of another Borgia from its horrors. One only object rears itself above the eddying waters; this is the mast of a vessel long since wrecked in attempting to cross the bar, and it still stands, a dismal witness of the destruction that has been, and a boding prophet of that which is to come. (De Caro and Jordan 21–22)[6]

For the writer, the best if not only way to make sense of the wetlandscape is through literary allusion, an appeal to Dante, the famous author of hell. Of all the things that Trollope sees on the river, only one human object sticks out in the physical environment. It is a shipwreck, hovering between the past and the future, not quite submerged, at least not yet. Trollope continues:

> Trees of enormous length, sometimes still bearing their branches, and still oftener their uptorn roots entire, the victims of the frequent hurricane, come floating down the stream. Sometimes several of these, entangled together, collect among their boughs a quantity of floating rubbish, that gives the mass the appearance of a moving island, bearing a forest, with its roots mocking the heavens; while the dishonored branches lash the tide in idle vengeance: this, as it approaches the vessel, and glides swiftly past, looks like the fragment of a world in ruins. (23)

This scene of horror, a kind of postapocalyptic and fleeting world, upside down and fragmentary, represents much of the local travel writing during the nineteenth century. But perhaps A. Oakey Hall says it best when he comments on the river's deltaic base and connects the environmental realm with the literary. The first paragraph of his *The Manhat-*

taner in New Orleans; Or, Phases of "Crescent City" Life (1851) consists of the following one sentence: "The 'Father of waters'—the tortuous and elastic Mississippi River—possesses a most unpoetical mouth" (2).

Unlike many of the Anglophone travelers to New Orleans who found a city in perpetual decline, a locale plagued by moral and environmental decadence unredeemable, a chorus of "unpoetical mouths," many native New Orleanians held a different interpretation of their city as a bastion of high literary culture forged and maintained through its association with France. These Francophone New Orleanians in the nineteenth century were not only those creoles who had lived in the city for generations. They were also French-speaking immigrants who had come from abroad, especially from Saint-Domingue, to escape the Haitian Revolution between 1791 and 1804, as well as from continental Europe itself.[7] The literary production of these Francophone New Orleanians signals a turn in New Orleanian literary history and helps to explain the place of decadence within the Enlightenment–romanticism dyad.

FRANCOPHONE POETS

The Francophone poets of mid-nineteenth-century New Orleans testify to transatlantic routes of intellectual exchange, trajectories that not only move westward from Europe to America but also circulate as a continuous feedback loop across the Atlantic. These French-speaking New Orleanians of both European and African ancestry traveled to the European capitals, Paris especially, to get what they considered a proper education, and they learned the literary trends. But their presence there would have inevitably influenced their European contemporaries as well. Indeed, one wonders how romanticism would have proceeded without the influence of the Americas, and especially of the Louisiana Territory, anchored by New Orleans, on the European imagination.

Twentieth and twenty-first century literary critics have often disparaged these poets as mere imitators.[8] A poem by Charles-Oscar Dugué called "Souvenirs du désert [Memories of the Desert]" (1847) does indeed use the romantic mold without much, if any, innovation. Perfectly representing the romantic sensibility, Dugué writes:

> O belle Louisiane, ô vastes cyprières,
> Où m'égaraient jadis des courses solitaires;
> Où j'allais, tout enfant, ainsi qu'en un saint lieu,
> Ouïr, déjà rêveur, la grande voix de Dieu! (56)

> O beautiful Louisiana, O vast cypress forests,
> Where solitary walks used to get me lost;
> Where I went, as a child, as if in a saintly place,
> To hear, already dreaming, the grand voice of God![9]

Louis Allard's "Au Moqueur [To the Mockingbird]," published in both Paris and New Orleans in 1847, likewise relates a romantic sensibility. He writes, "Je sens ravir tous mes sens à la fois" (4), or "I feel ravished by all my senses at once." And he continues:

> Comme le mal qui circule en nos veines
> Cède aux vertus d'un baume bienfaisant,
> Ainsi, toujours mes chagrins et mes peines
> Sont suspendus ou guéris par ton chant.

> Like the illness that circulates in our veins
> Cedes to the virtues of a calming balm,
> Then, all my sorrows and pains
> Are suspended or healed by your song.

These two poems are indicative of much French colonial literary language in their textbook romanticism, and many critics have therefore been skeptical of the literary merits of their authors, thinking them naïvely mimicking the romantic moves of the French originals, exhibiting all influence without any of the innovative anxiety.

Against this grain, it seems, Alfred Mercier was writing. Born in New Orleans in 1816 and educated in Paris, Mercier was very much a transatlantic writer, traveling widely and crossing the Atlantic to escape imminent war—first the revolution in France, in 1848, when he was living there, then the Civil War, in 1861, when he was living in New Orleans. After his permanent move back to the United States, Mercier became a founding member of the literary society *l'Athénée louisianais*, in 1876, and editor of its journal. He was thus a key figure in the New Orleanian postbellum literary scene. But it is an early poem, written in Paris and published in 1842, called "Patrie," or "Fatherland," that is especially significant for taking the city's pulse in the process of Americanization. In "Patrie," Alfred Mercier writes:

> Voici mon fleuve aux vagues solennelles:
> En demi-lune il se courbe en passant,
> Et la cité, comme un aiglon naissant,
> A son flanc gauche étend ses jeunes ailes.
>
> Meschacebé, tu me vis autrefois
> Jouer, enfant, sur ta rive sonore;
> Pére des eaux, tu me revois encore
> Bondir d'ivresse aux longs bruits de ta voix. (130)
>
> This is my river with its solemn waves:
> In half-moon it bends itself in passing,
> And the city, like a newborn eaglet,
> By his left side extends its young wings.
>
> Mississippi, you saw me another time
> Playing, as a child, on your bank sonorous;
> Father of water, you saw me again
> Bouncing with joy from the long uproar of your voice.

The poem then shifts dramatically in tone:

> Quelle est là-bas cette maison qui tombe,
> Vers le chemin qui mène à Gentilly?
> Sur son front plane un silence de tombe,
> Elle paraît condamnée à l'oubli.
>
> Rien, ce n'est rien qu'un squelette sans âme
> Pour l'étranger qui passe insoucieux;

Mais pour mon cœur ce toit silencieux
De jours heureux recoud toute une trame. (130)

What is over there that house in ruins,
On the road that leads to Gentilly?
On its front hovers a silence of a tomb,
She seems to be condemned to oblivion.

Nothing, it is nothing but a skeleton without soul
For the stranger that passes unconcerned;
But for my heart that silent roof
Sews up a thread of happy days.

He questions why he can no longer be "le jeune enfant de la vieille forêt" (130), the young child of the old forest. Romanticism here is contained in poet's passion and isolation, the fleeting nature of his happiness, the adoration of his childhood. He sits by Lake Pontchartrain and reads Jacques-Henri Bernardin de Saint-Pierre's *Paul et Virginie* (1788), an important touchstone for Jean-Jacques Rousseau and many other romantics, and weeps. It is the book that brings the tears to his eyes. It is important to underscore here that Mercier is writing this poem in Paris, about New Orleans. The poet longs for home; he does not look to Europe for redemption, à la Laussat, but to New Orleans.

A familiar story about New Orleans in the nineteenth century involves a central tension between two opposing groups: the Anglo-Americans, shrewd businessmen and developers of the American Sector, and the French creoles, lacking a Protestant work ethic and devoid of the spirit of capitalism, whose lack of industriousness weakens their success until they wither away, becoming only a flickering glimmer of their former, glorious selves. But those populations often came together; their interests combined, especially in the upper classes—the owners, operators, and beneficiaries of the slave plantations.

Other groups besides the Anglo-Americans and French creoles also are important to remember in the story of nineteenth-century New Orleans. The poets of *Les Cenelles* (1845), the first published anthology of poetry written by African Americans in the United States, formed literary societies in New Orleans that were connected to both Port-au-Prince and Paris, and they focused not only on local issues of freedom and oppression but also on global issues of independence related to the African diaspora.[10] The first Spanish-language newspaper in the United States began publication in New Orleans in 1808 as *El Misisipí*, and the large German population of New Orleans further complicates such a straightforward narrative of the century.[11] In order to make this case more clearly, I would like to explore a key nineteenth-century novel that places transatlantic decadence front and center, Ludwig von Reizenstein's *The Mysteries of New Orleans* (1855), a novel that appeared decades before decadence as a self-conscious movement came about in the Parisian 1880s.

LUDWIG VON REIZENSTEIN

Born in Germany in 1826, the aristocratic Baron Ludwig von Reizenstein moved to New Orleans in 1851 and began writing a long novel, set in the city, that was published serially as *Die Geheimnisse von New Orleans* in the German-language newspaper *Louisiana Staats-Zeitung*, from 1854 to 1855. Although this novel would remain lost for more than a century, it holds immense significance for transatlantic literary history. "The German-American urban mystery novel," Steven Rowan writes in his introduction to the English translation, "is an interesting witness even beyond its obvious function of describing the immigrant experience in the pre–Civil War era." For Rowan, "The German writers showed much more sensitivity than their English-speaking contemporaries to the ethnic diversity of the United States. The novels teem with Creoles and foreigners, and the black population of America, both free and slave, is described with a detail and a lack of false sentimentality that is unique for the time" (xxvii).

While Reizenstein's novel is indeed unique, it also fits squarely in the literary history of the city by registering and expanding a particular image of New Orleans that became popularized nationally a generation later in the "local color" fictions of George Washington Cable and

Lafcadio Hearn. Like many writers who come before and after him, Reizenstein begins his novel with a provocative picture of the setting: "New Orleans is now the prima donna of the South, the whore insatiable in her embraces, letting go of her victims only after the last drop of blood has been drained and their innermost marrow of life sucked dry" (3). The city as vampiric is a common trope with the rise of industrial capitalism—indeed, it would become one of Karl Marx's favorites—but Reizenstein here figures the city as a vampiric *female*. His vision is one of prostitutes, sex workers, the forbidden agents of the pleasure industry; and in case readers miss the point the first time, Reizenstein repeats the claim once again: "It is a vast grave for poor immigrants and the homeless, who can never extract themselves in time from the arms of this prostitute" (3). For travelers to New Orleans, there is only a short window of opportunity in which they can enjoy their stay without losing themselves.

For Reizenstein, the particular vice of New Orleans seems to be birthed from the landscape itself. The city is "the palmetto boudoir of Louisiana, with its poisonous miasma" (420), and its surrounding swamp consists of "crippled palmettos instead of stately, feathered palms, and sick giants of a lost time instead of a forest primeval" (168). Despite all the sickliness of the flora and the poisonousness of the air, however, there is still a seductiveness to the city: "New Orleans is the tree with the forbidden fruit; here the old snake extends its three-forked tongue as far as the Gulf shore and licks its frothy waves. Here life and death dance continuously with each another, each inking into the other's arms. Whoever has not yet seen sin, come hither!" (3–4).

What follows is a remarkable tour de force into the "hiding places and dens of vice" (47). Readers of the novel will encounter crossdressers and homosexuals, thieves and murderers, prostitutes and madams, all represented unsentimentally as a matter of fact. Furthermore, like the European and American naturalists who will come after him, Reizenstein does not simply present this decadent picture for pure titillation; there is also an epistemological motivation: "Vice, when painted in its nakedness, leads to a knowledge of human beings; mere allusion and gentle veiling leads to confusion" (48).

Reizenstein explores the knowledge that naked vice affords through the context of transatlantic exchange. He writes of the city, "Here the nations buzzed together like an anthill. Black, yellow, white, brown, and red families—all colors mingled together like a colorful mosaic" (19). The people coming together in nineteenth-century New Orleans—their bodies, their languages, and their literatures—do not enter the mix as equals, of course, so Reizenstein's decision to figure the city as an anthill begs close reading. To begin, Reizenstein does not describe the mixing of language as a babel of voices; he does not hear multilinguistic or even heteroglossic sound, nor does he hear the complex language game by which pidgin evolves into creole. Instead, he hears a *buzzing* of nations, a buzzing sans lingua, a nonhuman noise without tongue. A buzzing is, after all, a single sound repeated with varying degrees of frequency, and one, at least from the perspective of the outsider, with questionable communication between individuals. Like the rattler of the snake or the hum of the hornet's nest, the buzz of nations may be prefiguring disaster. So Reizenstein's readers can read the image in very different ways. On the one hand, the anthill can signify the epitome of uniformity, happy harmony, and efficiency, but on the other hand, the image can also generate a more violent interpretation. Ants, the most Spartan of insects, wield hidden weapons.

Even among the Europeans, there is cultural and linguistic conflict. Consider the marriage of the German Albert and the French Claudine. "Although he spoke excellent French," Reizenstein writes of Albert, "he usually failed to strike on the most spirited phrases" (30). The lesson of this linguistic dissonance, for the novelist, is the following: "It is extraordinarily rare for spouses to be happy when they do not speak the same language. They normally function as little more than automata on public display, bound together by an arbitrary contract, and the children of such parents are always odd, at best traitors to their national self-awareness" (31). What Reizenstein does not exactly spell out here is that linguistic difference is not the only problem in the marriage. Indeed, the bigger issue is that Claudine is a lesbian living in New Orleans—a lesbian, that is, living in her natural habitat—and she is in love with a woman named Orleana.[12]

As Reizenstein describes in great detail, the buzzing together of nations follows strict codes, both temporally and geographically. The organization of time—especially creating an irrefutable mark between day and night—is an absolute necessity in a place where the biopolitical distinction between slave and free always teeters on the edge of catastrophe. "The Negro cannon," Reizenstein reports, "fired at eight o'clock during the winter months, signaling the white race's monopoly of the streets of New Orleans from this hour on, had always ordered home all slaves who did not have written permission from their master to remain away" (61).

If time is organized clearly to police the line between free and unfree, spatial distinctions are more complex. On the upriver side of Canal Street, Reizenstein identifies the St. Charles Hotel as "the crucible of speculation and politics of the American portion of our population" (60). Like the French and creoles of color, the German immigrant is not especially drawn to this area, writing, "There is nothing here for the romantic, who must direct his steps to the streets of the French District, where people play *Domino à la poudre* and where the color line is not so strictly observed" (61).

Canal Street marks the separation between the First and Second districts, the Anglo-Saxon and the French. "In the Second District," Reizenstein reveals, "the skin color grows browner, the hair shinier, the eyes darker and more curious, the necks shorter and fuller, the noses shorter, and (since elegance and gallantry have brought chewing tobacco into discredit) the teeth whiter" (379). The Third district is farther downriver. "In this district," Reizenstein writes, "live most of the pale chino cholas, whose deadly qualities are well known to any denizen of New Orleans. Most women of this coloration are free, since they are useless to their masters as slaves and they have a dreadful effect on children entrusted to their care" (380).

The most sensual of all the beings that populate this novel are, unsurprisingly, the characters descended from Africa. The German baron seems especially captivated by "the untrammeled frivolity of African beauties, who boldly leap over the boundaries of decency set by civilization and innocent nature, drowning in the white-hot steam of a throbbing volcano of sensuality" (48). In one of the most remarkable passages in the novel, Reizenstein attempts a full classification of all these persons of color in the city. To illustrate the vastness of the vocabulary, the sheer aspiration for completeness, Reizenstein writes:

A zambo Negro is the offspring of a Negro and a female mulatto. A *zambo negresse* is the *non plus ultra*, a ragingly insatiable sensual being. Owing to the crossing of the colored blood, one can call a *zambo negresse* "man-crazy" with emphasis. The other shadings vary in sensuality according to the following sequence: *zambo,* resulting from the impregnation of an Indian woman by a Negro; *mulatto,* the child of a white man and a Negro woman; *dark mulatto,* the child of a Negro and a mestiza; *mestizo,* the child of a white and an Indian woman (also possible with a colored quinteroon—otherwise a pale mestizo); *chino,* the child of an Indian and a Negro woman; *copperchino,* through colored inheritance on the male side; *quadroon,* the child of a white man and a female mulatto; *zambo chino,* the child of a Negro and a chino woman; *pale chino zambo,* unnatural coloration of the dominant shade; Creole (in its colored variety), the child of a white man and a mestiza; *black mulatto,* the child of a Negro and a quinteroon; *dark chino,* produced by the impregnation of a mulatto woman by an Indian of good race; *dark zamba,* the child of a mulatto woman and a zamba; *chino chola,* child of an Indian and a chino; and *pale chino zambo chola,* a colored creation with the dreadful confusion of species (a pitiful race). (236–237)

It is difficult to know the extent to which these terms were actually used in New Orleans in 1853 and how exactly they were being translated from one language to another at the time. After all, Reizenstein immigrated from Germany only a couple of years before writing *The Mysteries,* and readers have a right to question the true scope of his knowledge of the city. But this passage is astounding on a number of levels, especially in contrast to the era after the *Plessy v. Ferguson* decision of 1896, during which New Orleans was divided neatly into black and not-black.

What marks the passage is Reizenstein's attempt to bring a Linnaean order, a fully developed classificatory system, to a chaos of bodies. On the one hand, the passage dramatizes the dangers of doing so. Classificatory systems are never innocent but instead are symptomatic of precise modes of valuation and devaluation of the entities under consideration. But, on the other hand, the passage dramatizes the limits of such a classificatory system. Perhaps against the will of the author, here is a system of signs—almost a self-contained language, with one sign referring to the others—that cannot maintain the logic it purports to represent. Here is a system of signs that is on the verge of breaking down under the pressure of its own obsessive weight.

Speaking of Merlina, the madam of a particularly perverse brothel, Reizenstein writes, "Despite the animalistic formation of her face, this female *zambo negresse* could still be called beautiful. It is not just symmetry of members, or pure harmony of facial features, but also the violent bestiality of a predator which is beautiful—even if only animalistically beautiful, or devilishly beautiful!" (242). The "zambo negresse," the female offspring of a native mother and an African father, represents for Reizenstein the creolized New Orleanian body par excellence. The coming together of transatlantic bodies yields a beautiful viciousness. On the one hand, those bodies may be considered inferior or bastardized copies of some imagined ideal, but on the other hand, those bodies may be considered *decadent* in the fullest sense of the term.

Despite Reizenstein's figuration of Africans, especially beautiful African women, as more animalistic than their European counterparts, the author does insist throughout the novel on the fundamental injustice of slavery and racial oppression. In fact, *The Mysteries* should be considered alongside the other, more famous abolitionist novels of the antebellum period. In one passage in particular, Reizenstein compares New Orleans to that other port city, Venice, and the debilitating effects that slavery has had on one but not the other. Reizenstein argues:

What Venice was in its days of glory, New Orleans would long since have become—the queen of the seas, the monopolist of world trade. The merchant of Venice would be just as much at home here as he once was in the city on the lagoons. There is no lack of Shylocks, with the sole difference being that the Shylocks here are not Jews but orthodox Christians who thirst not just for their pound of flesh but for whole shiploads. Yes, New Orleans would long since have become a Venice if an invisible hand had not punished it in many a year for a crime that meanness and selfishness has held to be a necessary evil. (193)

At the heart of Reizenstein's *Mysteries* is a prophecy. For a city so focused on the crimes and glories of the past, such a preoccupation with the future is unusual in the literary history of the city. A black messiah will arrive as the American Toussaint L'Ouverture and will liberate the descendants of Africa through apocalyptic and magical violence in the year 1871—that is, seventeen years after the novel was being published. This messiah slouches not from Bethlehem but from the base of the Red River, where a decadent German impregnates a mulatto prostitute. This locale, the Red River in Louisiana, is coincidentally the setting of Solomon Northup's autobiography *Twelve Years a Slave,* which appeared in 1853, the same year as *Mysteries.* This German character, Emile, is in possession of a "mythological nudity," repeated twice in Reizenstein's text (457, 464). He "was pretty," Reizenstein writes. "Perhaps too pretty for a man" (18).

What stands out in these descriptions is Emile's decadence; his character twists and turns spectacularly from the image of the ideal citizen. In this vein, Reizenstein philosophizes:

True beauty always deserves our wonder, whether it gleams from a woman or a man. It's all the same. Whether it is a whim or a perversity of Mother Nature, she bestows her full gifts only on those who are regarded in social life as decadents and ne'er-do-wells, who waste their lives wandering from one day to the next in careless indifference. Who has ever seen a beautiful banker, a beautiful grocer, a beautiful established citizen, a beautiful newspaper editor, and so on? Certainly no one. (18)

Decadence in Reizenstein's *The Mysteries of New Orleans* emerges as a transatlantic phenomenon, in stark relief to the economical and profitable business of slavery and racial oppression. And yet decadence cannot maintain axiological certainty; its value will always prove relative. The decadent characters exhibit a "careless indifference" to the world even if they are generating the only hope amidst the vast hopelessness in New Orleans during the 1850s. Their value, both aesthetic and political, stems from their animalistic beauty, creolized deformity, or egomaniacal aloofness. As both symptom and cure, these characters become emblematic of the decadence of the city itself and form part of the *longue durée* of the city's three-hundred-year literary history.

Reizenstein's themes will be evolved into George Washington Cable's *The Grandissimes* (1880), Kate Chopin's *The Awakening* (1899), Nelson Algren's *A Walk on the Wild Side* (1956), and Michael Ondaatje's *Coming Through Slaughter* (1976), to name just a few of the most famous novels. According to Reizenstein, "It is an indubitable mathematical truth, established according to the reasoning of a human erotic, that wherever the highest moral decadence has marked the character, there the spirit also has its greatest triumph" (287). New Orleans decadence, for Reizenstein and for many other writers who come after him, ought not be read simply as decline, or even *beautiful* decline, but as the city's greatest triumph, the city's most expressive form of life and vitality, especially in the face of some *other* threat. That other threat changes, of course, with each new generation, with different writers of the same generation, and with the same writer at different moments of life. But the fact of decadence as having some sort of salvation often remains, in one form or another.

THE WAR

Reizenstein's text works as a counterpoint to the white supremacist dreams of the future that were circulating privately and publicly in New Orleans in the 1850s, when there was still hope that slavery's future would be secured, that the South would win the war of ideas and its beliefs would be vindicated. The real war began, however, and the capture of Confederate New Orleans came relatively quickly, in April 1862. Seventeen-year-old George Washington Cable, himself a "blasé" Confederate soldier in training in New Orleans at the time (415), witnessed the events and published his experience later, as an adult, in "New Orleans Before the Capture" (1885).

In that text, he writes of the condition of the city between secession and fall. In the South's mad dash to maintain its oppressive autonomy at any cost, New Orleans teetered on economic collapse, with Confederate currency rendered virtually useless. "Decay had come in," Cable writes of the period. "In that warm, moist climate it is always hungry," he continues, "and wherever it is allowed to feed, eats with a greed that is strange to see" (417). The human population was thrown into sheer chaos after the Union captured the city, according to Cable's recollections: "You have seen, perhaps, a family fleeing with lamentations and wringing of hands out of a burning house; multiply it by thousands upon thousands; that was New Orleans, though the houses were not burning" (418).

A ten-year-old Grace King likewise witnessed the events of 1862 firsthand and published her account, later in life, as *Memories of a Southern Woman of Letters* (1932). "Alarm bells were ringing all over the city," King writes, describing the "enemy" invasion. She continues with her narration of the chaos: "Crowds were running through the streets below, shouting and screaming. The flames would die down every now and then, only to start up fiercer than ever, lighting up the heavens." The young King is terrified; the sights and sounds of the capture cause her imagination to run wild: "Will they kill us all when they take the city, I wondered vaguely, recalling pictures of captured cities of the Bible, where men and women were cut through with spears and swords, and children were dashed against the walls" (38).

None of this biblical destruction came to pass, of course. Like many New Orleanians of means, King's family escaped the city and lived for the remaining four years of the war on their plantation in rural Louisiana. Despite the relative well-being of her family, however, the fall of New Orleans was nonetheless a momentous event for King. It was a sign of abject failure, a shattering of morale and morality, a descent into deep decline without a flicker of hope. History turned that day as a vast agent of destruction came to the city in the form of a beast slouching from the North, named Benjamin Butler, and his Union troops.

Three years after Cable and King witnessed the Union troops taking the city of New Orleans in 1862, and a few months after the Confederacy throughout the South finally failed and the bloodiest war on American soil came to its official end in the spring of 1865, a poem appeared in *La Tribune*, the city's black newspaper, on September 24.[13] Signed with only the first name Henry, the poem is called "La rebellion du sud en permanence [The South's Permanent Revolt]." Henry begins by stating that his poem is being written in response to a friend who has asked if his poetic muse is silent. "Oui," he says, "ma muse est muette en ces jours d'epouvante" (90). Yes, he says, his muse is mute in these days of terror. Henry knows that those in power and in profit do not give up so easily. King Cotton and the institution of slavery, oppression and exploitation, will not fade so easily into the past. The rebellion against equal rights and a biracial government was *en permanence*.

Henry ends his poem:

> Voilà pourquoi ma muse est muette et violée,
> Car elle pressent bien plus d'un nouveau combat,
> Et l'esperérance, ami, de son sein envolée,
> La laisse morne et triste, et son destin l'abat.
> Quoi qu'on fasse, mon luth ne peut vibrer de rage,
> Il prêche la concorde et la fraternité;
> Aux opprimés il dit: Frères, debout, courage,
> L'heure est près de sonner, sauvez la liberté! (92)

> This is why my muse is mute and violated,
> Because she strongly senses more of a new combat,
> And the hope, friend, from her breast has taken flight,
> Leaving her dreary and sad, and her destiny cut down.
> Whatever you do, my lute cannot be stirred from rage,

He preaches concord and fraternity;
To the oppressed he says: Brothers, stand up, courage,
The hour is nearly sounding; keep liberty safe!

Henry is saying that in times of social catastrophe—in times of decline, regress, utter horror—the literary muse goes silent, and yet his very literary production evidences the opposite. The muse may go silent, but the lute continues to call out.

The subject of the first four lines of the stanza, internally connected through the *abab* rhyme scheme, is the *muse*, gendered as feminine in the French language. This muse is mute, silent, and *violée;* she is violated morally and sexually, desecrated, raped. The muse in trauma, uneasiness, and anxious fear of the future, cannot maintain hope; her destiny is *l'abat*, shot down, destroyed, slaughtered. The subject of the stanza then switches to the masculine *luth*. This switch in the stanza also involves a shift from person metaphor (muse) to thing metaphor (luth), from human to instrument, from mythical anthropos to practical tool. The rhyming words in French also shift, moving from *rage* to *courage*, from *fraternité* to *liberté*, as if to tell an inspirational story of transformation in the city. But the poem, written by a man whose identity is only partially disclosed, and addressed to an unnamed friend, cannot encourage publicly, or not fully publicly, in the face of the catastrophe, a catastrophe *en permanence* that is social and political, of course, but that is also deeply bodily, linguistic, and literary. As the war ends and as other battles grow within the city itself, as the fin de siècle draws nearer, what will the writers do? How will they respond to the decline, the rot, the disintegration?

4

THE CIVIL WAR TO THE
FIN DE SIÈCLE, 1865 TO 1900

Ce sont de vieux Français; ils font vingt fois le tour
Du jardin, le regard noyé de rêverie,
Heureux de retrouver vaguement la patrie
Dans ces illusions d'un lointain souvenir.

These are the old Frenchmen; they go twenty times around
The garden, the glance drowning in dream,
Happy to retrieve vaguely the fatherland
In these illusions of a remote memory.

—GEORGE DESSOMMES, "Un Soir au Jackson Square
[An Evening in Jackson Square]" (1880), 54

In George Dessommes's "Un Soir au Jackson Square," the poem's narrator sets off alone after dinner to stroll in the small public park at the city center. In front of St. Louis Cathedral, he encounters characters of all sorts—young and old, rich and poor, black and white, drunk and sober—but it is the old Frenchmen whom the poet finds the most remarkable. They walk in circles around the square in a kind of haze, caught in their minds between the past and the present, all the while at home in neither. They amble "au milieu des promeneurs joyeux," in the midst of joyous walkers, but unlike these other people they are "muets et seuls," mute and alone (54). These old Frenchman are:

Flétris par la misère et l'exil, sans familles,
Mal vêtus, mais gardant encore sous leurs guenilles
La dignité des jours meilleurs, morts sans retour. (54)

Withered by misery and exile, without families,
Poorly dressed, but still keeping under tattered garments
The dignity of better days, dead without return.

As flâneur or romantic isolato capable of seeing without being seen, the young male poet, who would have been in his midtwenties when the poem appeared, in 1880, strolls out in health after a nourishing dinner to witness the physical and mental deterioration of the old Frenchmen. What he sees is a form of decadence, a beauty in decay, that rises and falls across the city's three-hundred-year life span. Unable or unwilling to speak, the poor souls the poet sees can only live miserably in the past. Because they have no connection to others and they have produced no offspring, they have no ontological claim on the present and future. Like smoke, their very essence is being erased from the endlessly unfolding story of New Orleans, and their bodily forms are quietly dissolving into thin air. Their misery is all the more exaggerated by the happy families that surround them, characters enjoying the bliss of the present and the pull of the future.

At the center of "Un Soir au Jackson Square" is the drama of historical change understood as a progressive transformation from one epoch to the always more modern next, and the decadence that seems to come necessarily with that transformation. Some of the figures represent the vanguard of this transformation: the young and the healthy, participating together in the public square. Other figures represent what remains, what is left over in this epochal shift: the old Frenchmen, withering and sickly, out of place and out of time, yet lingering on still. The poet, for Dessommes, is there to witness these figures in the transformation from one epoch to the next, to walk invisibly among them, and to sit quietly in judgment.

The title of the poem is the first hint at this epochal transformation, beginning as it does with the French "Un Soir au" and ending with the English "Jackson Square." In 1880, when the poem appeared, Dessommes could no longer use the former place name, the French Place d'Armes, or even the Spanish Plaza de Armas. He must use the English place name in currency, Jackson Square, commemorating the American military general Andrew Jackson, who fended off a British invasion in 1815, during the Battle of New Orleans. The linguistic shift from French to English that for Dessommes occurs in the waning hours of daylight—a temporality so central to the decadent imagination—also signifies a political shift in the city. As the day draws to a close, the old Frenchmen not only end up lost in an Anglophone world but also are left literally revolving around the statue of an *Américain*, the wartime hero and seventh president of the United States, Andrew Jackson.

The poem concludes with a turn from the third person to the second person plural, a turn from the poet talking about the old Frenchmen to addressing them directly:

> Pauvre gens! tout-à-l'heure il faudra revenir
> A la réalité sinistre de la vie;
> Mais dans votre âme, au spleen quelques instants ravie,
> —Au fond du gite obscure où vous vous abritez,—
> Pour cette nuit, malgré le faim, vous emportez
> Un éclair d'allégresse, un rayon d'espérance,
> Ce rêve inoubliable et sacré de la France. (54)

> Poor men! soon they will have to return
> To the sinister reality of life;
> But in your soul, that escaped from your melancholy for an instant,
> —Deep in the obscure refuge where you have found shelter,—
> For this night, in spite of your hunger, you carry
> A flash of happiness, a ray of hope,
> This dream unforgettable and sacred of France.

Dessommes's miserable exiles are suspended in a kind of temporal and spatial limbo, neither here nor there, neither now nor then, caught between illusion and reality, between dreaming and waking life. The only upshot, the only possibility of escape that Dessommes offers them, is their dream of France. He does not offer them France exactly, it is important to stress, but the *dream* of France.

Why can they not go back to the genetic and linguistic source? Why must France remain merely a dream? For at least political reasons, which Dessommes does not disclose in the poem, these old Frenchmen could not really return to the homeland to protect their withering bodies and languages. Because France, like the United States at the time, was itself deeply in the throes of bloody division, the European nation could not possibly offer what the old Frenchmen sought. It could not offer them stability, safe retreat, and sanctuary. They are left, then, with nothing more than a flash of hope inspired by an imaginary object of comfort.

In the second person plural, the twenty-five-year-old Dessommes directly addresses his audience, which presumably consists of Francophone men of a certain age and class, men who read the *Comptes-rendus de l'Athénée louisianais*, the journal where the poem appeared. Edited by Alfred Mercier, who would have been in his midsixties at the time, this journal was the lifeline of the New Orleanian French literary elite, but one also beginning to enter into its own twilight. Dessommes's imagined audience, moreover, consists of men not only of a certain age and class but also of a certain race: white Francophone men. His subject, as well as his audience, in other words, does not include the many Francophone creoles of color, men and women who were facing a loss more profound than that of the old Frenchmen he sees circling the square in increasingly enfeebled form.

The Francophone creoles, marked by the "shadow of the Ethiopian," had much more to lament, in fact, than their white counterparts circling in Dessommes's poem.[1] Their profound difficulties included the weakening of their educational systems, the pushback against their voting rights, the violent overthrow of their participation in the new and biracial government, and their agonizing decisions to leave the city to escape from these oppressive conditions. The loss of their major newspaper, the dual-language *Tribune de la Nouvelle-Orleans*, was an especially hard cultural blow. According to literary historian Anna Brickhouse, the loss of this newspaper, the first African American daily newspaper in the United States, signaled a distinctly political loss, a loss of the "discourse of critical internationalism [and] a model for political alliance beyond the boundaries of national statehood" ("L'Ouragan" 1109).[2] Unlike these Francophone creoles of color, the old Frenchmen that Dessommes sees and addresses in his poem were all free before the Civil War and continued to be free after. They also had their whiteness as a vital asset, both before and after the war, in the face of explosive social relations, domestic terrorism, political oppression, and extrajudicial killings.[3]

George Dessommes was a white New Orleanian lamenting a major shift that was occurring in the tumultuous period after the Civil War. Some of these white Francophone writers found solidarity in a shared vulnerability with other previously oppressed groups. The trilingual Adrien Rouquette, who channels Chateaubriand's romanticism in *La Nouvelle Atala* (1879) and other important works, for example, found compatriots in the Choctaw Nation and lived among the Choctaw in the Bayou St. John area of New Orleans and on the north shore of Lake Pontchartrain. Alfred Mercier, like Rouquette, also presented an unflinching indictment of racism and the plantation system of exploitation, in *L'Habitation Saint-Ybars* (1881).[4]

Many others, of course, chose not sympathy and political affiliation but a very different path, aiming instead to join the larger world of unmarked white Americans and to take advantage of all the rights and protections afforded by that distinction. This different path, however, was not a straightforward one. Indeed, the legal history of the French language in the Louisiana constitution, summed up in the next chapter, shows the stumbling nature of this endeavor to achieve equal footing as unmarked white Americans.

When Dessommes writes that the human subjects of his poem, as well as his audience of white Frenchmen, must return to "la réalité sinistre de la vie," what reality does he mean exactly? Does he mean the explosive social relations that came with warfare and reconstruction? Is this the sinister reality of life to which they must return? Or is the sinister reality, for them, a loss of their own power, a loss of their youth and vigor, their wealth, their physical and mental health, their capacity to dominate? What is the cause of their poetic decline, their spectacular torture performed for all to see in the most public of public spaces in the dead center of New Orleans? Surely, Dessommes's is not a simple poem of growing older, of aging human bodies and minds caught equally in the progressive throes of time. There must be an identifiable source of the old Frenchmen's particular pain. In the poem, these crucial etiological questions go unanswered. Yet they seem to linger, haunt, and help shape the complex aura surrounding decadence in the city.

Dessommes's poetic vision of old and childless men walking around in circles, dreaming in foreign languages about other times and places fading now into memory, plays into a larger myth, so precious and useful, of French decadence in New Orleans. Weakness and strength, after all, are not unambiguous opposites, for weakness and its associates—vulnerability, debility, incapacity—may enact power in its fullest form, especially when feigned and performed in spectacular contexts. For this reason, the myth of French decadence in New Orleans, the narrative of the decline and fall of a people who are always on the verge of taking their last gasps of life, has a remarkable ability to survive. It is a death story that refuses to die. Perhaps this is part of the reason why the city seems so conducive to housing the fictional dead and undead, beings who push through the natural limits of the biological life cycle and who remain always tethered to some state of thanatological limbo but cultivating a power of their own. In the remainder of this chapter, I trace Dessommes's brand of decadence as it is translated from French into English by two of the city's most famous nineteenth-century writers: George Washington Cable and Lafcadio Hearn. I end with a discussion of endings at the fin de siècle.

GEORGE WASHINGTON CABLE

At the very beginning of George Washington Cable's *The Grandissimes* (1880), an immigrant family arrives on the coast of Louisiana and travels upriver along the Mississippi to New Orleans. In describing the ascent of the Frowenfelds, Cable foregrounds the threatening nature of this "land hung in mourning, darkened by gigantic cypresses, submerged; a land of reptiles, silence, shadow, decay" (9). The environment not only impinges on the senses and imagination; it also literally enters the immigrants' bodies as they are bitten by the swarming mosquitoes and become infected with the virus that causes yellow fever. If the deltaic plain appeared as an external threat before, it now bores into their bodies and proves its capacity to kill. The German immigrants become sick and they all die, except for the young Joseph. Left alone in an unknown land, Joseph Frowenfeld must fend for himself, and as an outsider, he becomes Cable's objective commentator on the city in its particular place and time.

Set in the early nineteenth century, just after the Louisiana Purchase of 1803, the novel revolves around the troubling story of the creole Grandissimes family. At the center of their story are two half brothers, one white and one black, who share a name and a father but whose different mothers set their racial fate. On one side of the Atlantic, while being educated in Paris, they are truly brothers, and the white Grandissimes brother extends affiliation and affinity to his darker kin. On the other side of the ocean, however, while establishing themselves as adults in the socioeconomic world of New Orleans, they are categorically different. They may still be kin, but they are no longer kind. Cable writes of the white brother, "Returned to Louisiana, accepting, with the amiable, old-fashioned philosophy of conservatism, the sins of the community, he had forgotten the unchampioned rights of his passive half-brother" (279). As in Antoine-François Prévost's *Manon Lescaut*, Marc-Antoine Caillot's *Relation du voyage*, and many other texts, the transatlantic move from Paris to New Orleans involves a kind of moral degeneration, an ethical decay, among other kinds of falls. Here, specifically, the moral degeneration happens when the white sibling loses his capacity to recognize the equal political subjectivity of his black counterpart.

Cable describes the moment Joseph Frowenfeld, the German immigrant to New Orleans, lays eyes on the black Grandissimes brother, "a man who seemed, in some respects, the most remarkable figure he had yet seen in this little city of strange people" (41). Cable continues with a lengthy description of the man's appearance:

> A strong, clear, olive complexion; features that were faultless (unless a woman-like delicacy, that was yet not effeminate, was a fault); hair *en queue*, the handsomer for its premature streakings of gray; a tall, well knit form, attired in cloth, linen and leather of the utmost fineness; manners Castilian, with a gravity almost oriental—made him one of those rare masculine figures which, on the public promenade, men look back at and ladies inquire about. (41–42)

Cable's description radiates out from the man's face to include his hair, attire, and bodily movements. These attributes hover between male and female, and they are attractive to both. When the man signs the name Grandissimes as his own, Frowenfeld is shocked to read on the paper "what the universal mind esteemed the synonym of enterprise and activity" (42). Even though Grandissimes is a wealthy rentier, he does not or cannot live up to his name's reputation. A character prone to melancholy, he falls in love with a woman who loves his white brother, and he ultimately commits suicide. Such an unfortunate character, and one who carries all the negative marks of decadence with little of its redeeming qualities, will cause Charles Chesnutt to revise this tragic figure in *Paul Marchand, F.M.C.* (1921).[5]

The Grandissimes family and its genealogical vicissitudes brings into relief the narrative of decadence and progress in the context of New Orleans. Some family members are described as strong, others as increasingly enfeebled. One cousin, for example, is described as "a rather poor specimen of the Grandissimes type," insinuating that their breeding is not as flawless as they pretend (100). Playing the role of authoritative scientist, Dr. Keene says:

> They are an old, illustrious line, and the strength that was once in the intellect and will is going down into the muscles. I have an idea that their greatness began, hundreds of years ago, in ponderosity of arm—of frame, say—and developed from generation to generation, in a rising scale, first into fineness of sinew, then, we will say, into force of will, then into power of mind, then into subtleties of genius. Now they are going back down the incline. (101)

Dr. Keene presents a concise narrative of the Grandissimes family as they have progressed from physical to mental fitness over multiple generations, but a family's biological fitness cannot rise forever, he suggests. The Grandissimes's story has reached a turning point, the action is falling, and their denouement inevitable.

If Cable's understanding of beautiful decline wraps around the New Orleanian bodies he narrates in his novel, it also relates to the languages used and the literatures developed in the city. Six years after *The Grandissimes* was published in 1880, Cable's transcription and translation of "Creole Slave Songs" appeared in *The Century Magazine*. Cable's work in this important text, as well as Lafcadio Hearn's in his writings on the New Orleanian patois, corresponds to a prominent trend in the literary history of New Orleans—the profound interest in folk language and literature—that came in the wake of the Civil War and, especially, the publication of the monumental *Slave Songs of the United States* in 1867. When Cable's "Creole Slave Songs" appeared, it followed from and reinforced the assumptions, aims, and methods crystallized, if not altogether inaugurated, by the editors of *Slave Songs* two decades before. What were those assumptions, aims, and methods, and how did they fit into the paradox of progress and decadence in the New Orleanian contact zone?

When *Slave Songs of the United States* was published, it contained seven songs that were from Louisiana, out of 136 in total. Unlike most of the other songs collected after the Civil War, the ones from Louisiana were not sung in English, and they did not take Scripture as their primary subject. Instead, they were secular in nature and were sung in the vernacular creole of the Good Hope Plantation, located about twenty-five miles west of the French Quarter, along the east bank of the Mississippi River, in what is now the town of Norco. Along with the musical scores, the lyrics of the seven songs were transcribed in the volume in their original form, without English translation.

In their introduction, the three editors of the volume—William Francis Allen, Charles Pickard Ware, and Lucy McKim Garrison—declare that the moral imperative at the heart of their project is historical preservation, because these songs "should not be forgotten and lost." They write, "These relics of a state of society which has passed away should be preserved while it is still possible." The editors, furthermore, foreground the authenticity of the songs they have located and preserved by specifying the body part and race from which the songs emanate: "The music here presented has been taken down by the editors from the lips of the colored people themselves" (iii).

In the songs of "these half-barbarous people," the editors find two opposing elements or rhythms (ii). One rhythm, the "chief part," they write, "is *civilized* in its character—partly composed under the influence or association with the whites, partly actually imitated from their music" (vi, emphasis in original). The other rhythm, the "barbaric element," reverberates across the Atlantic from its source on the African continent (vii). What makes the slave songs so significant, what gives them their value for the editors, is this ontological duality, their uncanny ability to shift between their two continental rhythms and to synthesize them into a single and unique sound on American soil.

Far from denigrating the linguistic aptitude of the race, the editors of *Slave Songs* in fact go to the opposite extreme and aim to document the special "musical genius" of people descended from Africa (i). "The negroes keep exquisite time in singing," they write, "and do not suffer themselves to be daunted by any obstacle in the words." They continue, "The most obstinate Scripture phrases or snatches from hymns they

83

will force to do duty with any tune they please, and will dash heroically through a trochaic tune at the head of a column of iambs with wonderful skill" (iv). For the editors, black oral talent exceeds expectations when the mouth is literally free to open and the black voice is free to ring out, always in tune, with some glorious musical power. The most complicated linguistic utterance is no match for the black tongue.

On the one hand, editors Allen, Ware, and Garrison are performing the essential work of recuperating black literary aesthetics, wresting it from the racist logic by which black literary production is deemed indecent, as a perverse agent of decline in language, both English and French, as inappropriate company in the canon. And yet their way into this work, this recuperative evaluation, is through the orality of the people, the sound of black musicality. One assumption of this work is that black talent excels the most, is the most aesthetically advanced, in the realm of oral and aural musicality. Black talent is at its most true when it moves from the oral to the aural, from the mouth to the ear.

But there is a double bind here in which the black artist whose medium is primarily language is caught. The black literary artist is black and true to the extent that he or she works against the grain of writing, for it is writing that institutes calcification, dissipation, and death. The true mark of black genius thus would not reside in the New Orleanian poets of *Les Cenelles* writing in proper French, imitating a language and literary aesthetics that is supposedly not their own, but in the black singer and animated storyteller of the plantation. The benefits of the volume, in other words, may also have unintended costs, perhaps most significantly the active forgetting of the poets who were working in writing, silently in the printed field of language, because these individuals carried with them a suspect authenticity.

In "Creole Slave Songs" (1886), Cable seems to follow the trajectory established almost two decades before in *Slave Songs.*[6] For Cable, the creole language forms in the contact zone "wherever the black man and the French language are met" (807). To put Cable's claim another way, the creole language comes to be when the African body, whose own language is not specified, meets European language, whose body is elided. This ontological situation generates axiological ambiguity, and thus the creole language will have value, but that value will always be suspect and will require much qualification. The creole language, Cable writes, "is not merely bad or broken French; it is the natural result from the effort of a savage people to take up the language of an old and highly refined civilization, and is much more than a jargon" (807). Notice the arrangement of the three claims Cable makes here. Between the two positive evaluations of the language, which bookend the passage—i.e., the creole language is not "bad or broken" and it is "more than a jargon"—Cable inserts the mark of language's debasement. It is an *effort* on the part of the lowly African to attain the civilized nature of Europeans, one of the good things to come of the horrors of the transatlantic slave trade.

Cable continues with his linguistic narrative and claims that the supposedly easygoing natures of the African slaves, as well as of their French owners, relaxed in "the languorous climate of the Gulf," brought this new creole language into existence. Cable concludes with a final evaluation of the language: "Its growth entirely by ear where there were so many more African ears than French tongues, and when those tongues had so many Gallic archaisms which they were glad to give away and get rid of, resulted in a broad grotesqueness all its own" (807). A linguistic miscegenation that unevenly favors black ears over white and careless tongues yields something grotesque for Cable, but that grotesque language nonetheless deserves meticulous preservation and dedicated admiration.

LAFCADIO HEARN

Like George Washington Cable, Lafcadio Hearn comes to the creole language and literary expression of New Orleans with many of the same assumptions, aims, and methods that are operative in *Slave Songs*. He assumes that what has been devalued historically ought to be valued highly instead, he wants to preserve that valuable body of work for future generations, and he does so through careful transcription and translation from the authentic speakers of the language.[7] Unlike Cable, however, Hearn's extraordinary multilingualism allows him to approach his subject with much more complexity than does Cable, not only in the texts that specifically address creole but also in the novel *Chita* (1889) and his other writings. Hearn's background in Greek, English, French, and Chinese before his arrival in New Orleans; his thinking in non-English languages while residing in the city, such as his translation of Théophile Gautier's decadent short stories for an 1882 publication; his researches into Senegambian language and culture; and his study of Native American folklore all bear on his work.[8] His texts exhibit extraordinary philosophical and cultural range, and they also show complexity on every linguistic level: phonologically (in the sounds contained in words), morphologically (in the words themselves), and syntactically (in the arrangement of words). Hearn's brand of literary production simply would not have been possible before the Civil War, and it certainly would not have been able to achieve the broad contemporary and subsequent acclaim that has elevated him to his status as one of the city's most gifted writers.

For Hearn, the novelty that New Orleans presents to the foreigner, the stranger in the city, is not really something new. It is instead the recollection of something from the deep past that surfaces, a kind of déjà vu, an uncanny experience in which familiarity is found in what was supposed to be exotic. In a November 1877 piece for the *Cincinnati Commercial* called "At the Gate of the Tropics," Hearn writes that the city of New Orleans "actually resembles no other city upon the face of the earth, yet it recalls vague memories of a hundred cities." He continues, "Whencesoever the traveler may have come, he may find in the Crescent City some memory of his home—some recollection of his Fatherland—some remembrance of something he loves" (670). Hearn repeats this claim a month later for the same Cincinnati newspaper, in "New Orleans in Wet Weather." Hearn asks, "I wonder whether something of the old pagan faith of the elder civilizations does not yet linger in our midst despite eighteen centuries of Christianity—something of a vague idea that the manes of the dead must be appeased by offering at the sepulcher?" (683).

In a seminal piece called "New Orleans," published in December 1877, again in the *Cincinnati Commercial*, Hearn theorizes about the process by which human bodies and languages come together in the transatlantic contact zone. "This strange blending of nations seems always productive of strange results," Hearn begins. He continues, "One would suppose, from comparing those results in various lands, that the more good blood is mixed, the more savage it becomes" (690–691). Goodness and savagery, of course, are always in the eye of the beholder, and not every observer will hold the same evaluation as human bodies from four continents intermingle sexually in the city of New Orleans.

In Cable's *The Grandissimes*, for example, the family patriarch and chief racist, Agricola Fusilier, "the aged high-priest of a doomed civilization" (324), illustrates a slightly different approach to the subject. For Agricola, any intermingling—social, political, affective, sexual— between European and African peoples is a sign of decline. It is a decadence understood in purely negative terms, a degradation of the white race. And yet the character proudly speaks French and Choctaw. His "most boasted ancestor," in fact, is a Tchoupitoulas princess named Lufki-Humma, who was born in 1673 and inhabited the land before the city became the city. Cable underscores this irony when he writes, "It appears the darkness of her cheek had no effect to make him less white, or qualify his right to smite the fairest and most distant descendant of an African on the face" (18). Agricola demonstrates the paradoxical effort of maintaining white supremacy even while admiring one's own native heritage as the historical cornerstone of one's strength.

Indeed, understanding this evaluation of transracial sex as the genetic incorporation of Native America—that paradoxical conjunction of nobility and savagery—into the civilized bloodline of the French, helps us to see the surprising choice, at least to me, of one of the city's and the state's most blatantly racist lobbies, the Choctaw Club of Louisiana, to adopt a native tribal name in 1896 as the mark of their affiliation. Believing that "the Indians had always been friends of the white man [and] blacks constituted a corrupting element in state politics," the white supremacist organization maintained transracial affiliation as long as that affiliation did not include people of African descent (Haas 21).[9]

Like human bodies, for Hearn, languages, too, register the surprising and decadent transvaluation of value in the New Orleanian contact zone. "The languid speaker of the patois simply declines to change the termination of his verb according to tense at all, and refuses to endure the tyranny of subjunctive or potential moods," Hearn suggests. Like Bartleby, who "would prefer not to," without any fuss, the creole speaker quietly "acknowledges only the primary tenses—past, present and future—and adapts these to all his wants, not perceiving the usefulness of the secondary tenses." The simplification of temporal complexity—expressed linguistically in the conjugations of verbs and presumably experienced phenomenologically in the speaker of the language as well—bastardizes the proper French from which it is formed. And yet, for Hearn, "there is certainly no European patois owning greater curiosities of construction, greater beauties of melody and rhythm than this Creole speech; there is no provincial dialect of the mother country wealthier in romantic tradition and ballad legends than this almost unwritten tongue of Louisiana" (694).

In "The Creole Patois," published in January 1885 in *Harper's Weekly*, Hearn continues to investigate the linguistic paradox of progress and decay in the city. Using self-consciously loaded imagery, he claims, "The creole patois is the offspring of linguistic miscegenation, an offspring which exhibits but a very faint shade of African color, and nevertheless possesses a strangely supple comeliness by virtue of the very intercrossing which created it, like a beautiful octoroon." Nowhere is the ontological and symbolic relationship between human language and the human body made more clearly. The story of the creole patois as linguistic type and octoroon as bodily type go hand in hand; their origins and fates are one. Always aware of the cognitive associations that come with certain words, especially words like *octoroon*, Hearn continues, "That word reminds one of a celebrated and vanished type" (746). The emergence of the word and its referent in human evolutionary history is but a fleeting moment. Just as quickly as it appears, it disappears.

Hearn's discussion of language as bodies moves quickly into a discussion of bodies as such. The passage is worth quoting in full, to see the way in which Hearn's logic moves from one paragraph to the next:

> Uncommonly tall were those famous beauties—citrine-hued, elegant of stature as palmettos, lithe as serpents; never again will such types re-appear upon American soil. Daughters of luxury, artificial human growths, never organized to enter the iron struggle for life unassisted and unprotected, they vanished forever with the social system which made them a place apart as for splendid plants reared within a conservatory. With the fall of American feudalism the dainty glass house was dashed to pieces; the species it contained have perished utterly; and whatever morality may have gained, one cannot help thinking that art has lost something by their extinction. What figures for designs for bronze! what tints for canvas!
>
> It is for similar reasons that the creole tongue must die in Louisiana; the great social change will eventually render it extinct. But there is yet time for the philologist to rescue some of its dying legends and curious lyrics, to collect and preserve them, like pressed blossoms, between the leaves of enduring books. (746–747)

Not only are Hearn's octoroons a distinct type, a variety of human bodily form, but also they seem to have achieved complete species differentiation. Hearn does not clearly identify the source of their speciation, the human violence perpetrated by white male slave owners against their black female slaves, but he does allude vaguely to the "social system" that made them. In the end, their extinction is an extraordinary aesthetic loss, an indisputable moral gain, and an occasion for the decadent preservationist to get to work.

In his approach to the octoroons of New Orleans, Hearn seems to be prefiguring the Transylvanian-Jewish-American Andrei Codrescu, theorist and practitioner of decadence. Codrescu, in "My City My

Wilderness" (1995), describes the "specific life-form" that is the New Orleanian as "a dreamy, lazy, sentimental, musical one, prey to hallucinations (not visions), tolerant, indolent, and gifted at storytelling." Counting himself one of these remarkable individuals, Codrescu continues, "We, and our ways, are marked for elimination; there is no room in an efficient future for what we embody" (135).

It bears repeating that this decadent drama of bodies, languages, and literatures takes place against the backdrop of the southern Louisiana landscape. The fragility of that environment is given life nowhere more fully than in Hearn's novel *Chita*. Revolving around the devastating hurricane of 1856, the novel paints a stunning picture of the storm, its effects on human, animal, and plant life, and its lingering traumas in the minds of those human beings who are forced to come to terms with its effects. The first sentence of the novel reads, "Traveling south from New Orleans to the Islands, you pass through a strange land into a strange sea, by various winding waterways." This sentence begins the liquid style and imagery of Hearn's novella, always on the brink of being swept away by the current, in the mood of languor, finding oneself "floating through sombre mazes of swamp-forest—past assemblages of cypresses all hoary with the parasitic tillandsia, and grotesque gatherings of fetich-gods" (77).

Hearn's description of the landscape does not relent; it does not let the reader go, as layer upon biological layer is piled up in the narrative: "The quaggy soil trembles to a sound like thunder of breakers on a coast: the storm-roar of billions of reptile voices chanting in cadence—rhythmically surging in stupendous *crescendo* and *diminuendo*—a monstrous and appalling chorus of frogs!" (77). One of the multiple climaxes of the narrative ends in this way: "And finally all the land melts down into desolations of sea-marsh, whose stillness is seldom broken, except by the melancholy cry of long-legged birds, and in wild seasons by that sound which shakes all shores when the weird Musician of the Sea touches the bass keys of his mighty organ." Besides all this biological fecundity, "the place is bleakly uninteresting," Hearn writes, "a wilderness of wind-swept grasses and sinewy weeds waving away from a thin beach ever speckled with drift and decaying things—worm-riddled timbers, dead porpoises" (79).

One of the earliest literary representations of coastal erosion in southeastern Louisiana may also be found in the novel. But, for Hearn, these representations are never objectively laid out; instead, they are full of subjective and affective complexity that follow from his decadent aesthetics. "On the Gulf side of these islands you may observe that the trees—when there are any trees—all bend away from the sea," Hearn writes, "and, even on bright, hot days when the wind sleeps, there is something grotesquely pathetic in their look of agonized terror." The author then identifies the cause of their agony and terror: "They are being pursued indeed—for the sea is devouring the land." Hearn describes the process in this way: "Forever the yellow Mississippi strives to build; forever the sea struggles to destroy—and amid their eternal strife the islands and the promontories change shape, more slowly, but not less fantastically, than the clouds of heaven" (81). Hearn continues:

> Year by year that rustling strip of green land grows narrower; the sand spreads and sinks, shuddering and wrinkling like a living brown skin; and the last standing corpses of the oaks, ever clinging with naked, dead feet to the sliding beach, lean more and more out of the perpendicular; as the sands subside, the stumps appear to creep; their inter-twisted masses of snakish roots seem to crawl, to writhe—like the reaching arms of cephalopods. (82)

Locked in a battle between creation and destruction, life and death, land and water, the Mississippi River and the Gulf of Mexico wage war on each other along the withered toe of Louisiana. The result is an environment constantly in flux, a wetlandscape that more resembles the moving sky than the stable earth.

In a scene reminiscent of Edgar Allan Poe's "The Masque of the Red Death" (1842), Hearn describes the horrifying moment when the hurricane of 1856 hits an island hotel housing four hundred occupants. Amidst the lavish decoration, amidst the expensive food and drinks and music and dancing, the revelers believe they can escape the enormous death agent that is the Gulf of Mexico. But the waters begin to rise nonetheless. "Someone shrieked in the midst of the revels," Hearn writes, "some girl who found her pretty slippers wet. What could it be? Thin streams of water were spreading over the level planking—curling about the feet of the dancers" (93). With the rising Gulf the chorus of human screams rises too: "Then rose a frightful cry—the hoarse, hideous, indescribable cry of hopeless fear—the dying animal-cry man utters when suddenly brought face to face with Nothingness, without preparation, without consolation, without possibility of respite" (94).

Of the very few survivors is a young girl discovered by rescuers, clutched in the arms of her dead mother. Her father is nowhere to be found, and she is too young to identify herself and where she comes from. Despite the rescuers' best efforts, "diligent inquiry and printed announcements alike proved fruitless" (114). The young girl's crisis is not hers alone. Like the other victims of the hurricane, she must suffer the aftermath in the form of erasure. Hearn writes:

> Sea and sand had either hidden or effaced all the records of the little world they had engulfed: the annihilation of whole families, the extinction of races, had, in more than one instance, rendered vain all efforts to recognize the dead. It required the subtle perception of long intimacy to name remains tumefied and discolored by corruption and exposure, mangled and gnawed by fishes, by reptiles, and by birds—it demanded the great courage of love to look upon the eyeless faces found sweltering in the blackness of cypress-shadows, under the low palmettos of the swamps—where gorged buzzards started from sleep, or cotton-mouths uncoiled, hissing, at the coming of the searchers. And sometimes all who had loved the lost were themselves among the missing. The full roll-call of names could never be made out—extraordinary mistakes were committed. Men whom the world deemed dead and buried came back, like ghosts—to read their own epitaphs. (114)

One of these men deemed dead is the young girl's father. When he returns to his home in New Orleans, Hearn writes, "He had come back to find strangers in his home, relatives at law concerning his estate, and himself regarded as an intruder among the living" (118). The father, then, is left alone in New Orleans, knowing his wife is dead and assuming that the same fate has befallen his daughter.

On the Louisiana coast, the young girl is adopted by a Spanish-speaking couple, and "a new name had been given to her with that terrible sea-christening" (122). The girl becomes Conchita, or Chita for short. The story then moves forward in time, from the horrific hurricane of 1856 to the year 1867. During this time, Chita has transitioned from French to Spanish, and from city life in New Orleans to life on the coastal islands. Hearn asks, "What had she lost of life by her swift translation from the dusty existence of cities to the open immensity of nature's freedom? What did she gain? [. . .] With her acquisition of another tongue," Hearn writes, "there came to her also the understanding of many things related to the world of the sea." From her adopted mother, Hearn continues, "she learned the fables and the sayings of the sea—the proverbs about its deafness, its avarice, its treachery, its terrific power" (126–127). But she also learns that "the sea lived: it could crawl backward and forward; it could speak!—it only feigned deafness and sightlessness for some malevolent end" (130). Mixing the terror contained in the Gulf of Mexico with its beauty, Chita becomes the romantic young girl of the sea: "For the strength of the sea had entered into her; the sharp breath of the sea had renewed and brightened her young blood" (133).

If the southern coast of Louisiana below the city presented much danger with the hurricane in 1856, little relief was found in the city itself, for New Orleans in 1867 was experiencing an outbreak of yellow fever. "Such were the days," Hearn writes, "and each day the terror-stricken city offered up its hecatomb to death; and the faces of all the dead were yellow as flame!" (134). At this point, the girl's father returns to the island. He sees Chita, recognizes her as the daughter he thought dead, and then dies of yellow fever.

"Tombs ruin soon in Louisiana," according to Hearn (125). So what becomes of cities that cannot bury their dead? How does place attachment hover in limbo? The difficulty does not arise from the burial of the bodies themselves, not from the flesh and bones that enter the earth, but from the enclosures placed around the bodies to protect them from the elements, the airtight coffins that defy decay. Those are the things that break free from their resting place below ground, that rise with the rising saturation of the earth and bring the bodies contained within them up again. The regular and irregular floods of southern Louisiana put pressure on both the living and the dead, the present and the past, and for this reason, on the future, the unborn, those impossible beings whose ethical claim, whose face, is not yet known. The dead return often in New Orleans, in dreams and in waking life, in memory, in likenesses walking down the street or cast in bronze on the pedestal. Sometimes the coffins that hold them, the enclosures made to keep the dead underground, are the very things that bring them back when the water rises and the airtight containers break free from their viscous homes. In such a situation, one can only ask: Where is Dionysus when you need him? When does Bacchus roll again?

FIN DE SIÈCLE

In the very last year of the nineteenth century, a landmark work of literature appeared that consolidated the moods and sensibilities of the times: Kate Chopin's *The Awakening*. This famous novel tells the story of Edna Pontellier, an American woman translated into the creole society of New Orleans and left alone to read and interpret the foreign texts before her. She is an aspiring painter, an emotional woman always moved passionately and irrationally by the piano playing of Mademoiselle Reisz. She also listens intently to the folktales of the Gulf of Mexico, told to her on Grand Isle.

Married with two children, she is constantly presented with tests of her character, of her ability to fulfill her assigned role of wife and mother, but she does not conform, either by choice or by compulsion, despite occasional flashes of dutiful excitement. In her dreamy languor, a state often repeated and vividly described throughout the novel, she loses touch with reality and ultimately becomes the victim of her own imagination. She is swept away by her romantic attachment to other men, the visual landscape of the city and the coastal islands below, the climate of southern Louisiana, and the weather. The soundscape, too, impinges on her body and mind as the music of wind and water, of the plants and animals of the coast, mix together with the soft, multilingual voices of human people. These "drowsy, muffled sounds lulling her senses" eventually get their way, and she submits to the decadent temptations surrounding her (84).

"The voice of the sea is seductive," Chopin writes, "never ceasing, whispering, clamoring, murmuring, inviting the soul to wander for a spell in the abysses of solitude; to lose itself in mazes of inward contemplation" (57). This loss of self, Edna's retreat into the world of fantasy, the world of music and literature and visual arts, comes to a head in her relationship with the Gulf. Edna's interpretation of the Gulf proves to be a fatal misinterpretation, and she enters its body unable or unwilling to keep her head above water. The suicide is described thus:

> The foamy wavelets curled up to her white feet, and coiled like serpents about her ankles. She walked out. The water was chill, but she walked on. The water was deep, but she lifted her white body and reached out with a long, sweeping stroke. The touch of the sea is sensuous, enfolding the body in its soft, close embrace. (175–176)

What kind of temptation is this? Why does Edna's decadence occur? Why does she fall away from the progressive narratives of health and fitness and even basic survival? If Hearn's young girl-child of the forest is the romantic figure swimming above the decadent undercurrent, Chopin's no-longer-young woman only has one choice: to submit to her fate, to swim into the Gulf and test the waters. Edna is no René and Chopin is no Chateaubriand, and so, despite the dismalness of the story, the decadent character and her author will feel no guilt, and they will always maintain composure because *c'est* after all *la vie*.

In the interval between two endings—the end of the Civil War, in 1865, and the end of the nineteenth century—literary critics and historians have rightly identified a golden age of New Orleans literature, a kind of beginning of literary New Orleans in the English language, as the city gained national attention through the local color writings of some of the city's most famous writers. If the city's old Frenchmen were walking in circles around an American Andrew Jackson in increasingly enfeebled form in 1880, in George Dessommes's "Un Soir au Jackson Square," by 1899 they were joined by Chopin's suicidal woman. This would be the kind of city that New Orleans would be and would become for at least the next century.

5

THE FIN DE SIÈCLE TO
WORLD WAR II, 1900 TO 1945

Hardest of all, though, was when Grandmère sternly bade him cease
speaking the soft, Creole patois that they chattered together, and forced
him to learn English. The result was a confused jumble which was no
language at all; that when he spoke it in the streets or in school, all the
boys, white and black and yellow, hooted at him and called him "White
nigger! White nigger!"

—ALICE DUNBAR-NELSON, "The Stones of the Village" (ca. 1905), 133

Alice Dunbar-Nelson's short story "The Stones of the Village" traces the
life of Victor Grabert as he makes his way from rural Louisiana to the
city of New Orleans. Part of that transition involves the psychosocial
trauma of being suspended in linguistic limbo and taunted by his peers.
Caught between linguistic worlds, the young creole of color degener-
ates in his capacity to communicate verbally. His too-many languages
have the paradoxical effect of creating none, his multilingual tongue
marks his body as the illicit product of transracial sex, and the lie of the
color line rears its ugly head in a final insult: his unelected appellation
as a "white nigger." When he is old enough to parse and utilize his languages effectively and be out on his own, his grandmother, herself a
creole of color from the West Indies, sends him to New Orleans, where
he can start a new and successful life passing for white. The story thus
traces a number of related displacements as Victor moves from rural

to urban life, from creole French to English, from poverty to wealth, from black to white, and the heavy tolls these displacements take on his mental and physical health.

Written around 1905, how does "The Stones of the Village" fit into larger histories of human bodies and their languages as the nineteenth century turns into the twentieth? One way to chart those larger histories is through the shifting position of the French language in the state's ten constitutions. Beginning with its first constitution, in 1812, the state of Louisiana maintained a kind of schizoid bilingualism. Written in French, the 1812 constitution unequivocally mandated English as the official language of Louisiana law. For the next century and a half, as nine more state constitutions were written and adopted, the last one in 1974, Anglophone legislators whittled away at the Francophone presence in Louisiana. Although the political pendulum did swing in both directions vis-à-vis the English–French power struggle, with give and take on both sides, the broader trajectory tended toward English monolingualism.

The second (1845) and third (1852) constitutions were written in English but allowed for laws in both English and French, while the fourth (1864) specified English as the single language of law and instruction in the public schools. The fifth (1868), required after the Civil War, reiterated the fourth, and again specified English as the only language of law and public education. The sixth (1879) provided for English as the official language of law but opened the possibility of laws being translated into French. It also allowed for French as the language of education in the public schools at the primary level. The seventh (1898) and eighth (1913) expanded the possibility of French to all levels of public schools, while the ninth (1921) drastically changed course and specified English only in law and education. The tenth (1974) included a general statement for the rights of any linguistic community to preserve its language.[1]

The Victor Graberts and other creoles of color in New Orleans were caught up in this linguistic drama dictated by constitutional law. Many of them chose Victor's path and adopted English voluntarily in order to join the Anglophone world and take advantage of all its personal, professional, political, and financial opportunities. In his 1911 polemical history *Nos Hommes et Notre Histoire [Our People and Our History]*, however, the creole of color Rodolphe Lucien Desdunes sees this move away from Francophone culture as a kind of decadence, and one cast in purely negative terms. More specifically, Desdunes connects three forms of decay in the postbellum period: the withering of the French language in New Orleans, the loss of the language's literary resources, and the moral deterioration of the *gens de couleur*.

"The Latin influence among our people," he writes, "disappeared with the death of Armand Lanusse," the poet and editor of the groundbreaking anthology *Les Cenelles* (1845), who died in 1868. Desdunes continues, "With his passing away we are bereft of his example, of the stimulating force provided us by the classics. No longer do we occupy ourselves with reading La Fontaine, Boileau, Fenelon, Racine, Corneille. No longer are we ardent students of the masters. Lanusse led us in the study of these brilliant lights of civilization." These classic authors of French literature, according to Desdunes, helped the young creoles of color resist "the temptations of self-interest" and "material pleasures." Without them, the New Orleanian creoles of color "can never preserve their distinctive character"; without them, they are "yielding to the inclinations of the present, particularly to the modern interest in politics." Politicians, for Desdunes, represent the opposite of poets; the politician's desire springs primarily from egotism and opportunism, and they think of nothing more than how they can take advantage of the ambiguous and ever-changing present. "For us," he concludes, "rejecting the influence of the classics has meant condemning ourselves to live without the knowledge of certain principles indispensable for the formation of character" (15–16).

The way Desdunes characterizes decadence as a triple decline—linguistic, literary, and moral—is extremely clear in his writing. But there is an irony here that is not so obvious. All the while that Desdunes is criticizing the modern creoles of color for their decadence, he sounds in fact very decadent himself. He sounds, in other words, very much

like the self-identified decadents of Paris, those individuals who con-
signed their lives to literature, learning, and art and who spurned the
political exigencies and economic opportunities of the present. In this
way, Desdunes shows the tu quoque route that decadence often takes
when it is conceived in purely negative terms: although one may actually be accused of the same thing, decadence is projected outward as
the affliction of another person.

If Desdunes criticizes the disinterest of the creoles of color in the
French language and its literary lessons, many Anglophone writers
began to show a profound interest in exactly that. George Washington
Cable, Lafcadio Hearn, Kate Chopin, Alcée Fortier, and Jules Choppin,
among many others, turned to the creoles of color for material in their
own work. Their interest in the creoles of color, however, was highly
selective. They did not turn to Armand Lanusse or the other highly
educated individuals writing in highly literary French. Instead, they
turned to the poor and uneducated, the former slaves, speaking and
singing in the creole French patois.

Their motivations for their selected interest were many: they wanted
to preserve what they thought was being lost, the use of vernacular
speech was becoming a common literary technique on a national scale,
and they probably thought the writers who were already successful did
not need more exposure. But it may also be that they were caught—
consciously or otherwise—in the ideological trap of white supremacy
and black inferiority. After the emancipation of the slaves, as people
of African descent were achieving more rights, categorical differentiation and hierarchy became all the more imperative. The supposed
sophistication of highly literate poets writing in highly literary French
would have posed a fundamental threat for those worried about their
moves for full equality under the law. The white Anglophone writers
who turned to the Francophone creoles of color for material were thus
caught in a double bind, a contradictory impulse to show black intel-
ligence, capability, and talent, on the one hand, and black difference,
debility, and inferiority, on the other.

This chapter traces decadence in this time of double bind as a form of individual and social illness through two literary texts: Alice Dunbar-Nelson's "The Stones of the Village" and Charles Chesnutt's *Paul Marchand, F.M.C.* (1921). Decadence in these texts comes out of the understanding that human beings are haunted not by some supernatural spirit or demon but by their very selves. One is haunted from within one's own mind and body and the surrounding social structures. For Dunbar-Nelson and Chesnutt, the signs of decline that make up decadence are individual and social illnesses. They are psychoses, dangerous obsessions with the self, that result from a profound uneasiness regarding the ambiguous nature of the color line. They come when the color line is revealed to be nothing more than a color lie with grave consequences. Dunbar-Nelson's and Chesnutt's texts are part of the decadent tradition in New Orleans, but for these African American writers there was very little that was redeeming in the concept of decadence. In this way, this chapter explores another question: To what extent is decadence itself a white European and Euro-American phenomenon?

ALICE DUNBAR-NELSON

"The Stones of the Village" is unusual in the literary history of New Orleans and the larger nation, for it tells the story not of the tragic mulatta—that most beautiful and feminine creature formed through illicit human desire and fated for death—but of the transracial male, a figure that has been given considerably less space in both the primary texts and the critical literature. The drama of mixed, and often mistaken, racial identity in a female character is recounted in many fictional texts set in New Orleans during the late nineteenth and early twentieth centuries. George Washington Cable's "'Tite Poulette" and "Madame Delphine," collected in his *Old Creole Days* (1879), as well as Grace King's "The Little Convent Girl" (1893), are among the most famous.

Behind these fictional texts is also the so-called Toucoutou Affair, or the case of *Anastasie Desarzant v. P. LeBlanc and E. Desmaziliere, his wife* (1858).[2] Anastasie Desarzant, also known as Toucoutou, had been passing for white, until she had her whiteness called into question on the street. She subsequently sued her accuser for slander, but she lost her case and was proved to be of African descent. Toucoutou was thus legally and socially reclassified as a person of color and became part of famous folk song with the refrain: "Ah, Toucoutou, we know you! / You are a little Mooress. / Who does not know you? / No soap will make you white."[3] She was also resurrected as the titular character in Edward Larocque Tinker's novel *Toucoutou* (1928). The staying power of Toucoutou's story can be traced back to its purpose; it is a cautionary tale for budding Toucoutous, demanding that they not abandon the race (from the perspective of their black peers) or that they stay where they belong (from the perspective of their white counterparts).

Alice Dunbar-Nelson does something different in "The Stones of the Village." It is not the beautiful female mulatta that interests the author, and especially not her public shaming. Instead, Dunbar-Nelson presents the character of a transracial male, Victor Grabert. In doing so, the author explores one's decision to pass for white in early twentieth-century New Orleans and the ways in which that decision is never completely voluntary, even though one would wish it to be so.

While Dunbar-Nelson lends a sympathetic ear to her character, other black writers of the period were not as willing to listen and understand. For Desdunes, writing in 1911, for example, the creoles of color who choose to pass for white "have fallen to such a point of moral weakness." Desdunes continues, "They live in a moral depression that seems to represent the last degree of impotence." This state of decadence or "deterioration," for Desdunes, has no redeeming value (18). There is no transvaluation of value here; instead, the moral failure is final. Dunbar-Nelson would agree with Desdunes's diagnosis of passing, and indeed "The Stones of the Village" traces exactly that narrative of decline, but she asks why a person, in the character of Victor, would take the route that leads to decay (moral, mental, and physical), to depression and impotency, to deterioration.

"The Stones of the Village" was written and set in the wake of *Plessy v. Ferguson* (1896), when the progressive doors that had opened during Reconstruction were slammed shut by the white supremacist establish-

ment. Historian Donald E. DeVore presents a horrifying list of the challenges African Americans faced during the period: "white hatred, racial
injustice, lynch law, inferior schools, slum neighborhoods, rigid racial
segregation, white-on-black violence, crop lien laws, peonage, white
primaries, grandfather clauses, residential segregation laws, white-only
ads, colored-only signs, back doors, back alleys, and white-men-only
government" (57).[4] There were, however, opportunities for black New
Orleanians to seek positive social good, and DeVore explores the many
"voices of black dissent" in the era of segregation (viii). Victor could
have joined those voices; in fact, as a highly educated man, he would
have been in a particularly good position to effect positive change, but
he chooses a very different path.

To trace Victor's decision to pass for white, the story begins with
his childhood in a small village in rural Louisiana. His grandmother is
"crooning a bit of song brought over from the West Indies years ago;
but when the boy sat silent, his head bowed in his hands, she paused
in the midst of a line and regarded him with keen, piercing eyes." Herself a woman of color still carrying the cultural remnants of the West
Indies, Victor's grandmother looks suspiciously at her grandson. She
detects some hidden misery there and "laid a sympathetic hand on his
black curls, but withdrew it the next instant" (131). The sympathy that
turns to revulsion in touching the young boy's hair illustrates the grandmother's own struggle with her racial identification. In fact, she has
internalized the racism of her lifeworld so completely that she spurns
herself and her own family.

In an important scene that precedes this chapter's appalling epigraph, Victor is playing in the street with the other little boys when his
grandmother grabs him.

> "What you mean?" she hissed at him. "What you mean playin in de
> street wid dose niggers?" And she struck at him wildly with her open hand.
>   He looked up into her brown face surmounted by a wealth of curly
> black hair faintly streaked with gray, but he was too frightened to question.
>   It had been loneliness ever since. For the parents of the little black
> and yellow boys, resenting the insult Grandmère had offered their off-

spring, sternly bade them have nothing more to do with Victor. Then
when he toddled after some other little boys, whose faces were white
like his own, they ran away with derisive hoots of "Nigger! Nigger! And
again, he could not understand. (132–133)

Both her body and her language betray her racial past, but still she
presses her racist demands on Victor. Eventually, he is ostracized by all of
the other children, regardless of their color, ridiculed as a "white nigger"
and interpolated into a world in which referentiality itself seems to be
breaking down (133).

Grandmère Grabert sends Victor to live with her friend Madame
Guichard in New Orleans, and the populous city allows Victor the ano-
nymity to start a new life: "Never in all his life had he seen so many people before, and in all the busy streets there was not one eye which would
light up with recognition when it met his own." He gets a job at a rare
book store on Royal Street, and the years of working there have a peculiar effect on the young man. Dunbar-Nelson writes, "Victor had grown
pale from much reading. Like a shadow of the old bookseller, he sat day
after day poring into some dusty yellow-paged book, and his mind was a
queer jumble of ideas. History and philosophy and old-fashioned social
economy were tangled with French romance and classic mythology
and astrology and mysticism" (133–135). Like Tennessee Williams's
Blanche DuBois in A Streetcar Named Desire (1947), whose decadent
signature includes the marks of a literature teacher whose imaginative
play goes too far, Victor begins to have difficulty distinguishing between fact and fiction, and his moral compass goes haywire as a result.

After Victor is many years in his employ, the old bookseller dies and
leaves Victor with a large inheritance that he intends for Victor's education
at the segregated Tulane University. Upon hearing this news from his
benefactor's lawyer, Victor is shocked and is prompted to ask "Why—
why—why—" before changing his course of action. "Then he stopped
suddenly," Dunbar-Nelson explains, "and the hot blood mounted to
his face. He glanced furtively about the room. Mme. Guichard was
not near; the lawyer had seen no one but him. Then why tell him? His

heart leaped wildly at the thought. Well, Grandmère would have willed it so" (135). Paled by his years spent indoors, jumbled by his eclectic and unmonitored literary education, willed into whiteness by his West Indian grandmother, and outside the purview of those who could testify against him, Victor makes his fateful decision to pass.

The story then advances quickly in time to Victor as an older adult, a successful lawyer, married to his white wife, Elise, and the proud father of a son. Having been accepted by the white young men and desired by the white young girls, Dunbar-Nelson writes, "he had passed through the portals of the social world and was in the inner circle." His grandmother has died, and all ties to his past life as a young creole of color have been erased. "And yet," Dunbar-Nelson writes, "as he sat there in his cosy study that night, and smiled as he went over in his mind triumph after triumph which he had made since the old bookstore days in Royal Street, he was conscious of a subtle undercurrent of annoyance; a sort of mental reservation that placed itself on every pleasant memory" (137).

This "subtle undercurrent of annoyance" comes to a head one day when he is in court and a white employee utters the word *nigger*. "At the forbidden word, the blood rushed to Grabert's face, and he started from his seat angrily," Dunbar-Nelson writes, and Victor is forced to hide the emotion on his face with a newspaper. This scene has a powerful effect on the character, and he begins to separate himself from the African Americans in his company. Of one employee, Dunbar-Nelson explains, Victor "found himself with a growing sympathy towards the man, and since the episode in the courtroom, he was morbidly nervous lest something in his manner betray him" (138). As Victor becomes more and more paranoid, he realizes that his threat is increasing not only externally from those outside himself who would do him harm but internally as well. Victor recognizes that he is a danger to himself.

In subsequent events, Victor's sympathy becomes more and more of a liability, and instead of caving in to it, instead of using his position as a judge to institute justice among the races, he swings in the opposite direction and becomes more racist than the racists. "When it came to a question involving the Negro," Dunbar-Nelson writes, "Victor Grabert was noted for his stern, unrelenting attitude; it was simply impossible to convince him that there was anything but the sheerest incapacity in that race." For his racist approach to African Americans under the law, Victor "was liked and respected by men of his political belief, because, even when he was a candidate for a judgeship, neither money nor the possible chance of a deluge of votes from the First and Fourth Wards could cause him to swerve one hair's breadth from his opinion of the black inhabitants of those wards" (145).

His very success—personal, professional, social, and financial— causes his anxiety, making "him tremble more, for he feared that should some disclosure come, he could not stand the shock of public opinion that must overwhelm him." Increasingly paranoid at the possibility of being found guilty from association, Victor dismisses all of his "dar-kies" and tells his wife that "old mammies just frighten children, and ruin their childhood." This anxious paranoia begins to take a toll on his mental and physical health: "His eyes had acquired a habit of veil-ing themselves under their lashes, as if they were constantly conceal-ing something which they feared might be wrenched from them by a stare. He was nervous and restless, with a habit of glancing about him furtively, and a twitching compressing of his lips when he had finished a sentence" (143–144).

The relationship Victor has with his new family—his unsuspecting white wife and their young son, who would be deemed black, according to the laws of segregation, if his truth were revealed—is particularly troubling for him. "Elise loved him because she did not know," Dunbar-Nelson writes. But if she did find out, there would be so many barriers to their union—legal, social, psychological—that Elise would probably flee from her husband in horror. Victor thus oscillates between utter rage and enfeebled incapacity: "He found a sickening anger and disgust rising in himself at a people whose prejudices made him live a life of deception. He would cater to their traditions no longer; he would be honest. Then he found himself shrinking from the alternative with a dread that made him wonder" (141).

Revenge is the affective form that this oscillation between indigna-
tion and resignation ultimately takes. In the final scene of the story,
Victor is invited to a banquet in his honor. The other white judges of
New Orleans want to celebrate Victor's lifetime of achievements, which
include, not least of all, his resolute support of segregation and other
systems of black oppression from his privileged seat on the bench.

How does Victor believe he has achieved revenge against the boys
from his childhood? From her character's point of view, Dunbar-Nelson
explains:

> Oh, what a glorious revenge he had on those little white village boys!
> [. . .] He had taken a diploma at their most exclusive college; he had
> broken down the barriers of their social world; he had taken the highest
> possible position among them and, aping their own ways, had shown
> them that he, too, could despise this inferior race they despised. Nay,
> he had taken for his wife the best woman among them all, and she had
> borne him a son. Ha, ha! What a joke on them all!
>
> And he had not forgotten the black and yellow boys either. They had
> stoned him too, and he had lived to spurn them; to look down upon
> them, and to crush them at every possible turn from his seat on the
> bench. Truly, his life had not been wasted! (150)

Dunbar-Nelson's final sentence, the ironic exclamation, shows just
how delusional she believes her character to be. Victor's delusion can
be read within the literary trajectory of decadence in New Orleans. He
is in a position of power, privilege, and prestige; he is abject, tortured,
mentally and physically ill; and these afflictions are chosen by and sus-
tained through himself alone. And yet Victor's author does not approve
of his decadence; there is nothing transvaluated in his decline and fall.
In the end, she kills him off.

At his banquet, Victor steps up to address the assembly, and in the
chairman's place he sees his grandmother "as she had wont to sit on
the steps of the tumbledown cottage in the village" (151). What he has
repressed has returned. Dunbar-Nelson paints the scene:

"Grandmère," he said softly, "you don't understand—" And then he was
sitting down in his seat pointing one finger angrily at her because the
other words would not come. They stuck in his throat, and he choked
and beat the air with his hands. When the men crowded around him
with water and hastily improvised fans, he fought them away wildly
and desperately with furious curses that came from his blackened lips.
For were they not all boys with stones to pelt him because he wanted to
play with them? He would run away to Grandmère who would soothe
him and comfort him. So he arose and, stumbling, shrieking and beat-
ing them back from him, ran the length of the hall, and fell across the
threshold of the door. (151–152)

Caught between anger and debility, wanting to speak the truth but unable to relinquish the benefits of his lie, Victor is forced into effective
silence. Even if he is able to shriek the unintelligible with his dying
breath, he can no longer make sense. In his last moments, he turns to
the memory of his grandmother, but she cannot solve his crisis. Indeed,
she was its source from the very beginning. Unable again to make true
language, unable to find comfort in the arms of his dead grandmother,
Victor dies in utter horror. The secret of his African ancestry is kept
secret from his white wife, his son, and everyone else. Perhaps, Dunbar-
Nelson suggests, this son, too, will grow up and follow in his father's
footsteps as the legal arm of segregation. In the story's denouement,
Dunbar-Nelson puts her decadent and unfortunate character in his
place, with dead and "blackened lips." But the specter of race in the big
uneasy continues to haunt the city's inhabitants, as well as the literary
imagination.

CHARLES CHESNUTT

Like "The Stones of the Village," Charles Chesnutt's late novel *Paul
Marchand, F.M.C.* is one of those literary texts tormented by the specter
of race in the segregated city. Written in 1921 and set a century before
in New Orleans, the novel traces the life of its titular character, Paul
Marchand, a free man of color in a slave society. If Dunbar-Nelson

analyzes her black character's decision to pass for white, however, Chesnutt does something a little different. As the novel unfolds, Paul, too, makes a categorical move from black to white, but unlike Victor's, Paul's move comes not through a conscious decision to lie but instead through an elaborate backstory that reveals the long-kept family secret of his white parentage. If this sounds like an uplifting story of Paul's good luck, it is not. As he makes that supposedly positive move from black to white, there are grave consequences in store for Paul and those who surround him.

Paul Marchand grows up thinking that he is a quadroon orphan, "an inferior but not entirely degraded class," with an unknown benefactor (6). Educated in Paris, "where a man is a man," Paul experiences a level of *liberté, egalité,* and *fraternité* unimaginable in his native country (28). "There was no color line in France, nor ever has been," Chesnutt writes, "and in that country men of color even at that epoch had occasionally distinguished themselves in war, in art, in letters and in politics" (22). Upon his return to New Orleans, however, Paul finds the social situation vastly different. His "strain of African blood" follows him everywhere, the mark of his debasement in a socially stratified society. Despite this horrific situation, Paul nevertheless marries another free person of color, has two children, and prospers financially within the legal confines of his caste. But because of his very success, Paul becomes an easy target for the Beaurepas cousins, "champions of the white race [who] were always on the alert to rebuke presumption on the part of any mulatto or quadroon" (24).

The Beaurepas family represents the old and powerful elite of New Orleans. Their ancestors "had helped Bienville lay the foundations of the colony, and had profited by valuable land grants and trading monopolies." The family had invested in John Law's company, sold their shares before the bankruptcy, and established their wealth. Later generations, too, had benefited financially and "by successive accretions, due to conservative management, natural growth and wise and fortunate investments had attained large proportions." By the time of Paul Marchand's story, in 1821, the family patriarch, Pierre Beaurepas, is "the wealthiest Creole in New Orleans" (36). But the great patriarch Pierre is old and dying, and he must name an heir to his fortune. Because he is childless, he must choose one of his five nephews, young men whose parents were killed during the Haitian Revolution, before the boys were able to escape and immigrate to New Orleans.

Pierre's five nephews had grown up with the knowledge that one of them would become Pierre's heir, but the effect of this prospect on their lives was not positive. Chesnutt explains:

> Had old Pierre specifically designated any one of his nephews as his successor, the remaining four would in all likelihood have applied their fair native abilities to business with the hope of finding through this channel the way to wealth and honors. But how could one reasonably expect a Creole, of Gallic blood and imagination, softened by the languors of a subtropical climate, to struggle painfully toward the heights of life, while there was one chance in five that he might ride thither in a golden chariot, behind a black driver in livery? (38)

The Beaurepas men represent one side of New Orleanian decadence. These wealthy and lazy young creoles are fond of drinking, women, gambling, and not much else. Languorously letting the good times roll, they avoid work at all costs and would prefer instead to ride in luxury on the backs of others.

Chesnutt presents the character of Paul Marchand as the antithesis to the Beaurepas men. His interest in family, hard work, and patient success distinguishes him among the other New Orleanians, but he cannot escape his social classification as a quadroon. In an important passage, Chesnutt writes of the quadroon balls and speculates on their place in New Orleans history and society:

> This institution, for many years a feature of New Orleans life, was an outgrowth of the exotic civilization of a pioneer race, who, bringing with them no wives, before the advent of their own race, had mated, more or less like the birds, with the Indian and Negro women. Though frequently severe and even cruel slaveholders, the Latins have nevertheless always shown a marked affinity for the darker races, for whom

they had never the harsh Anglo-Saxon contempt. Recognizing their own blood, too, even when mingled with that of slaves, it had always been the fashion in Latin America to manumit the children of these left-handed unions, and to provide for their support. There had thus grown up in New Orleans the large class of free colored people known as the quadroon caste. (64–65)

Chesnutt continues by describing the psychosocial state of this caste. "The quadroon men were, as a rule, of amiable disposition and cheerful temperament," he writes. "While they regarded their social treatment as cruel and unjust," he continues, "and discussed it among themselves with much animation, the cruelty was mainly a matter of feeling and might be ignored" (78). Chesnutt attributes this relatively calm personality to the quadroon's genetic makeup: "The pleasure-loving French temperament, superimposed upon the easygoing African, produced a usually placid acceptance of the situation" (79). The quadroons' amiability and cheerfulness also stems from their pride and feelings of superiority over the more darkly complected New Orleanians, who carried with them the clearest mark of bondage. Indeed, even Chesnutt himself does not seem immune to this brand of colorism when he writes, for example, that "the proud blood of French gentlemen, even when mingled with that of slaves, sometimes clamored for its birthright" (125).

Paul Marchand grows up thinking that he is part of this quadroon caste, but, like Victor Grabert, he does not feel himself to be one of them exactly. "Whether it was the fiery spirit of some adventurous European ancestor," Chesnutt writes, "or the blood of some African chief who had exercised the power of life and death before being broken to the hoe, or whether the free air of revolutionary France had wrought upon him—whatever the reason, he had chafed more than most under the restriction of his caste" (78–79). Paul's position as a perpetual outsider, Chesnutt suggests, comes from some atavistic echo from the deep past. Like Victor, Paul, too, is caught between races, mixing a kind of sympathy for both, based upon his own genetic history, but distrusting both as well—the whites for their oppressive systems of slavery and segregation, the quadroons for their easy willingness to accept their lowly fate. The distrust goes both ways, moreover, as Paul is distrusted by the whites for his black ancestry and by the quadroons for his "truculence" and ability "to stir up feeling against the rest of them" (31).

In this impossible position between white and black, Paul finds himself. At one point in the novel, Paul must go to a quadroon ball in order to retrieve his niece and save her reputation. Because these balls were exclusively the domain of white men and their potential quadroon female lovers, Paul would have to pass for white. Chesnutt describes the character's appearance in detail:

> The elegance of his attire, the clear olive of his complexion, so far as it was visible around the small black mask, in contrast with the straight, brown hair which fell to his shoulders; his slender but sinewy hand, with the nails carefully trimmed and polished and bearing several rings set with precious stones, made up a *tout ensemble* which no one would have suspected as belonging to other than a gentleman of the first social rank. (71)

Surrounded by the decadent extravagance of the ballroom are Paul's beautiful body, impeccably dressed, and his handsome face, seductively hidden by a small mask. His perfect hands, accentuated with expensive jewelry, epitomize the life of lavishness, leisure, and luxury. At the center of this decadent scene, however, is the sheer absurdity of the situation. Chesnutt is describing Paul Marchand, a white man who thinks he is a black man passing for a white man. But despite this epistemological mess, there is an ultimate truth here for Chesnutt. Paul looks like a white "gentleman of the first social rank" because he is exactly that. Even if he thinks he is passing, he in fact is not; he is the ontological thing he pretends to be. Indeed, Paul is able to fool everyone at the ball—perhaps even himself, as well as his author—because he is not fooling anyone.

If Chesnutt uses this scene to open up, epistemologically, the sheer absurdity of racial classification only to close it down, he is not as flippant or playful in his description of Paul's wife, Julie. She is a black woman, and nothing can change that fact. Critical readers may detect, moreover, a blatant racism in Chesnutt's description of his character. "She was a beautiful woman," Chesnutt writes, "dark-eyed, petite, on whom the slight strain of African blood left its mark more in a certain softness and pensiveness of expression than in any pronounced Negroid feature" (89). Julie's beauty seems to stem from the absence of the "Negroid," and one would wonder, then, how a more African genetic marker would affect the author's estimation of his character's beauty.

Unlike her husband, Julie could never pass for white:

> Her parentage was well known, and she bore upon her shapely features, in the warmth of her tint and the wave of her hair, the faint though quite distinguishable imprint of her mother's race. No matter how sweet or desirable she might be as a woman, no fairy tale could make her white, nor could she be a white man's lawful wife in Louisiana. (169)

As the novel unfolds, the reader is made aware that there is more to the story of the old and childless Pierre Beaurepas: "There was, of course, an underlying romance. The air of New Orleans was full of romance. The old world superimposed upon the new; the careless mingling of races, the flux and reflux of governments—these and a dozen other things had made the city a center of adventure which pulsed with romance" (94). In a romance too convoluted to summarize here, Paul is proclaimed the biological son of Pierre Beaurepas, "white *pur sang*—of the pure blood," and the legal inheritor of the great fortune that had been accumulating over four generations, since the family's arrival in New Orleans (97). The lawyer "declared him fitted in all respects to wear the mantle of the late Pierre Beaurepas, and hand on the traditional glory of his race" (105). "The power of wealth," Chesnutt philosophizes, "is nowhere more manifest than when wielded by a dead hand" (95).

Gaining "legal title of admission" to the white world changes everything for Paul (107). He is now completely free from both the written and the unspoken—indeed, the unspeakable—rules of social relations that he needed to follow. But despite these clear and immediate gains, he also has much to lose. Because he is now a white man, Paul's marriage to Julie is null and void in Louisiana, and his children illegitimate.

Like Victor, Paul has a monumental decision to make based on his racial fate in the white supremacist world of New Orleans. In the end, he relinquishes his inheritance and chooses his cousin Philippe, the only honorable one out of the five cousins, as his successor. With Julie and his two children, he embarks on the transatlantic move to France.

Before moving to Paris, however, Paul learns of another elaborate story, in which one of his cousins is in fact a quadroon, that same position he had formerly occupied for his entire life. Chesnutt describes the scene in which Paul asks the five cousins if they want him to reveal which one of of them "was of quadroon birth" (182). Chesnutt explains:

> They looked at one another furtively, and studied their own reflections in the mirrors which lined the walls of the dining room. One perceived in another a certain breadth of the nostril, but in himself a certain fullness of the lip—in one a certain thickness of the eyelid, in himself a certain wave of the hair. They examined their fingernails furtively for the telltale black streak. For a moment no one spoke. (183)

The five cousins are in a room together, surrounded by mirrors, so they can see one another and themselves. The dimensions of the nose and lips, the heft of the eyelid and behavior of the hair—the supposedly material manifestations of a conceptual race—are all brought into the psychological realm of paranoia. Each of these cousins, in comparing his own appearance to the four men next to him, makes a thousand alliances and disavowals in the blink of an eye. Each one knows that he must carefully study himself in the mirror, but each one is also terrified of what he will find. But notice that Chesnutt mentions nothing about the color of the skin. The only blackness, in fact, that Chesnutt identifies is a supposed streak in the fingernail, prefaced with the ironic "telltale."

The word *furtively* appears twice; it is also a word that surfaces many times in the period's literature of creolized confusion, including Dunbar-Nelson's "The Stones of the Village." Furtively, secretively, stealthily stealing glances, the five cousins work to differentiate the one from the others. The suspense builds with silence. When asked if they want to know which one of them is the quadroon, which one is a stranger even to himself, they all respond as one, and at once, with a resounding *no*. Why do they make this communal decision? Despite the foundational racism in this scene, each cousin is willing to let another pass if he himself can escape the microscope. Blackness in the creole city remains both omnipresent and repressed, everywhere and nowhere at once. It seems to reside just below the surface, cultivating a strength of its own, and, despite diagnoses of decadence, it resurfaces again and again where and when one least expects it.

Chesnutt concludes *Paul Marchand, F.M.C.* with a short history from 1821, when the novel is set, to 1921, when the novel is written. The chance that one of the Beaurepas cousins "was of quadroon birth" did not change their white supremacist work, Chesnutt writes. In fact, like Dunbar-Nelson's Victor, they and their descendants "were ever in the forefront of any agitation to limit the rights or restrict the privileges of their darker fellow citizens" (184). Their racist work was immense:

> They helped procure the passage of a law forbidding the manumission of slaves and lead an abortive movement to expel all free colored people from Louisiana. They fought gallantly for slavery in the Civil War, were leaders and advisers of the Ku Klux Klan, and prominent in the "redemption" of Louisiana and the nullification of the Fifteenth Amendment. A grandson of Henri Beaurepas not long since introduced into the Louisiana legislature an amendment to the criminal code, making marriage a felony between a white person and a person of colored blood to the thirty-second degree inclusive. (184–185)

The irony that a man of African descent could sponsor such racist legislation is not lost on Chesnutt and his readers.

Charles Chesnutt finished *Paul Marchand, F.M.C.* at the very beginning of the 1920s, the decade when "bohemian New Orleans" was in full swing and the city was experiencing a period of heightened literary production. This was the decade during which William Faulkner, in particular, famously described New Orleans, in his novel *Mosquitoes* (1927), as a prostitute. "Outside the window," Faulkner writes, "New

Orleans, the vieux carré, brooded in a faintly tarnished languor like an aging yet still beautiful courtesan in a smokefilled room, avid yet weary too of ardent ways" (262). Alongside Faulkner, this was the decade during which Sherwood Anderson, Lyle Saxon, and Hamilton Basso, among many others, wrote their most famous work in the city and used the figure of a decadent New Orleans in their texts. What these eminent names all have in common is that they attach to people of the white and male variety. For John Shelton Reed, in *Dixie Bohemia: A French Quarter Circle in the 1920s* (2012), the racial situation was stark. The city's "Bohemia was for whites only," he writes. "It's true that black New Orleanians helped to make it possible and were very much a presence (both actually and in art and literature), but they were not themselves allowed to be Bohemians" (56). Reed's claim about these bohemian writers raises an important question about race and decadence.

The characters of Victor Grabert and Paul Marchand come out of the decadent tradition, and yet, unlike Antoine-François Prévost's Chevalier des Grieux in New Orleans, Chopin's Edna Pontellier on Grande Isle, or J. K. Huysmans's Jean Des Esseintes in Paris, their authors find very little to celebrate in their stories. If decadence often transvaluates value, whereby the supposed opposites of progress and degeneration, beautiful and ugly, good and bad, end up switching places, it does not do so here. Indeed, the decadence contained in "The Stones of the Village" and *Paul Marchand, F.M.C.* ought to be avoided at all costs, for if one does catch it, there will only be two ways to escape: death or the transatlantic journey back to Paris.

If Dunbar-Nelson and Chesnutt emphasize the harmful aspects of decadence, there are other cultural traditions in the city that are more sympathetic. Indeed, the advent of jazz in the early twentieth century ought to be understood in such an air of embrace. Michael Ondaatje's fragmented and hallucinatory novel *Coming Through Slaughter* (1976) tells the story of jazz cornetist Buddy Bolden, insane at the age of thirty-one and institutionalized in 1907. The legendary and unrecorded black artist died in 1931. Through a mysterious narrator, Ondaatje describes

Bolden's musical style as he plays on the street and in the Storyville brothels:

> Thought I knew his blues before, and the hymns at funerals, but what he is playing now is real strange and I listen careful for he's playing something that seems like both. I cannot make out the tune and then I catch on. He's mixing them up. He's playing the blues and the hymn sadder than the blues and then the blues sadder than the hymn. That is the first time I ever heard hymns and blues cooked up together. (81)

Bolden's jazz, his musical style, may serve as an important rejoinder to the decadence of Dunbar-Nelson and Chesnutt. For Ondaatje, Bolden represents the decadent artist par excellence, whose very life moves not in reality but through the aesthetic realm. He beautifully describes one particular decadent moment when Bolden's brain and fingers travel out of joint for the sake of pure self-indulgence: "Every note part of the large curve, so carefully patterned that for the first time I appreciated the possibilities of a mind moving ahead of the instruments in time and waiting with pleasure for them to catch up" (93).

Natasha Trethewey's book of poems called *Bellocq's Ophelia* (2002) is set in the same place and time as Ondaatje's novel. Looking back on Storyville, the book opens with an ekphrastic rumination on one of E. J. Bellocq's famous photographs. The poet compares the New Orleanian's picture with the British John Everett Millais's 1852 painting of Shakespeare's tragic character Ophelia. Through this temporal splintering and referential fracturing, the poet resurrects the Storyville prostitute of color. Trethewey writes:

> The small mound of her belly, the pale of hair
> of her pubis—these things—her body
> there for the taking. But in her face, a dare.
> Staring into the camera, she seems to pull
> all movement from her slender limbs
> and hold it in her heavy-lidded eyes.
> Her body limp as dead Ophelia's,
> her lips poised to open, to speak. (3)

And speak she does. The book then proceeds in the voice of the Storyville prostitute of color, who is no longer merely and meekly the object of Bellocq's camera but is now the subject of her own discourse.[5] Forced into a decadent lifestyle not of her own choosing, the prostitute sits and tells her story.

Perhaps even more so than Ondaatje and Trethewey, Zora Neale Hurston thoroughly demonstrates that Europe's claim on decadence is by no means absolute. In "Mother Catherine" (1934), Hurston describes the priestess's chapel in the Lower Ninth Ward. It was a "place of barbaric splendor, of banners, of embroideries, of images bought and images created by Mother Catherine herself; of an altar glittering with polished brass and kerosene lamps" (854). Hurston continues:

> Catherine of Russia could not have been more impressive upon her throne than was this black Catherine sitting upon an ordinary chair at the edge of the platform within the entrance to the tent. [. . .] She might have been the matriarchal ruler of some nomad tribe as she sat there with the blue band about her head like a coronet; a white robe and a gorgeous red cape falling away from her broad shoulders, and the box of shaker salt in her hand like a rod of office. [. . .] It seemed perfectly natural for me to go to my knees upon the gravel floor, and when she signalled to me to extend my right hand, palm up for the dab of blessed salt, I hurried to obey because she made me feel that way. (855)

Mother Catherine sits in her extravagance amidst environmental ruin. In *Gumbo Ya-Ya: Folk Tales of Louisiana* (1945), Lyle Saxon, Edward Dreyer, and Robert Tallant describe Mother Catherine's complex as a "jumble of decaying frame buildings" (207). And yet in this place, in this decadent place, the black queen wields her profound power.

6

WORLD WAR II TO HURRICANE KATRINA, 1945 TO 2005

WRITER (*his speech slurred by drink*): God, but I was ignorant when I came here! This place has been a—I ought to pay you—tuition . . .

MRS. WIRE: One drink has made you drunk, boy. Go up to bed. We're goin' on tomorrow like nothing happened. (*He rises and crosses unsteadily from the kitchen light.*) Be careful on the steps.

—TENNESSEE WILLIAMS, *Vieux Carré* (1977), 869

In the late winter of 1938, Tennessee Williams moved from his family home in Saint Louis to a new life in New Orleans. His late autobiographical play *Vieux Carré*, written just a few years before his death in 1983, recounts that time period from 1938 into the spring of 1939 when, at twenty-eight years old, he took up a room at 722 Toulouse Street. In the heart of the French Quarter, the writer receives his aesthetic education, decadently administered and tuition free, from the severely disturbed Mrs. Wire, his landlady, and the other tenants of the boardinghouse. That group includes drunks and drug addicts, hardened bouncers, gay-for-pay male prostitutes, bat-crazy women, orgy enthusiasts, and transvestite artists. No one has any money, and many have fallen into such a state of illness that they can no longer recognize their affliction. One character is dying of tuberculosis, for example, and the blood spots that appear every morning on his pillow he blames on the building's bedbug infestation. Although each of the characters is in a different stage of their mental and physical deterioration, they are all headed in the same direction. And yet they continue on, stumbling up and down their French Quarter stairs as if nothing is wrong.

Behind the scenes of *Vieux Carré* is the increasing presence of the many tourists who sometimes barge into their private courtyard, which Mrs. Wire has entered into the Azalea Festival in order to make a little extra money. This was the period, after all, coming in the wake of the Great Depression, that the city of New Orleans began to see the rise of tourism as the new basis for its economy.[1] As a port city, New Orleans had long been a place for visitors, and the large archive of the city's travel writing testifies to its power to attract, and oftentimes subsequently revolt, those from afar. But it was in the era after World War II, especially, that the French Quarter—its supposed decadence and Old World charm—became an attraction for the common vacationer. New Orleans dressed and undressed for the stranger and offered itself as a place of pleasure where revelers could indulge in vice on a magnitude of their choosing—privately, publicly, or the many places in between—without guilt or shame.

One short story that intimately portrays the experience of two tourists to the city is "No Place for You, My Love" (1952), by the Mississippi writer Eudora Welty. Like the author, who is from Jackson, the two characters are outsiders, "strangers to each other, both fairly well strangers to the place, now seated side by side at luncheon—a party combined in a free-and-easy way when the friends he and she were with recognized each other across Galatoire's" (561). The "*degrading heat*" of the Sunday afternoon lulls the tourists' senses as they walk through "the bath of July" (562–563, emphasis in original). In their languorous mood after lunch, the two nameless characters—he from Syracuse, New York, and she from Toledo, Ohio—decide to drive down the withered toe of Louisiana from New Orleans to the southernmost town of Venice.

As they drive south toward the Gulf, the two characters attempt to read and interpret their surroundings, each other, and, indeed, themselves: who they are, what they want, and how they present themselves to the other to be read. The story can thus be read as an "allegory of reading," to borrow a phrase from Paul de Man.[2] Welty's readers, in other words, are reading her characters reading. Nothing is obvious, however. No text—whether literal or figurative, human or otherwise—presents itself transparently. Like the thick vegetation and dark bayou water of the wetland through which they are traveling, the characters are openly and intentionally impenetrable to each other. Welty calls it "deliberate imperviousness" (562).

"Of all human moods," Welty explains, "deliberate imperviousness may be the most quickly communicated." In a flash, one knows when the other person does not want to be known, and yet the communication of "imperviousness," the transmission of affective impenetrability from one person to another, need not end the interpersonal relation. For Welty, "two people can indulge in imperviousness as well as in anything else" (562). Indeed, communicating "deliberate imperviousness" to another person may sometimes go by another name: flirting.

As they go down Louisiana, Welty reveals more about her male character than her female one. The unnamed man is married, with a wife back home in New York, but the romantic situation of her female character is left undisclosed. The drama, then, revolves around the central question of desire: Does he want to have an affair with her, and what does she want? And this question is couched within the landscape south of New Orleans on the drive toward Venice. Welty describes the scene thus: "It was a strange land, amphibious—and whether water-covered or grown with jungle or robbed entirely of water and trees, as now, it had the same loneliness. He regarded the great sweep—like steppes, like moors, like deserts (all of which were imaginary to him); but more than it was like any likeness, it was South" (577).

The loneliness of the landscape, of course, does not actually reside there. It is instead projected by its (overly?) imaginative reader. Indeed, Welty emphasizes that the character does not see the landscape at all as it is in itself. It is filtered through images of steppes, moors, and deserts that the character has not actually seen in person but that has been read and represented by others. Despite all this cognitive and interpretative commotion, in the end there is still a simple fact: "it was South." For Welty, New Orleans and its vicinity is located in the seemingly simple but always troubled signifier of the South. To make matters worse, however, the place is located "far down here in the South—south of South, below it" (578).

Welty also describes the insects in this fabled land: "There were thousands, millions of mosquitoes and gnats—a universe of them, and on the increase" (564). If, on the one hand, the landscape can be imagined through projection and romantic interpretation, it is also, on the other hand, very real and can exert a will of its own. The threatening nature of the environment comes to the forefront even in the form of tiny mosquitoes. "His wife," Welty warns, perhaps suggesting other diseases as well, "would not be at her most charitable if he came bringing malaria home to the family" (565). If the mosquitoes and gnats are bad, there are other creatures, too, with more obvious power:

> More and more crayfish and other shell creatures littered their path, scuttling or dragging. These little samples, little jokes of creation, persisted and sometimes perished. The more of them the deeper down the road went. Terrapins and turtles came steadily over the horizons of the ditches.
>
> Back there in the margins were worse—crawling hides you could not penetrate with bullets or quite believe, grins that had come down from the primeval mud. (565)

If the characters thought they were degraded by the heat before they left the city, they were wrong. Welty writes:

> No, the heat faced them—it was ahead. They could see it waving at them, shaken in the air above the white of the road, always at a certain distance ahead, shimmering finely as a cloth, with running edges of green and gold, fire and azure.
>
> "It's never anything like this in Syracuse," he said.
>
> "Or in Toledo, either," she replied with dry lips.
>
> They were driving through greater waste down here, through fewer and even more insignificant towns. There was water under everything.

Even where a screen of jungle had been left to stand, splashes could be heard from under the trees. In the vast open, sometimes boats moved inch by inch through what appeared endless meadows of rubbery flowers. (568–569)

In this environment, the body is compromised and the mind does not quite work. The characters conclude their drive in Venice, at the very tip of the withered toe of Louisiana. Welty describes the scene thus: "The end of the road—she could not remember ever seeing a road simply end—was a spoon shape, with a tree stump in the bowl to turn around by." Welty continues, "Around it, he stopped the car, and they stepped out, feeling put down in the midst of a sudden vast pause or subduement that was like a yawn" (571).

The Venice of Louisiana is a very different kind of place than the great Italian city it is named after. Indeed, all the American locales mentioned in the text—New Orleans, Toledo, Syracuse—are very different than their original European referents. Within this doubled world, suspended in temporal limbo, punctuated with the threats of death at every turn, the two characters finally make contact with each other. At a dilapidated restaurant in Venice, they dance:

Surely even those immune from the world, for the time being, need the touch of one another, or all is lost. Their arms encircling each other, their bodies circling the odorous, just-nailed-down floor, they were, at last, imperviousness in motion. They had found it, and had almost missed it: they had had to dance. They were what their separate hearts desired that day, for themselves and each other. (576)

This scene of touching, bodily connection swaying in unison and motion, shows two people with different pasts and separate futures meeting just for a moment, a very brief moment, in sensual contact. Welty's story is a marked contrast to the decadence of Mardi Gras, the city's most prominent tourist attraction, with all its excessive pageantry, debauchery, ancient Greek and Roman imagery, indiscriminate consumption and waste. The subtleness of Welty's story plays against this picture of New Orleans: "strangers, they had ridden down into a strange land

123

together and were getting safely back—by a slight margin, perhaps, but margin enough" (579).

"Going back," Welty continues, "the ride was wordless, quiet except for the motor and the insects driving themselves against the car" (577). He drops her off at her hotel, and they each go their separate ways, neither one knowing how the other will continue with the evening, the rest of the trip, or life back home. "As he started up the car," Welty writes, "he recognized the smell of exhausted, body-warm air in the streets, in which the flow of drink was an inextricable part, the signal that the New Orleans evening was just beginning" (579). The story concludes: "As he drove the little Ford safely to its garage, he remembered for the first time in years when he was young and brash, a student in New York, and the shriek and horror and unholy smother of the subway had its original meaning for him as the lilt and expectation of love" (579–580).

Williams's play and Welty's story are both narratives of escape, of outsiders coming into the city to look for one thing or another and safely leaving. The writer at the end of *Vieux Carré* is a young man who, like many others during the Great Depression, goes west to sunny California. With a charming musician refreshingly named Sky, he is able to escape from the decadence of Mrs. Wire's boardinghouse in the French Quarter.

The two characters in "No Place for You, My Love" are likewise able to escape. But even if Welty herself is able to go back to Jackson and her characters are able to return up North, the writer stresses this point about leaving: "The stranger in New Orleans always sets out to leave it as though following the clue in a maze" (563). Some are not as lucky as her characters and remain in the maze, for something lurks behind "the Southern mask" (562), as Welty puts it, behind the romance and sweet olive hedges and confederate jasmine, behind the wrought iron fences and ancient brick walls. The dreaminess captured in so much of New Orleans literature can be a trap, for what dreams may come when lucidity begins to fail?[3]

New Orleans can be a gift to writers, but it can also be a "burden," as literary critic Thomas Bonner Jr. puts it.[4] Indeed, the author of the great comic novel *A Confederacy of Dunces,* John Kennedy Toole, found the burden too great to bear and committed suicide in 1969, at the young age of thirty-one.[5] And Toole is only one example of the pain and violence circulating at all levels of the psychosocial world of New Orleans. If decadence points to some uneasy relation between progress and decline, one of the major signs of decline in the postwar period is the city's unconscionable murder rate and shocking disregard for human life. With one of the highest murder rates in the nation, New Orleans witnesses, on a daily basis, how quickly one human being can shoot and kill another, how effortlessly a person can viciously injure or permanently disfigure another person for drugs or gang retaliation, for an insult, for a phone or a few dollars, and sometimes for no reason at all.[6]

One of the most impressive literary treatments of this murderous violence is Tom Dent's play *Ritual Murder,* written in 1967, performed in 1976, and published in the journal *Callaloo* in 1978. Although these years point to a New Orleans that existed decades ago, the play has not lost any relevance. At the very beginning, Dent specifies the play's time frame simply as "now," and it indeed and unfortunately is (67).

TOM DENT

The main character of Tom Dent's *Ritual Murder* is not a tourist. He is not an outsider or a stranger to the city looking for some decadent education or romantic experience. He does not want a nice lunch at Galatoire's, or his one true love, or anything else. If he is looking for something, it is an escape from his surroundings, and indeed from the dreamy trap of the city itself. But Joe Brown Jr. is not as lucky as Williams's writer or Welty's mobile characters zipping around in their Ford. A young black man, he is stuck in a New Orleans jail, awaiting trial for the murder of his best friend, James Roberts, whom he stabbed to death at nineteen years old.

The play revolves around the mystery of detection, the question of motive, after Joe Brown Jr. has already been arrested and confessed to his crime. The facts are clear: the two friends were drunk at a bar, they got into a seemingly insignificant argument, and Joe stabbed his friend James once in the chest, killing him instantly. But something lurks below the surface, and the play's narrator acts like a documentarian, interviewing a cast of characters, each of whom represents an essential aspect of Joe's psychosocial life: his wife, parents, homeroom teacher before he dropped out of school, psychiatrist, boss, social worker, the city's police chief, and the ghost of the dead friend James Roberts. Each character interprets Joe's reason for murdering his friend in a different way.

Interviewed while enjoying her daytime soap operas and praying for a bigger television in the Florida Avenue projects, Joe's wife, Bertha, explains the reason for Joe's anger and his violent lashing out. She says Joe "wouldn't settle down and accept things as they are." Mrs. Brown, Joe's mother, blames the murderous act on Joe's refusal to go to church and accept the protection of the Lord. Mrs. Williams, the teacher, says Joe did it "because he was headed that way in the beginning," even though she cannot remember him individually, and he is amassed in her mind with all her other misbehaving students (69).

The police chief has a different interpretation of the situation: "The rate of crime in the streets in New Orleans has risen sharply. We know that most of our colored citizens are wholesome, law-abiding, decent citizens. But the fact remains that the crime wave we are witnessing now across the nation is mostly nigger crime. Stop niggers and you will stop crime." For the police chief, the problem with Joe is simple: Joe is not a "colored citizen" but a "nigger." If the problem for the police chief is simple, so is the solution: "The police must have more protection, more rights, and more weapons of all types to deal with the crime wave. We need guns, machine guns, multimachine guns, gas bombs, and reinforced nightsticks. Otherwise America is going to become a nightmare of black crime in the streets" (71–72).

Unlike the police chief, the black psychiatrist Dr. Brayboy has a more nuanced and historical view: "At the core of Joe Brown's personality is a history of frustrations. Psychological, sociological, economic." These frustrations compound to create "ritual murder": "When murder occurs for no apparent reason but happens all the time, as in our race on Saturday nights, it is ritual murder" (70). Dr. Brayboy explains further: "When a people who have no method of letting off steam against the source of their oppression explode against each other, homicide, under these conditions, is a form of group suicide. When personal chemistries don't mix, just a little spark can bring about the explosion. Ice picks and knives, and whatever happens to be lying around" (80). The audience of *Ritual Murder* witnesses a total system failure of the fundamental psychosocial structures that are designed to keep the individual afloat: the family system, the educational system, the criminal justice system, the economic system, and the mental and physical health systems.

At first glance, the play seems to be so sadly and unexceptionally American that its setting and the New Orleanian background of its author may seem irrelevant. Dr. Brayboy, the black psychiatrist, in fact, tells the audience that he has seen similar acts of violence in New York City. Dent mentions a number of neighborhoods in New Orleans— Pontchartrain Park, the Florida Avenue projects, and the Ninth Ward— but none are vividly or significantly described. There are no accents, furthermore, no clear marks of linguistic anomaly. Although some characters speak in their professional languages, the play is presented with the barest minimum of the heteroglossia particular to New Orleans.

Nonetheless, *Ritual Murder* forms an integral part of the city's larger decadent tropology. There is a dreamy quality, a drowsy atmosphere, to the play. In the background, behind the voices speaking on stage, the song "Summertime" is being played, but the narrator is quick to note that this "Summertime" is not the "Summertime" composed by George Gershwin. "It is blusier [*sic*], darker, with its own beat and logic, its joys unknown to the white world," Dent writes (67). Here decadence emerges not so much as a beauty in decay but as a will toward death, a thanatological obsession, that is part of the city's reputation.[7]

One glaring omission that travels throughout *Ritual Murder* is the complete lack of grief and mourning over the death of James Roberts, the character stabbed to death, or even a passing pause over the imprisonment of Joe Brown Jr. The narrator tells the audience that the murder has received some mention in the city's two newspapers—the black *Louisiana Weekly* and the white *Times-Picayune*—but the city's many other crimes have overshadowed its coverage. The narrator prompts each of the interviewees to think deeply about the murder, but none of them expresses anything that resembles sadness over the misfortune of either person. The loss of Joe and James is not figured as a loss at all.

Death in New Orleans in *Ritual Murder* seems, then, to encompass a double decadence. Not only is the death event itself a sign of decline that is not without its appealing spectacle, but so is the aftermath, the nonchalance and unmeaningfulness of its ethical consequence. The narrator asks the ghost of James Roberts, "Do you feel you died for anything? Is there any meaning in it?"

"Yes," he replies, "I died for something. But I don't know what it means"

The narrator then turns to Joe Brown Jr. and asks him a similar question: "And did your act mean anything?"

"I suppose so," he answers. "But I can't imagine what" (79).

Ritual Murder presents the horrifying climax of New Orleans on the decline. Against a backdrop of the social movements of the 1960s and 1970s, and after all the political gains and ethical progress expressed in *Brown v. Board of Education* (1954), the Civil Rights Act of 1964, and many other events, the play is still firmly located within a theater of seemingly interminable and uncircumscribable violence.[8] Indeed, a real murder that recently occurred in the city eerily resembles the play's fictional rendition. A journalist for the *New Orleans Advocate* begins his reporting of the murder in this cold and horrifying way: "After being told he had to move out, a 31-year-old Broadmoor man went out for a walk with his roommate and shot him to death."[9]

Tom Dent's play *Ritual Murder* is part of a much larger thanatological trajectory in the city. At a crucial juncture in Tennessee Williams's famous *A Streetcar Named Desire* (1947), the entwined themes of death and desire and New Orleans become most explicit. The bilingual Blanche DuBois, fluent in French and English, encounters a blind

Spanish-speaking woman as her suitor Mitch confronts her about her many past "intimacies with strangers," including with a seventeen-year-old student. As she is explaining herself to Mitch, the Mexican woman calls out "Flores. Flores. Flores para los muertos," layering her own voice into Blanche's speech about Belle Reve and its pervasive aura of death (546). Williams writes:

MEXICAN WOMAN: Flores.

BLANCH: Death—I used to sit here and she used to sit over there and death was as close as you are. [. . .] We didn't dare even admit we had ever heard of it!

MEXICAN WOMAN: Flores para los muertos, flores—flores . . .

BLANCH: The opposite is desire. So do you wonder? (547).

One woman is trying to sell her cemetery flowers; the other is trying to sell herself as a good potential wife; they both, however, are quickly realizing that no one is buying their wares and that death, whether real or symbolic, is the only way out.

Brenda Marie Osbey's "Peculiar Fascination with the Dead" (1985) likewise addresses the thanatological obsession of the city. The poem begins with a compendium of rituals designed to instruct the living in the ways of honoring the dead, and it offers the following directive: "live among your dead, / whom you have every right / to love" (25). Later in the poem, Osbey emphasizes this point: "i have never avoided / the tombed cities i was taught to tarry in. / and i have not let my dead lie" (33). The creole of color poet Sybil Kein presents another view, however, and her work may be understood as an important rejoinder to Tom Dent, Tennessee Williams, Brenda Marie Osbey, and the chilling ubiquity of death in the city. Kein recuperates the linguistic diversity of literary expression in New Orleans as an act of community healing and positive political action.

In the postwar period, the city of New Orleans changed in a number of significant ways: it moved into a new economy based on tourism, it shifted from being primarily a transatlantic contact zone to a site of global exchange,[10] and the school system began the seemingly impossible work of desegregation.[11] When the Supreme Court ruled on *Brown v. Board of Education* in 1954, it did not provide a timetable for the schools to become racially integrated, and it was not until November 14, 1960, after much legal battling, that first grader Ruby Bridges braved the horrifying taunts and the ugly faces of white supremacy to enter William Frantz Elementary School at 3811 North Galvez Street in New Orleans.

In the postwar period, the city also witnessed a new approach to language diversity that corresponded with other identity-based social movements. The Conference on College Composition and Communication, held in New Orleans in 1973, developed a specific policy on linguistic diversity. Chaired by Melvin A. Butler of the historically black Southern University in Baton Rouge, and consisting of a total of thirteen members from across the country, the committee asserted "the students' right to their own patterns and varieties of language—the dialects of their nurture or whatever dialects in which they find their own identity and style" (2).[12]

But one of the major obstacles to such a cultivation of linguistic diversity is the city's stubborn reputation. In *The Katrina Papers* (2008), Jerry W. Ward Jr. reminds us of a terrible fact: "New Orleans is one of the few cities in the United States where the cultivation of ignorance is thought to be a part of its charm" (93). One symptom of this charming ignorance may be heard in the city's most impoverished communities, where the most beautiful of linguistic gymnastics sound off in the street for the lucky, and where, for the unlucky, the most debased forms of illiteracy, mental illness, and substance abuse combine to form some of the most horrible human utterances, barely intelligible as such.

In the dual-language *Gumbo People* (1981), a book that does indeed cultivate the linguistic diversity of New Orleans, Sybil Kein harnesses the power of an ecstatic decadence found in many works about the city, including Marcus Christian's *I Am New Orleans* (1968) and Arthur Pfister's *My Name Is New Orleans* (2009). In *Gumbo People*, Kein includes a poem called "Les Cenelles" that explicitly channels the nineteenth-century creoles of color:

Les cenelles. Yé répousée
ferme et beau, comme
to fidéle, amour Créole.

The holly berries. They grow
once again, strong and beautiful
like your faithful Creole love. (22)

But the creole language represented here is not the high-literary French
of the original nineteenth-century anthology. Kein writes in the creole
and then renders her poetry in English translation. The poets of *Les
Cenelles* are not resurrected in Kein's poem alone. In 1942, in fact, the
poet Marcus Christian organized a literary group called *Les Cenelles*
Society of Arts and Letters.[13]

SHERYL ST. GERMAIN

A poem by Sheryl St. Germain makes explicit the connections among
bodies, languages, literatures, and environments, with regard to decadence, that have been the touchstones of this book. The first stanza of
"Getting Rid of the Accent" (2007) reads:

I thought I had gotten rid of it
after I moved to Texas: speech classes
and twelve years in another state, but I'd
still fall back into it like into the gutter
whenever I visited, even on the phone,
whenever my mother called, forgetting
I was a college graduate, forgetting
I was an English major, saying things
like wheah ya at sweethawt, or
dat doan mean nuttn, ya awta seen
da way she pawks dat caw, the sounds
I was fed like milk as a child, the aw
sound predominating as if it was just
too much work to pronounce the r. (146)

From the very beginning of the poem, the accent is characterized as something bad—an STD, maybe, or lice, or black mold, or a rat infestation, or something else to be exterminated. St. Germain does not use the phrase "my accent" or "our accent" or even "an accent" in her title. It is *the* accent—the definite article, the definitive articulation—that must be eradicated because it exposes so much: the place of one's birth, the social condition of one's present reality, the direction of one's future, the whole trajectory of one's life. We all know it in New Orleans; we all know exactly the accent she is talking about. It is a kind of linguistic oddity, sounding at once foreign and familiar. It has a charm, to be sure, but this charm can quickly degenerate into the butt of a joke and signal something infantile or stupid. The poem, in fact, revolves around the *aw* sound, the linguistically degenerative sound of the *r*. What linguists call *r*-lessness, *aw* is a diminutive, almost puerile sound and one often directed at the faux pas of babies or young children when a mistake becomes cute.

The accent for the poet is seemingly incurable. Defying all her attempts to repress it once and for all, the accent returns as if it were a constantly haunting presence. It returns especially, and ironically, during those moments of linguistic pride when she thinks she has gotten rid of it and lets down her guard. The accent acts like a ghost, materializing and making itself known every so often through a kind of linguistic mist. The poet tries her best to escape it by moving to Texas, engaging in speech classes, and becoming an English major. But still it returns. The accent cannot not stay put, as it were. It cannot keep up residence on Williams Boulevard.[14] "Even on the phone" talking to her mother, the poet's voice will fail again and fall "into the gutter," as if on cue (146). Here, the accent has traveled hundreds of miles and across state lines in order to alter her own as if by magic. The New Orleanian way of speaking not only has lodged itself squarely within the home language community and its ostensible English but also has done so permanently within herself and threatens always to resurface.

If the first stanza deals specifically with the sounds of the accent, the second stanza calls forth all its associated sights and smells.

> I tried hard to get rid of it,
> to make my voice sound
> as if I had nothing to do with
> the black smell of the Lake,
> nothing to do with my mother's
> beans and rice,
> nothing to do with my father's breath,
> my brother's track marks. (146)

The poet's goal in this stanza is to disassociate the sound of the voice, the vulnerable subjectivity of the "I," and the sights and smells of home. But St. Germain knows that all her attempts to sequester and hold in check each part of this triad will always prove insufficient. The best she can hope for is to speak and live "as if" these three things *could* be separated. So the poet twists her tongue, contorts her lips, and deforms her mouth "into unnatural positions" because she does not want to be marked as New Orleanian. She does not want to be marked as unsophisticated, backward, ugly, and smelly. She wants to protect herself, the "I," from the pungent nastiness of lake water, from the spice of creole cooking and its unwelcome rancidness on the human breath, from the disgusting traces of excrement left on the underwear. She tries hard to escape it all.

Unlike other writers in the long literary history of multilingual America, this poet does not assert her language rights. Sheryl St. Germain does not stand with James Baldwin, for example, or with Gloria Anzaldúa, who argues, in "How To Tame a Wild Tongue" (1987), that "attacks on one's form of expression with the intent to censor are a violation of the First Amendment" (76).[15] She is not out and proud, so to speak, with her speech. There is a sense, implicit in the poem, that dovetails with Martin Heidegger's figuration of language as "the house of Being," but St. Germain does not seem to set as her task the protection of that house.[16] Her response is not to shore up the inherited house of Being or to assert any kind of property rights, as it were, but to pack up and move. Of course, she probably has good reason to make this decision to relocate linguistically. Years of shame and embarrassment, self-consciousness and self-doubt, can do that to a person, especially in the absence of a James Baldwin or a Gloria Anzaldúa.

St. Germain's trouble with her language, with her house of Being, is not her trouble alone. It points to the uneasy dynamism that bodies in general necessarily have with their languages. When Heidegger presents the house as a figure to describe language, he helps us to recognize the centrality, the great and empowering potential, of that technology for our species. But that figuration also helps us to see why uneasiness about one's language can be so debilitating. The house is supposed to protect the individual and the collective self—it is supposed to offer shelter from the elements; it is supposed to provide sanctuary and the *chora* of communion—and so when an outside force draws attention to the house-language, regardless of the motivational temperature, there will automatically be thoughts and feelings of vulnerability.

Outside forces, however, are not the only threat to the house-language. Vulnerability can be generated from the inside, as well, and the uneasiness is produced from within when one realizes that one's own voice may betray oneself. The best, if not the only, way to feel comfortable at home is to take the protective function of the home for granted. To think too deeply, or perhaps even to think at all, about the house— what it separates, what it keeps in and what keeps out, its material and figurative realities—is to invite speculations about its own fragility.

Contemporary colloquialisms such as "Spanglish," "Ebonics," and "Chinglish"—to name just a few of the less offensive ones—testify both to the fact of linguistic mixing and variation, on the one hand, and to the implicit understanding of societal disambiguation and valuation, on the other. The words themselves speak to etymological bastardization, unholy mixtures of linguistic elements, that demonstrate some real process that is both highly serious and the deserving object of ridicule. Those variations and valuations change within different contexts, of course—on the street, in the marketplace, on the academic panel, among others—but even in these less offensive terms, one can sense the extent to which one's self is dependent, often fragilely so, on one's language use.

St. Germain's "Getting Rid of the Accent" moves to the beat of trans-atlantic decadence in at least four ways. First is the way that the poet foregrounds the ease with which one's language can fall into disrepair and disrepute. The rhetoric of linguistic decay is as commonplace in New Orleans as red beans and rice. Interpreted as echoes from the early colonial world—Anglophone and Francophone, Afro-Caribbean and native—and filtered through the warm and humid climate, the New Orleanian accented voice is said to intimate the lazy easiness by which languages meld and mesh and coevolve. This voice can never be com-pletely controlled, even in the face of education and training, care and self-consciousness. It can always and easily slip back "into the gutter."

Second, and relatedly, is the way that the poet figures such a fall as not only easy but also in some sense desirable. Even with volitional and steadfast repudiation, there is still a longing, of more-or-less equal power, to partake in the linguistic sinfulness. This dynamic of repudi-ation and longing surfaces, especially, in the following stanza:

> I was not going to sink
> as my mother had, lower
> and lower into this spongy
> land, I would not have my words
> sound like the drunken streets,
> the ditch-water
> that runs by our house still,
> infectious, addictive (147)

The poem is ostensibly about the desire to get rid of one's accent, to grow up and individuate, to have one's words "rise / strong and true, separate." And yet the true heart of the poem—the aesthetic center around which all the other pieces revolve, as well as the prime mover of the poetic plot—is the accent, the marked words, the *dat* for *that,* the *aw* for *r,* the *layg* for *leg,* the *rum* for *room,* and so on. These pronuncia-tions and the larger speech patterns that make up the accent are tanta-lizing and seductive. Filtering through a complex matrix of desire and disavowal, they are "infectious, addictive," despite their supposed signs of linguistic decay. The tenuousness of linguistic propriety becomes a tempting object with which to flirt. Despite, and often *because of* its figuration as disfiguration, its debasement and perversion of reputable speech, the accent still taunts and tempts, inviting speakers to partake in its depravity. And that depravity, in the end, may end up morphing into a language of incomparable beauty.

Third is the way that St. Germain entwines linguistic decadence with bodily decadence. Languages and bodies seem to be ontologically fused for the poet, as if one can stand for the other. In one moment, the connective tissue between "the voice of my father, / the blood of my brother" becomes explicit as these two seemingly disparate things are cast as different parts of a larger ontological whole. How should St. Germain's readers think about this connection exactly? Bioconceptually speaking, at least, it is the breath that connects the voice to the body. It is the conduit by which the human body exhales air in order to form sounds and their relations—utterances, syntaxes, and rhythms—in the creation and communication of meaning. But like the body itself and its language, the breath can attract or repulse. It can aromatize or it can stink. It can fill a room with the sweetness of new growth or the dankness of matter decomposing. It can demonstrate the progressive influences of higher education or it can atavistically conjure ancient history, against one's will. It can incite pride or it can reanimate the lingering shame of one's past.

Fourth is the way the poet juxtaposes the ostensibly unfiltered nature of speech—here, the New Orleanian "yat" accent—with the the ultra-refined status of poetic writing. The philosophical depth of the poem hinges, in fact, on that lacuna, that conceptual gap, between the spoken and the written language. The immediacy of the accent is cast within the temporal latency of the poem, of poetic writing, in which every sound and syllable, every word and connotation, every cadence and mark of punctuation, is carefully planned and executed. Published poems never just happen. Decadence vis-à-vis language can here refer to a set of opposites—to the lowest and to the highest forms of cultural expression—to the raw, lazy linguistics of New Orleanian speech, on the one hand, and to the refined, contemplative complexity of poetic writing, on the other.

There is also an elegiac tonality to the poem, as if the accent can only be preserved within the essentially ironic universe of writing or exploited within the confines of the commercial industry—especially restaurants and football teams, who love the *dis* and the *dat*, the *ain'ts* and all the fecundity of double negatives, the things dat ain't dere no more, all those expressions and sounds that betray the close proximity of white, black, and other dialects as they have evolved in easy and uneasy relation. Decadence can name the hiccups that occur in the fall from authentic unself-consciousness to ironic self-consciousness. Once the poet hears the accent in others, once she hears the accent in herself and tries to get rid of it, she will never be able to get back into the naïveté of her former language use, despite her newfound admiration for its sights and sounds. The self-conscious voice of the poet could never regain a voice that would be anything other than alien. That, then, would be the other side of the decadence.

7

NEW ORLEANS AFTER KATRINA, 2005 TO THE PRESENT

CAMILLE: We need to know what we are dealing with.

SUGAR: I'll tell you what we're dealing with—water, plain and simple.

—JOHN BIGUENET, *Rising Water* (2006), 14

The character of Sugar in John Biguenet's play *Rising Water* thinks he knows what's what when he responds to his wife's concern about their situation. That "what" is water. He is a practical man, and there is only one thing they can do as the floodwaters quickly rise from the floorboards and inch up the walls of their home. They must climb the rickety ladder into the attic for safety. But, truth be told, there is nothing plain and simple about their situation: neither the cause, nor the thing itself, nor its consequences. They are in the pitch dark and they have no way of knowing what has happened in the city and what will happen to them in the future. They have no way of knowing how high that enormous agent of death—it does *resemble* water—will climb.

During the course of the play, the two lone characters sit in their attic, look back on the story of their lives, and hope they can live some more. By the end of the play, Camille has managed to escape through the attic vent and has perched herself on the roof. Sugar is not thin or lucky enough, and his body gets stuck in the vent. His upper half makes it to the temporary haven of the roof, while his lower half is trapped in the attic and its waters. What ultimately becomes of these two characters is left undisclosed by the playwright. As the final curtains are drawn, the audience sees them close together still. Something is about to happen, but nobody knows what.

Along with his subsequent work in *Shotgun* (2009) and *Mold* (2013), Biguenet, in *Rising Water,* captures the *longue durée* of uneasiness that plagued the city in the intense days, weeks, months, and years after Hurricane Katrina made landfall on August 29, 2005.[1] It is a play that captures the anxious fluctuation between two distinct poles—absolute confusion and appalling moments of realization—in which New Orleanians still living within the city limits, those of the diaspora, and others out in the world with a keen interest in the city were all caught.

The characters of Camille and Sugar dramatize an astonishing will to survive between these two poles. They want to live on, and they do, at least during the temporal frame of the play. They push their aging bodies up through the hole in the ceiling and claw their way through the dark heat and stifling humidity into the attic. There they sit, faced with utter and unrelenting horror. Camille imagines her friends and neighbors, and strangers too, who are experiencing the rising water. She imagines "Miss Jeanfreau, all those people in pitch-dark rooms, balanced on a chair, a coffee table, standing on their mattresses with water up around their mouths—old people, parents holding up their kids against the ceiling." She asks her husband, "How many men, how many women, how many children—children, Sugar—trapped in rooms so dark they can't even see the water drowning them?" (27). Through his characters and their disturbing imaginations, Biguenet demonstrates not only the human will to survive but also a more profound will to meaning, a struggle to make sense of the senseless, a fight to establish purpose despite the glaring fullness of its absence.

Besides being an essential document of life after the levees failed in 2005, of the hope and almost crippling pessimism that came in psychosocial waves in the wake of the storm, Biguenet's play also captures the *longue durée* of uneasiness that plagued the city *before* the storm. Spurred by long-established perceptions of decadence, the disaster of Hurricane Katrina could be figured as the most recent act in the long drama of the city, as the most recent ripping of more flesh from the already withered toe of southeastern Louisiana. The play, as well as many other literary texts under consideration in this chapter, could tap into a larger uneasiness and longer story about New Orleans as a decadent city, as a city marked by sins known and unknown, fated for destruction, enchanted, and for that reason enchanting.

It is important to remember that Hurricane Katrina inundated New Orleans on the Monday before Southern Decadence, the annual LGBT festival held every Labor Day weekend, so the disaster was also interpreted within that particular context. Immediately following the storm, many pundits with a penchant for moralizing and fueled by the specter of homosexual decadence cast the city as the modern world's Sodom and Gomorrah, a fertile nexus of sin and sex that deserved a healthy dose of divine retribution.[2] While the rest of the country was preparing to celebrate the fruits of its labor and laboriousness, New Orleanians were staying true to form and efficiently organizing for debauchery.

Even within the most sympathetic camps, it was hard to see clearly and to understand exactly what we were "dealing with," as Camille puts it. It was difficult to unravel the discursive threads—the seemingly biblical scale of the event, say, and the symbolic potential of water— from the facts of reality. Politically, culturally, even theologically, there seemed to be something more to this national tragedy. Despite Sugar's insistence, there was nothing "plain and simple" in the water.

Unlike other national tragedies of purely political genesis—the bombing of Pearl Harbor, for example, or 9/11 sixty years later—the national tragedy of Hurricane Katrina was a complex phenomenon that encapsulated the older scripts of New Orleans decadence that have evolved over the course of three centuries. But because it was not *purely* political, the storm was also able to encapsulate the anxieties of an older and more universal struggle of the human species battling larger forces—both natural and supernatural—that threaten death and destruction. It is for this reason that, in discussions of Hurricane Katrina, the most ancient of gods and goddesses, divinities invented even before the Christ figure, come back again. Katie Ford's book of poems called *Colosseum* (2008) is pregnant with such imagery of the ancient world: the biblical flood and Noah's ark, gods and goddesses, Roman ruins, and Greek mythologies.

Ford's poem called "Rarely," for example, concludes with the following final two stanzas: "Take your rarities. / Take your household gods. // If you have no gods: / make them" (12). It is almost as if the poet and other critical commentators cannot help but discourse in the realm of symbolic theology. The imperative is so strong, in fact, that Ford says bluntly that if you are among the unfortunate who had no theological commitments before the storm, now would be a good time to make some up. The making of gods, for Ford, corresponds with the larger symbolic images, theological drives, and mythological narratives of New Orleans. The city and its vicinity, Ford writes, is "a land where everything grows, and there are many killings" (32). This rich imagery of reproduction and destruction, fertility and death—contradictions condensed within mythological figures such as Shiva or Persephone— find a special home in New Orleans literature in general, but especially in the wake of the major storms of 2005.

The other key difference between Hurricane Katrina and other national tragedies is that those tragedies were not read as boiling down human existence to its barest of nature. The bombings of Pearl Harbor and 9/11 showed something about the species' propensity for murderous violence, to be sure, but that propensity was cast as a complex predicament of our political species-being. Those bombings involved sophisticated technology and ultramodern warfare and were *purposefully* carried out within the sphere of global power dynamics. If those bombings could be read as harbingers of an advanced and militarized future, there seemed to be something much more primal going on in Hurricane Katrina. Perhaps because of the prolonged nature of the tragedy, wherein human ontologically reality was spectacularly falling apart; perhaps because Americans could not come to terms with blatant national shame, wherein blame could not be placed abroad; perhaps because the event eerily corresponded to an expectation, the hurricane seemed to be revealing what the Italian philosopher Giorgio

Agamben has called *la nuda vita,* or bare life. From a Hobbesian perspective, one saw the violent anarchy that resulted in a state of nature
as humans let their criminality loose. From a Rousseauian perspective,
on the other hand—as, for example, in Rebecca Solnit's in *A Paradise
Built in Hell* (2009)—one saw peacefulness and cooperation. Either
way, Hurricane Katrina seemed to be exposing what human life essentially is.[3] The media, the talkers and the writers, the poets too, albeit
often with more nuance, all seemed to be asking the same question.

Katie Ford's poem "Tell Us" condenses this aspect of the hurricane's
power to expose the becoming *nuda* of human species-being, but there
are steps and stages for Ford in this biosymbolic trajectory. She writes,
"first the storm / will take all lanterns and flags." The hurricane, for
Ford, will in its first stage take the lanterns, one of the most fundamentally human technologies of fire and electricity. With the lanterns goes
the light and hence the ability to see. Flags, along with their psychosocial function for national identification, will be torn away, reducing
the human body to its essential corporeality sans political association.
The tense of the poem is anticipatory: "the storm / will take." It is ori-
ented toward a future, a future that is as certain as it is horrifying. Ford
specifies that future and continues, "it will begin at 600 hours / end
at 1300." The temporal framework is military rather than civilian. Its
clock is the clock of war, violence, and destruction. In the end, "your
absolute nakedness / the barest accident of you // will stand before its
organized eye." (11).

With extinguished lanterns and no flags for protection, with an inescapable fate set according to an authoritarian clock, the city's inhabitants
become *nuda.* They lose their own visual agency and become the visual
object of some monstrous other's gaze. The eye of the storm, the con-
centric calmness in the middle of chaos, becomes the stage upon which
the human stands in unsympathetic scrutiny. There is a moment of clarity and stillness, and then chaos is once again loosed upon the world.

The poet does not spell all of this out, of course. She works through
nuance and suggestion, through flashes of imagery and disjointed action, and my close reading here may be construed as being as imagina-

tive—for better or worse—as the primary text itself. The question becomes, then, a question about the function of poetry in disaster amidst
other forms of discourse. What does poetic language do in times of
crisis? What does it offer vis-à-vis the other, more ordinary kind?

The most famous writing on Hurricane Katrina—the writing that
in many ways has defined the terms of the debate—has been not poetry but expository prose for a general reading public. Diverse books,
ranging from Tom Piazza's urgent apologia in *Why New Orleans Matters*
(2005) to Dave Eggers's story of one man's struggle in *Zeitoun* (2009),
all fall under this category, as do the sociological studies of John Arena,
Kristen L. Buras, and many others.[4] These prose writers ask their audience to take them at face value. They mean what they say, and they say
what they mean. The word *prose*, in fact, originates etymologically in
the Latin word *prorsus*, meaning "direct," and suggests straightforward
and unadorned language, a language unconcerned with aesthetic style
in its revelation of truth. *Prose* may also be related to the word *porous*,
as if the meaning embedded in prose writing can flow unhindered from
writer to reader, from speaker to audience. There are reasons to be sus-
picious of the central truth claims of prose, of course—the controversy
surrounding *Zeitoun* is an important case in point—but the general goal
of the genre is to minimize that suspicion.[5]

Poets do something different in their writing. Because Hurricane
Katrina may be understood as a giant mythopoeic project, reflecting the
old and creating the new, poetry ought not to be considered as some
sort of adjunct to other and often more famous forms of analysis. Cities
and neighborhoods are built and destroyed through the impersonal
logics of capital accumulation and disinvestment; houses are made, and
are made to come undone; nations themselves rise and fall with the
long waves of time; and through it all are actual human lives with their
remembrances of things past, their *recherche* for those things, their
present moments that go by so quickly, and their desires for the future.
Poetry remains a realm of thought and writing that records those things
in indeterminate form. Poetry asks the other to read and to think not
once or twice about the text but over and over again.

But there is no guarantee. From both the reader's and the writer's perspective, there is no way to know for sure that something like intended meaning is being communicated. Unlike in nonfiction prose written for academic or general audiences, unlike even, to some degree, in the other literary genres—in fiction, say, or in drama—readers and writers of poetry are left with a text, a document, a testimony of thought that invites an ever-expanding web of interpretation. One reason that Biguenet's play can be so successful as a play, as a communal experience in the precise moment when actors act on the stage, is that it relies on determinate meaning. The play relies on authorial intention and shared interpretation. The words spoken on stage may trigger different memories and associations for different people, but the playwright's goal is to guide actors who call for a collective response.

Considering the full range of dramatic expression across disparate times and places, of course, the picture is much more complicated. There are many examples of prose writers operating like poets and vice versa—indeed, it is impossible to cast poetry and prose as a strict binary opposition—but let us suspend our disbelief for a moment and ask a crucial question about what poetry says that it does and why.

Poetry has at its disposal techniques that are more complex and unique than those usually associated with prose. Think of the major tropes, the use of irony and multivalent meaning, as well as all the auditory devices of sound repetition and rhythm. With these techniques come certain liabilities. Poetic writing—unprosaic language—may cause confusion. Readers of Ford may be left wondering what it is exactly that the poet means, what it is exactly that she intends to communicate, but such a question would rarely if ever enter Biguenet's theater.

Even more than poetry's propensity to confuse the mind of the reader, poetic writing has something else working against it. Poeticism may be understood as a liability with regard to the actual text's truth value. The more poetic the language, the skeptic will contend, the further it swerves from the truth. If prose writers such as Piazza, Eggers, Arena, or Buras are caught being too "poetic" in their language, their readers will fundamentally change the way they evaluate the author's truth claims.

The reasons for this skepticism have a long history—many of which go back at least to Plato—and have much to do with the dualistic casting of beauty *versus* truth and artifice *versus* reality. I will explore this issue in more depth during the course of this chapter, but I want to state firmly here that poetry matters in response to Hurricane Katrina. In fact, poetry may be the most appropriate kind of language for thinking through the disaster.

The poem as text appears in a manageable size. Like the hurricane itself, it can be charted and measured according to various parameters—the number of words and sounds, the arrangement of lines and stanzas, the spacing of marks on the page—but the poem often explodes, barely containing its meaning, or holding on to its meaning in uneasy ways. The poem bears its vulnerability seemingly always on the verge of breaking down. Also like the hurricane itself, the poem works its way into the mind with no clear beginning, middle, and end.

If the hurricane and the poem *appear* in manageable size, however, they are being deceptive. They beg for more and more response, for answers, for readers and communities of interpretation and reinterpretation. But if poetry calls for response, it also calls for responsibility. Whether it is hours, days, weeks, months, years, or even decades later, the words replay themselves in the mind, loosening the sediment of forgetful accumulation. The poem and the hurricane will not be quiet, and they do not sit still. Readers of poetry, like readers of the disaster itself, always return to the scene of the crime. In the remainder of this chapter, I will explore the work of two exceptional poets from Louisiana—Martha Serpas and Yusef Komunyakaa—to flesh out more carefully these theoretical claims.[6]

MARTHA SERPAS

Martha Serpas's *The Dirty Side of the Storm* (2007) may be read as one of the most quintessential works of wetland ecopoetics in contemporary literature. Many of the poems contained in the book were written before Hurricane Katrina, but they chronicle the withering toe of Louisiana that set the stage for the storm surge and levee failure that left New Orleans and its vicinity engulfed in 2005. Like Biguenet's *Rising Water* and Ford's *Colosseum*, Serpas's collection draws on the *longue durée* of uneasiness that has been developing in New Orleans for centuries. In many of her poems, that uneasiness is figured in double form—ecological and theological—and it is filtered through the paradoxical concept of decadence that I have been describing.

A poem called "The Discipline of Nonfulfillment" can serve as a representative example of this move. While meditating on the multiple significations of "Eastertide" in southern Louisiana, Serpas writes that the word "*tide* / means something different here" (24). The word in the swamps and bayous of coastal Louisiana becomes detached from its universal and catholic meaning, its referent to the Easter season commemorating the crucifixion and resurrection of an anthropomorphic godhead, and thus a symbol of the death and rebirth of us all. Because of its place specificity, the word does not suggest the annual commemoration of divinity becoming flesh and blood. The mind of the southern Louisianian attaches not to the prefixed *Easter*-tide but to the suffixed *Easter*-*tide*, the daily ebb and flow of Gulf waters.

Despite the clear divergence of the universal *Easter* from the place-specific *tide*—they are indeed two different words with two different meanings—Serpas poses the following question over the course of the next two stanzas:

> But wouldn't you say it's the same
>
> Sweeping abundance overtaking
> Shoals and inlets, joining lake and bay,
> Drowning everything in between? (24)

Although the grammatical form of these four lines is interrogative, Serpas intends a much more forceful and declarative proposition that the annual Eastertide and the daily tide are coterminous in their chief motions. The coming of Easter and the rising of the tides are both acts of overwhelming profusion; they are both powerful moments in which destruction and regeneration, uneasiness and rapture, become one. *Tide* may indeed mean something different in watery Louisiana than it does in Vatican City, but there is also a clear connection between these two place-based significations. For Serpas, the ecological meaning of *tide* in the wetlands and the theological meaning of *Eastertide* in the larger Christian world can converge, as if one can serve as an explanatory mechanism for the other, and theological principles (here the death and rebirth of the Christ figure) can help to explain ecological principles (the ebb and flow of moving bodies of water) and vice versa. This kind of figuration of an ecological–theological connection is recurrent in the long history of American environmental literature, and Serpas deserves a recognized place within that literary canon. But Serpas also approaches the ecological–theological dyad through a regionally inflected concept of decadence.

The title of the poem itself is an important feature of this decadence. "The Discipline of Nonfulfillment" revolves around a longing, an incompletion of fulfillment, an infinite deferral of satisfaction. But this type of longing requires extreme self-control—ascesis, to use a more theological term—in order to keep it going. One of the most decadent characters in literary history, whom I considered at length in the introductory chapter, is J. K. Huysmans's Jean Des Esseintes, who suffers from and seems to enjoy this type of desire without gratification. Much of *À rebours* reads as a contrapuntal reply to a supposedly natural inclination to get oneself satisfied. And yet the nonsatisfaction is precisely and paradoxically what satisfies more than anything else.

So decadence in this way names an elasticity stretching around the extremes of deprivation and engorgement, nonfulfillment and fulfillment. Serpas turns to water in order to figure poetically the conjunction of these extremes. On the one hand, readers will encounter in the water the starkness of "nonfulfillment," its stillness and absence. On the other hand, there is its "sweeping abundance." The liquid imagery throughout *The Dirty Side of the Storm* almost always flows between these two poles of lack and excess, too little and too much fulfillment, impoverishment and opulence. The imagery, furthermore and relatedly, is almost always ecstatic and mysteriously orgasmic, coming as it does in double waves of danger and pleasure.

The poetry of Martha Serpas indicates the value of poetic language in the face of social and environmental disaster because it helps to unpack the psychosocial charges of the situation. It helps to tease out the historical strains that form the affects and moods, the political positions and aspirations—in a word, the zeitgeist—of the contemporary moment. But there is always the risk that poeticism presents a fundamentally inaccurate picture of what it says it represents. There is always the risk that the poet's aesthetic sensibility will get in the way of pure ontological description.

Because Serpas writes about urgent matters in the context of South Louisiana, the stakes are especially high. Without a doubt, Serpas aestheticizes destruction and death simply by taking those things as her subject and presenting them in poetic language. Such a move raises many questions. For one, the poet's use of the word *drowning* in "The Discipline of Nonfulfillment" is especially curious, considering what it is, exactly, that the poet says "drowns." The "sweeping abundance" of water overtakes not animal and human life but "shoals and inlets, joining lake and bay." What is drowned is shoals, which seems to have the double meaning here of both shallows and schools of fish. Serpas claims that the shoals drown, as well as the water itself, raising the question of whether such entities actually *can* drown and suffer drowning. Poetry seldom calls a spade a spade, and the aesthetic drive always threatens to take priority and to trump the accepted meanings of things—in this case, of "drowning."

Critical readers of Serpas may also wonder how the poet would poeticize the event if she herself were caught in the rising water and drowned between lake and bay. For this poetry to work as aestheticized language, for the poet to find beauty in what many people would consider the horror of drowning, there must be a cognitive distance. Indeed, the poems in *The Dirty Side of the Storm* evince a detachment from their primary subject. There seems to be a spatial and temporal degree of separation between the initial event and the poetic figuration. Although Serpas is a native of Galliano, and although she cannot help but bear witness to the ecological disaster that renders the inhabitants of South Louisiana more and more vulnerable to hurricanes as the outer banks quickly dissolve into the Gulf, her poetry also dramatizes her separation from that place of origin. Her years of study and teaching outside of Louisiana, including at Yale Divinity School, are as readable in her poetry as her intimate knowledge of the wetlandscape.

Such a poetical detachment is especially striking in a poem called "Decreation." One section in particular stands out, although it is a part of a larger leitmotif of the human body becoming land becoming water. Serpas writes, over the course of two stanzas:

> If only the land would take me now,

> I would lie against the marsh grass and sink,
> muck enfolding me, and welcome the eroding Gulf—
> handful by handful, carrying us away. (79)

Two stanzas earlier, Serpas underscores this sentiment, in a line that likewise ends with the Dickinsonian dash: "If only I could give the land my body—." Readers could read Serpas here as romanticizing death purely and simply, as she had done so with the drowning. But notice that Serpas is not disclosing a straightforward desire for death. There is no "I" that wants, pure and simple, but instead the poet creates a conditional that would need to be met in order to allow the desire. That conditional begins the lines in the following way: "If only the land would" and "If only I could." Employing the anticipatory *if* without the corresponding *then,* and concluding the line with the Dickinsonian dash of interminability, Serpas stops in time and in thought. The romanticizing of death is put in check.

What also should be clear, I think, is that the poet and the reader desire not the thing itself—that is, the experience of the body dying and becoming land becoming water—but a poetic representation of the thing. Such a desire, a desire that is so fundamental to the concept of decadence, is not without its risks. Indeed, many a character, fictional and otherwise, has been seduced into the Gulf's embrace, the slow and deadly mixing of river and sea. Kate Chopin's Edna Pontellier may be just the tip of the iceberg.

In *The Dirty Side of the Storm,* Serpas figures something negative— the fact of coastal erosion in which thousands of years of amassed lands dissolve into the Gulf within a couple of human generations—as something positive, or at least desirable within the context of the quoted stanzas. The human body becoming land becoming water is reminiscent of a fantasy of return to the maternal womb, a fantasy that is something akin to Sigmund Freud's description of the "oceanic feeling," in *The Future of an Illusion* (1927).

Part of the reason why Serpas employs this kind of axiological play that hovers between the good and the bad, I believe, is that it gives her a chance to meditate on the psychosocial stakes of loss that wraps around both the human and the environmental. But in many of Serpas's poems—in "The Discipline of Nonfulfillment" and "Decreation" especially—there is little in the way of anthropogenic environmental destruction. If there is decadence, the paradoxical relation of decay and beauty, degeneration and regeneration, opulence and deprivation, that decadence is an ecological and theological reality outside the realm of human causality.

A poem called "The Water" is the paradigmatic example of this move. The water—the "it"—has a decadent life of its own, erotically rendered and dangerous, and also completely nonhuman. Serpas writes, "It is there under the wharf and soon under // the house, whoring with any swamp rat / or snake. It rings cypress knees with pearls—" (19). The rising tide of water is a morally questionable force, sexually engaging with the worst and proposing marriage in irony. It moves quickly, too, and has taken over the land and risen beneath the house before one knows it. And over the next three stanzas, Serpas goes further, pushing the water to its limits:

And then it is there, all gray length of it,

rich sex of it, it wants you so badly,
it pounds at the door, *let me take*

your smallness, your jetties, your broad
coasts, your loam. (20)

And here there is the unmistaken Freudian return of the repressed desire within dream work: "Its desire / thrums like an idling outboard. Ignore // it and it tows itself into your dreams. It's / everywhere, every chance, all the time" (20).

Although there is no anthropogenic mover of the water here, in many other poems, not only does the poet's insistence on human responsibility for environmental destruction become more pronounced, but so does her decadent sensibility. "A Corollary" stands out in this way. "The trees," Serpas begins, pauses for a stanza break, then continues, "stand dead but don't fall" (21). As discrete organisms, the trees fail to pass all the tests of the living and yet they exist still, standing beyond standing in a kind of undead living. Their standing, of course, was never legal, so their standing dead reflects their legal status in life. Over two stanzas, Serpas gestures toward the human to explain the cause of the trees' deadness: "Veins in the Gulf will swell, too, // carrying grayed-out swirls—ghosts—/ to greed's unbroken refrain" (21).

This stanza is one of the few in which Serpas calls for responsibility to account for environmental destruction, and even here that call is somewhat mystified. A "corollary" is a logical consequence of an event, an effect that cannot help but to follow. The corollary of greed is the poisoning of land, water, and air in the petrochemical corridor of southeastern Louisiana. The corollary of greed is dramatic loss of wetlands along the Louisiana coastline. The corollary of greed is the swelling of veins that can refer both to canals and to oil deposits. Swollen veins may show engorgement of the body in spectacular display of an *élan vital*, but it may also show the mark of an aging mammalian body and be a prelude to death.

The Dirty Side of the Storm may be approached precisely as a poetics of loss in a way that has been usefully theorized in Freud's "Mourning and Melancholia" (1917) and resurrected, among other places, in Judith Butler's *Precarious Life: The Powers of Mourning and Violence* (2004). "Freud reminded us that when we lose someone," Butler writes, "we do not always know what it is *in* that person that has been lost. So when one loses, one is also faced with something enigmatic: something is hiding in the loss, something is lost within the recesses of loss" (22). Although both Freud and Butler focus on the stakes of *human* loss, their insights are valuable in relation to Serpas, a poet who mines the something lost within loss and attempts to give that something a shape in the interstices between the human and the other-than-human world. Serpas in this way dramatizes the consequences of loss amidst the contemporary environmental crisis.

In an essay called "Melancholy Natures, Queer Ecologies" (2010), Catriona Mortimer-Sandilands teases out the implications of the Freudian-Butlerian conception of loss for the environmental humanities, and her words may help to unpack the psychosocial forces at play in Serpasian ecopoetics. Mortimer-Sandilands writes:

> At the heart of the modern age is indeed a core of grief—but that "core" is more accurately conceived as a condition of *melancholia*, a state of suspended mourning in which the object of loss is very real but psychically "ungrievable" within the confines of a society that cannot acknowledge nonhuman beings, natural environments, and ecological processes as appropriate objects for genuine grief. (333, emphasis in original)

The loss of a human person is difficult, without a doubt, and it is confusing because what it is, exactly, that one misses in the missing person is often extremely difficult to pinpoint let alone articulate. The event thus may morph into a prolonged and seemingly endless state of depression. But the difficulty of losing a human person is at least ameliorated by the social affirmation that one's pain is justified, that one has a right to mourn in the way one sees fit, and for however long. The loss of other-than-human beings and worlds, on the other hand, may prove even more difficult and confusing because that loss does not carry the weight of social legitimacy. That loss does not have the backing of grievability.

"In such conditions," Mortimer-Sandilands continues, "loss becomes displacement: the object that cannot be lost and cannot be let go, and as a psychoanalytic perspective reveals, such disavowed objects are preserved within the psyche in the form of identifications and incorporations" (333). This process is exactly what happens in *The Dirty Side of the Storm*. Because Serpas cannot seem to address the loss directly, the poet seems instead to take a different path by identifying with the eroding wetlandscape and desiring to be incorporated into it. Serpas's difficulty in directly addressing loss, of course, is not hers alone, and she joins many other inhabitants of South Louisiana in her poetic search.

YUSEF KOMUNYAKAA

The poetry of Yusef Komunyakaa, especially a poem called "Requiem" (2008), is important to read in conjunction with Serpas. Both poets are intimately connected with the psychosocial state of the state, but they originate from different backgrounds. Serpas hails from Galliano, in the bayous south of New Orleans, and seems to write primarily from a European American perspective, while Komunyakaa, hailing from Bogalusa in the drier lands north of the city, takes on the African American experience cum cosmopolitan *creolité*.

Serpas and Komunyakaa also diverge in significant ways on stylistic and thematic levels. In Serpas, the poetic language is supple, light on the tongue, and sensual. It is language that seems to flow much like the spongy bodies of water and people it describes. Although the themes that Serpas deals with are complex and there undoubtedly are layers of meaning that get refracted through *The Dirty Side of the Storm*, there is an apparent simplicity or naturalness of everyday speech. Across her work, Serpas does employ alliteration, assonance, and other kinds of repetitive sounds, but, more often than not, those sounds are couched within a relative accessibility of diction.

Komunyakaa is a difficult poet. In contrast to Serpas's sonorous softness and ease of pronunciation, Komunyakaa twists the tongue in a dazzling display of linguistic and cognitive acrobatics. If there are pauses
and breaks in Serpas, moments when the reader can catch a breath and
inwardly contemplate meaning, not so in Komunyakaa. "Requiem" is
all about hardball. Here are the first eleven lines of the poem:

> So,
> when the strong unholy high winds
> whiplashed over the sold-off marshlands
> eaten back to a sigh of saltwater,
> the Crescent City was already shook down to her pilings,
> her floating ribs, her spleen & backbone,
> left trembling in her Old World facades
> & postmodern lethargy, lost to waterlogged
> memories & quitclaim deeds,
> exposed for all eyes, damnable
> gaze & lamentation—plumb line (484)

The poem begins with the single word *so*, an anticipatory conjunction
that is intended to introduce the city's seemingly endless and sad state of
affairs. There is also something like gossip contained in the word. One
thinks of its usefulness in announcing an unbelievable—and yet completely believable—story about somebody, as in the common expression
"So, you will never believe what happened to so-and-so." That first word
can be elongated or shortened, depending on the intended intensity of
suspense. It also can be sharply exclaimed, as in the barked "So!," or
it can be quietly whispered. But there is also a ring of logical causality
to the word, a representation of corollary, if used synonymously with
the more formal *therefore*. When X exists, Komunyakaa says, so will Y.
The first line, so simple in its brevity and casualness, is deceptive; its
ease will not hold. So, beyond the "So," the poem lets loose.

The story that Komunyakaa tells in "Requiem" springs from his per-
ception of the blunt horror of social and environmental violence that
has been brewing for three hundred years. The way that violence gets

inscribed in writing, for Komunyakaa, has everything to do with the tropological avenues of decadence that have evolved kaleidoscopically over those centuries. Its major images are of decaying bodies ripped apart by a vicious predator, insides spilling out from the caverns of the body, almost devoured and trembling. This horror of social and environmental violence is nothing new for Komunyakaa. When Hurricane Katrina came aground in late August 2005, the city and the surrounding wetlands were already teetering on the edge.

The poem traces the whiplash and unholiness that ebbs and flows in the wake of capital accumulation and dispossession. Komunyakaa is especially interested in the physical landscape and its ecological history. The landscape yields and falls to human extraction. In the old-growth swamps Komunyakaa sees "a knelt-down army of cypress, / a testament to how men dreamt land / out of water" (485). And along the coast, he sees "the barrier islands / inherited by the remittance man, scalawag, / & King Cotton" (484). What is exposed when the heavy winds peel away the semblances of civilization and culture, the advertisements of progress and goodness, is "damnable." What is exposed is the uneven distribution of risk that is built into the logic of social stratification. Although it is always there, catastrophe dramatizes such injustices, the power structures that create uneasy social relations. Komunyakaa's poem is also a full frontal assault on the insidious optimism that seems to pervade the city and is epitomized in one of the city's most famously French sayings: "*Laissez les bons temps rouler*" (Let the good times roll). Komunyakaa's prime examples of the power of denial and the uglier underside of the ideology of hope come to the fore in "Requiem."

Such an assault is made in the context of transatlantic exchange. Komunyakaa begins one of his "already" anaphors with the following:

> already the last ghost song
> of the Choctaw & the Chickasaw
> was long gone, no more than a drunken curse
> among the oak & sweet gum leaves, a tally
> of broken treatises & absences echoing (484)

The Native American songs devolve into drink and cursing. Their bodies, like their languages, fall into impotence, according to Komunyakaa, and, as in Serpas, there is a provocative erotics to the destruction, a merger of Eros and Thanatos.

Here in particular, however, Komunyakaa's poetic claim ought to give his readers pause. Are the Native American songs truly gone? Have the ancient voices of the Choctaws and the Chickasaws been reduced to simple and enfeebled curses? The answer, if one were only to open one's ears, is simply no. "Indians," Ruth Salvaggio writes, "can be heard bringing the sounds of the lyric call to New Orleans as surely as they brought food to a fledgling colony often on the verge of starvation" (160).[7] The rich traditions of the Mardi Gras Indians likewise complicate Komunyakaa's claims, as do the writings of Joy Harjo, LeAnne Howe, Brenda Marie Osbey, Natasha Trethewey, and other writers who take up and amplify the voices of the Native American past, present, and future.[8]

Despite the poet's questionable claim on this issue, Komunyakaa's "Requiem" resounds powerfully in the human imagination, and he continues in his rich and provocative vein:

> already folklore began to rise up
> from the buried lallygag & sluice
> pulsing beneath the Big Easy
> rolling between & through itself,
> caught in some downward tug
> & turn, like a world of love affairs (484–485)

Such a merger of Eros and Thanatos returns again at the end of "Requiem." The final six lines read:

> already nothing but water
> mumbling as the great turbulent eye
> lingered on a primordial question,
> then turned—the gauzy genitalia of Bacchus
> & Zulu left dangling from magnolias & raintrees,
> already . . . (485)

Komunyakaa uses the word *already* six times in a relatively short poem of forty-nine lines:

1. "the Crescent City was already shook down to her pilings" (line 5)
2. "already the last ghost song / of the Choctaw & the Chickasaw / was long gone" (lines 13–15)
3. "already the sky was falling in on itself" (line 20)
4. "already folklore began to rise up" (line 30)
5. "already nothing but water" (line 44)
6. "already . . . " (line 49)

The final line, in fact, is only the single word *already* followed by an el-lipsis, a complex piece of punctuation that, in its excess, works against the purpose of the period. It is not the full stop that ends the sentence, the logical structure, but its opening. It is punctuation that punctures, opening things up and indicating not the end of discussion but its sus-pension. As aposiopetic technique, it is punctuation designed to spur the imagination and the continuation of thought.

Komunyakaa calls his Katrina poem "Requiem," a word that means a Mass or a religious song intended to put to rest the souls of the dead. Critical readers of Komunyakaa may wonder if the poet is being pre-mature in his evaluation. Everything and everyone is all ready, all pre-pared through prior knowledge. Like the concept of decadence itself, Komunyakaa's use of *already* can intimate a fatalism, as if the city were always already fated for doom and nothing can be done to prevent the disaster. The images the poet employs, furthermore, are almost hyperbolic: the skeletal remains of the city, the piers rising up from the ground with no house on top, sounds void of human voice and returning to the liquid of Gulf and swamp.

As is often the case, decadence here points to a set of dramatic opposites: great wealth and opulence (along with ruthless greed and ambition, horrific immorality, and ethical indifference in the face of suffering), on the one hand, and extreme poverty and all the psycho-social ills that result (violence and murder, addiction and self-loathing, *ressentiment*), on the other. Here, both sides of the coin seem to be a perversion of economic moderation, a necessary effect of the imma-nent laws of laissez-faire capitalism, of economic systems without any regulatory or redistributive mechanisms. The elite aristocracy can be decadent, and so can the dirt poor, but never the middle class. This is why the decadent adventure always seems to involve either the palatial residences of the Garden District or the ghettoes of Central City. New Orleans decadents very rarely flock to Gentilly or Lakeview.

As the globe warms and the waters rise, as fragile coastal habitat is reconfigured in response to sprawling human development, the ecopoetics of Serpas and Komunyakaa bears witness to the social and environmental changes, with all their indeterminate axiologies. The destruction and loss linger in the mind-body of the poets and their readers. But their work also fits squarely into what Frederick Buell has called a "maturer crisis literature," in his indispensable book *From Apocalypse to Way of Life: Environmental Crisis in the American Century* (2004). This "maturer crisis literature" is a literature that can no longer bear the urgency of impending doom and instead almost seems to ac-cept the fact of environmental destruction. It is a literature that comes in the wake of Rachel Carson's *Silent Spring* (1962), that does not so much deem environmental collapse as untrue but as a necessary evil, part of the deal, the trade-off for having the privilege to live as modern Americans. In this way, environmental crisis becomes a new normal, a way of life, just one more factor to consider in the calculation of risk.

Buell writes, "As never before, literature today represents deepening environmental crisis as a context in which people dwell and with which they are intimate, not as an apocalypse still ahead" (321–322). There can be no hard-and-fast solution to the crisis, in Buell's estimation of this mode of literary expression. This literature, Buell writes:

> does not ask for a look of panicked horror, an urgent effort to change, and then denial and forgetfulness until the next look. It asks that peo-ple gaze on and on without being able to avert their eyes or seize upon easy remedies or prescriptions for change. It asks that audiences realize just how deeply in the soup they themselves are and how difficult and

uncertain solutions are. [. . .] Stilled into form, yet persistingly ironic, moving, angry, chilling, and unresolved, this new literature of crisis silently awaits a meaningful collective response. It also fully acknowledges that this response may or may not come. (322)

Martha Serpas's *The Dirty Side of the Storm* and Yusef Komunyakaa's "Requiem" are precisely that kind of ecopoetry.

AFTER BRITISH PETROLEUM

The unique situation of a hurricane, as opposed to other disasters of pure politics, is that with a hurricane comes a sense of ultimate betrayal beyond cognitive and practical reparation. Jerry W. Ward Jr., for example, in *The Katrina Papers* (2008), writes of the deep despair without recourse or rectification that haunts him and others in the aftermath of August 29, 2005: "Thousands of us have been abused by Nature and revenge is impossible" (11). One can blame the political establishment; one can blame the Corps of Engineers and FEMA. One may even find oneself having one's day in court, pleading to a judge for redress and reparations. But there will also always be the nagging fact that something nonhuman, other-than-human, more-than-human was at work in the disaster, and "revenge is impossible."

In Hurricane Katrina, moreover, as Richard Campanella puts it, "ancient geographies of risk, supposedly subjugated by technology a century ago, came rushing back to life," thus compounding the dizzying preoccupation with historical origins and processual causality (333). As a genre, the ecopoetics of the storm works through a condensation or distillation of that fact of violence. The suffering of human and other-than-human beings and their worlds is suspended through time, with no hope of abatement.

There are epistemological difficulties in understanding a hurricane, its causes and effects. There are paradoxes and ambiguities and indeterminacies and so on; there are layers of voices and testimonies and controversies and disputed claims. But there is also a stark reality, a reality plain, and often horrifying in its plainness. Miss Jeanfreau is alive

159

or she is dead; the house either flooded or it did not; the old family photograph is either intact or it is lost somewhere forever. Violence has a way of doing that, of creating some absolute clarity amidst the dense of fog of confusion, even if that clarity comes in only one or two pieces.

The ecopoetics of Hurricane Katrina is drenched in the imagery of decadence that is both ecological and theological in nature, but the hurricane season of 2005 was prelude to a slicker disaster looming just off the coast, which blew up five years later, in 2010, with the Deepwater Horizon. In a hurricane, we can count the dead bodies, the corpses of people and pets and other wild animals. We can see the dead bodies floating in the water or trapped within the horrible tableaux of their deaths, when the waters recede. In an oil spill, most of the destruction is not immediate, and it often goes undetected by the human eye, although the video footage of 210 million gallons of black oil spewing out of an uncapped well at the bottom of the Gulf for eighty-seven days was a spectacular event. In such a disaster, the sign of decline was not about indulgence in food or sex or drink, the usual suspects in New Orleans. It did not parade itself half naked down Bourbon Street. Here, instead, those signs shone bright and plumbed the depths of so-called industrial progress. The decadents, cultivated in Paris and Vienna and Rome and Moscow in the nineteenth century, would have been nonplussed.

If a hurricane may be forgiven for its devastation because of the overdetermined nature of its meteorological force, forgiveness in the British Petroleum disaster comes with much more difficulty. Blame can be placed squarely on living people and corporate decisions. For this reason, because forgiveness does not come easily, forgetfulness seems to be the more prevalent mode of coping. The other significant thing to acknowledge is that the language of decadence, the language of loss and destruction, has the paradoxical consequence of invigorating the literary corpus. With the BP disaster, another wave of decadence came into the literary canon.

Serpas wrote *The Dirty Side of the Storm* and Komunyakaa wrote "Requiem" before the BP disaster. In many ways, that event would make no difference to Komunyakaa, because it had already been in the making for a very long time, but Serpas's poems operate according to a different ontology. The dirty side of the storm is dirty, to be sure, but its dirt is *pure* dirt. Its toxicity is low if not completely undetectable, so one may wonder about how Serpas would write a poem such as "Decreation" when the Gulf as womb becomes more toxic and less hospitable.

"Since 1930," the environmental historian Jason P. Theriot writes, "nearly two thousand square miles of Louisiana's wetlands have been converted to open water" (2).[9] Levee systems, canalization for many reasons (for petroleum, of course, but also for trapping, fishing, agriculture, and timber), soil subsidence, and hurricanes all bear responsibility. For this reason, assessing damage and assigning blame has been a notoriously difficult endeavor during the past fifty years. In the absence of a major spectacle such as the BP blowout, most environmental damage enacts what Rob Nixon describes as a "slow violence."[10] The damages accrue so gradually that they cannot be read as such. They are incremental and imperceptible, all the while having enormous effects. Theriot writes, "The quiet, slow-moving environmental crisis growing in coastal Louisiana over the decades has been a gradual, subtle deterioration of the ecosystem, nearly completely isolated from the eyes of the national public until the turn of the twenty-first century" (13).

One wonders about the future, as Theriot's book essentially tells the same old story over and over again. The industry works to create jobs and wealth by taking a risk in the business of extraction; the environmental impact of such extraction is either known and ignored, or not investigated at all; at some point, there is a critical turn and such knowledge can no longer be ignored. This is usually at the point of disaster. The industry vows to change; new technologies are developed that allow industry to work to create jobs and wealth by taking new risks in the business of extraction, and the cycle continues. Every now and again, industry must pay the piper, but this payment often seems to be factored into the bottom line from the very beginning. "The disaster ruins everything, all the while leaving everything intact," the French philosopher Maurice Blanchot presciently writes from his vantage in 1980 (1).[11] As disaster piles upon disaster, how will the poets and their readers respond?

8

THE DECADENT FUTURE OF
NEW ORLEANS IN LITERATURE

The future holds a simple promise.

—VALERIE MARTIN, *A Recent Martyr* (1987), 204

By the end of Valerie Martin's novel *A Recent Martyr*, the narrator has survived a number of disasters both large and small: a dead-end job, an unhappy marriage, a sadomasochistic relationship that turns into rape, bubonic plague, forced quarantine, and the loss of a friend who is a young Catholic nun murdered on her way back to the convent. New Orleans grounds and enlivens all this action, and yet, in the novel's denouement, the narrator chooses to remain in the city. "It's an odd sensation to recognize in oneself the need to be in a particular physical environment," Martin writes, "when one longs for the home ground no matter how terrible the memories it holds, no matter how great the efforts made to leave it behind" (204).

When the narrator does make those efforts to leave the city, she thinks herself "lucky to escape its allure, for it's the attraction of decay, of vicious, florid, natural cycles that roll over the senses with their lushness." But, try as she might, her efforts to escape always end in the same way, with her return to New Orleans. "Where else could I find these hateful, humid, murderously hot afternoons," she asks, "when I know that the past was a series of great mistakes, the greatest being the inability to live anywhere but in this swamp?" (204). For Martin's narrator, as well as for many New Orleanians, the decision to stay or go is caught up in this kind of circular dynamic between attraction and revulsion, topophilia and topophobia, in determining *oikos*.

This circular dynamic between -philia and -phobia plays out not only according to *topos* but also according to *chronos*. Indeed, the novel's denouement is best understood as a conjunction between topophilia-topophobia and chronophilia-chronophobia. For the narrator, there is pleasure and danger in "the threatening encumbrance of moss on trees, the thick, sticky plantain trees that can grow from their chopped roots twenty feet in three months, the green scum that spreads over the lagoons and bayous." But the pleasure and danger she finds in the place, and the specific life forms contained therein, are also caught up in the narrator's sense of time. After focusing on the past, especially on how New Orleans is associated for her with bad personal and social memories, a long "series" of haunting "mistakes," the narrator then moves outside that temporal frame. In the last three sentences of the novel, Martin writes, "The future holds a simple promise. We are well below sea level, and inundation is inevitable. We are content, for now, to have our heads above the water" (204).

While the novel's denouement remains fixed in one place, the city of New Orleans, it moves temporally from the past to the future, and then it backpedals into the present. The conditional contentment "for now" that ends the novel, in 1987, seems especially poignant, almost prophetic, looking back from our own now in the present. Its mood, a kind of good-enough-for-now apathy, recognizes a certain environmental disaster looming on the horizon without having the will to do anything about it.

Eighteen years after *A Recent Martyr* appeared, in 1987, the inevitable happened. During the devastating floods of hurricanes Katrina and Rita, in August and September 2005, the conditional contentment "for now" came to an end. The future's simple promise, that which was sent forward ahead of itself, became actualized in the present. A poem by Katie Ford called "Earth," quoted in full from her book *Colosseum* (2008), describes that moment just before the future keeps its promise, just before the inevitable inundation will come:

If you respect the dead
and recall where they died
by this time tomorrow
there will be nowhere to walk. (13)

Written in the wake of the 2005 hurricanes but seemingly set the day before the waters began to rise, "Earth" presents a haunting vision of tomorrow in the form of a syllogistic proof. If A (one has respect for the dead), and B (one is capable of memory), then C (within the next twenty-four hours, all ground will become unwalkable). Like all syllogisms, the poem works through a kind of rational clarity and certainty. As Ford writes it, the conclusion cannot help but follow from the combination of the two propositions. The logic, therefore, seems inevitable. As in Valerie Martin's novel, human agency seems to be rendered powerless to effect change within the span of the next twenty-four hours.

Such a view of the world is dark, but there is potentially an even darker interpretation in this short poem of four lines. What the poem does not exactly spell out is that, to avoid coming to the conclusion, to avoid C, one may undermine one or both of the two propositions. If one wants to walk, if one wants to have grounds upon which to walk tomorrow, one can undermine A or B or both. One can choose to cease respecting the dead, one can actively forget where they died, or one can do both. Because the imperative to walk is so great after the disaster, and because respect for the dead is so difficult to shake, as history has shown, the decision to forget seems to be the most popular avenue. The dead often go unrecalled.

In the context of southern Louisiana, one is faced not only with the loss of ground, spurred by the ethical imperative to avoid walking on the dead, if indeed they are recalled, but also with the literal loss of ground through environmental destruction, spurred by a variety of anthropogenic and non-anthropogenic forces: levee construction and soil subsidence, dredging and canalization, chemical poisoning and salt water intrusion, rising sea levels, whiplashing by major storms. All of these forces have the ultimate effect of dissolving the ground upon which one can walk and, by extension, perform that most meditative of philosophical and physical activities. The title of Ford's poem, "Earth," is general and planetary, moreover, as if to say that the future's promise in New Orleans does not apply simply there. It is the fate of the whole world.

The kind of ecological dread that surfaces in Ford, Martin, and many others in New Orleans can be traced back at least to the city's very founding, in 1718. The historian Lawrence Powell, in *The Accidental City* (2012), notes that during its very first spring of existence, the spring of 1719, the city was inundated by the regular flooding of the Mississippi River. Summing up the city's troubled relationship with its own future, even at that time, Powell writes, "It was a tacit admission that the only sure thing between the initial clearing of New Orleans in 1718 and the final order designating it as the new capital more than three years later was that it had no apparent future" (51).

This "tacit admission" persists even today, as the city prepares for its tricentennial in 2018, and yet those concerns now operate within a different temporal frame. In the early eighteenth century, the pressing questions were about finding ways to get through the seasonal wave of flooding at hand. Environmental risk, therefore, operated according to a very abbreviated conception of time. Chronophobia was monthly, annual, or at most stretched forward only a few years into the future. In the early twenty-first century, however, after the hurricanes of 2005, New Orleanians think very differently about time and place. Scientists and politicians now refer to the "hundred-year storm" that will come to impact the region with an intensity equal to a Katrina or Rita. The risk involved in the hundred-year storm is stretched out over the course of a century, and that risk is mathematically specified. The phrase uses the time frame of a century to understand risk, but it is also potentially misleading, referring as it does to a storm that will come not in one hundred years but to a storm that has a one percent chance of occurring every year. In this way, the phrase may be read as diluting, de-intensifying, or elongating the risk—and with it the dread—over the course of a century, but the phrase also refers to every present moment. It is thus fixed firmly within the perennially time-ticking structure of apocalyptic thought.

Apocalypse comes from the ancient Greek word *apokaluptein,* a combination of *apo-* (un-) and *kaluptein* (cover). The word's etymology helps to explain the uneasiness that arises in moments of its figuration. As an uncovering, it is as if some disaster lurks below what we perceive as reality and patiently waits for its time to surface. The disaster of the apocalypse is thus not temporally fixed in the future. Like the hundred-year storm, it spreads itself out unseen throughout the past and the present. It is here already but not yet known.

If one is tempted to write off the apocalypse as some unfortunate and hysterical offshoot of religious thinking, one should be quick to note that it extends widely into more subdued and secular manifestations. Many people and groups, including environmentalists, have been drawn to apocalyptic thinking for many reasons. In fact, Lawrence Buell, in *The Environmental Imagination* (1995), calls apocalyptic thinking "the single most powerful master metaphor that the contemporary environmental imagination has at its disposal" (285).

As environmental texts, Martin's novel and Ford's poem are not religiously derived or supernatural; instead, they are strictly naturalistic in their conceptualization. No literal god or devil will be coming in the environmental disaster. Ford mentions "the dead," but those entities have no real force in the world; they cannot dictate which grounds are walkable and which are not. It is only their memory, housed within the minds of the living, that has the power to haunt and compel the ethical question about where to walk with a clear conscience. There is no fire and brimstone in their visions of the future, but there is water, and lots of it.

One of the central questions that scholars and theorists of apocalypse are forced to ask is why people would want to live under such conditions. Why would people want to live under threat from a future whose seeds are already firmly planted in the present? Why does apocalyptic thinking exhibit such "extraordinary resilience," as Frank Kermode puts it in *The Sense of an Ending* (1966), capable of being "disconfirmed without being discredited" over and over again (8)? Why do people "hunger for ends and for crises" (55)? Indeed, it would seem that the fictions we tell ourselves would be those that are designed to make us feel safe and secure, calm and happy, and not those that are designed to produce the opposite feeling by marking an upcoming total catastrophe in the future.

In a new epilogue written for the 2000 republication of his classic work, Kermode looks back on the multiple apocalyptic threats that have arisen since the book's original publication in 1966. "The reason why any date, almost any excuse," he writes, "is good enough to trigger some apocalyptic anxiety is that apocalypse [. . .] represents a mood finally inseparable from the condition of life, the contemplation of its necessary ending, the ineradicable desire to make some sense of it" (186–187). The individual person, for Kermode, needs "fictions of beginnings and fictions of ends, fictions which unite beginning and end and endow the interval between them with meaning" (190). Apocalyptic thinking, in this way, is a collective expression of the individual desire for narrative unity and meaning. That psychosocial desire, however, like all desires, is not straightforward. It both satisfies and terrifies.

In *Poetic Closure* (1968), Barbara Herrnstein Smith offers an important caveat to Kermode's theory of apocalypse. We do not long for endings in general, Smith claims. Instead, we long for the ones that are more satisfying and less terrifying, and, in order to achieve those, we aspire to endings "that are designed" (1). Apocalypse, in this way, does not signal simply an ending, an ontological vanishing or some vague cessation of the world as we know it, but a conclusion to the individual and collective story, a "closure" in Smith's terminology. Smith writes:

> We tend to speak of conclusions when a sequence of events has a relatively high degree of structure, when, in other words, we can perceive these events as related to one another by some principle of organization or design that implies the existence of a definite termination point. Under these circumstances, the occurrence of the terminal event is a confirmation of expectations that have been established by the structure of the sequence, and is usually distinctly gratifying. (2)

The apocalyptic hunger, to expand on Kermode and Smith, is a symptom of the more general desire to achieve this gratification, to see the conditions of the past and present as ushering in a knowable and expected future.

Moira Crone's *The Not Yet* (2012), an unusual novel in the literary history of New Orleans that takes up some of these theoretical concerns, is set in the future, mostly in the year 2121, and may be classified as a "critical dystopia." This fictional genre, a particular expression of apocalyptic thinking, "is a negative cousin of the Utopia proper," as Fredric Jameson explains in *Archaeologies of the Future* (2005), "for it is in the light of some positive conception of human social possibilities that its effects are generated and from Utopian ideals its enabling stance derives" (198).[1]

In Crone's critical dystopia, not only is the physical world falling apart as the soil subsides and the Gulf of Mexico rises; the social world is collapsing, too, in the face of severe economic disparity and social stratification. This environmental and social decline comes in the aftermath of a stunning scientific breakthrough that allows a specific group of people, the Heirs, to live well past their natural life spans, for hundreds of years, if not forever. In this way, the disaster of the twenty-first century is generated when some good objective goes bad, when the desire to outwit death leads to a vigorous and destructive self-preservation at the expense of others. As a critical dystopia, in other words, Crone's novel takes the utopian impulse to figure out a better world in which to live and turns it on its head. The drive to improve the human lifeworld in fact engineers just the opposite.

The novel tells the story of twenty-year-old Malcolm as he makes his way to be "treated"—that is, surgically and psychologically transformed into an Heir—in the year 2121. In Crone's world of strict social classification, he is a "Nyet," shorthand for "not yet treated." Malcolm's benefactor is Lazarus, who has lived for two centuries and is holder of his Heir trust fund. His doctor is Lydia Greenmore, who is in charge of the treatment, part of which is pedagogical. Under sedation, Malcolm is educated on history and science from the time of the initial research into the prolongation of life in the 1960s; the "Reveal" in 2005; and the next century of social reclassification, total warfare, and, finally, relative peace brought about by the new world order. Behind the scenes is the ever-present WELLFI, the conglomerate in control of medicine, media, and politics.

The backdrop for Malcolm's adventure is the dissolving physical environment surrounding the city of New Orleans. The geographic location is the same as today, but many things have changed in the future, and these changes are reflected in new topographical names. The Mississippi River is now the Old River, after the major watershed jumped course to follow the Atchafalaya in a quicker route to the Gulf. Lake Pontchartrain is now the Sea of Pontchartrain. The city of New Orleans is now called the New Orleans Islands and is further subdivided into Audubon Island, the heavily guarded Museum City (presumably the former Garden District), and the Sunken Quarter.

Most of the Heirs have left the city for higher ground on the north shore of the Sea of Pontchartrain, lands protected by the United Authority and renamed Re-New Orleans. "It was crisp and pastel and full of turrets and verandas and pergolas—exquisite, clean, shining, and fashionable," Crone writes of this place on the north shore of the sea. Within their protected sphere, "Heirs waved their arms in greeting to each other, calling out, all smiles. They carried packages from the brosia merchants, the genenfabric stores" (45). This place, as Crone describes it, is a kind of suburban hell with a beautiful facade, where kin and kind are shielded from the others and where retail therapy works.

The scene south of the Sea of Pontchartrain in the New Orleans Islands, where the non-Heirs live, is quite different. Their houses stand half submerged in water, where once dry land had been. After "fending off the sea" for years, the non-Heirs could persevere no longer and "had succumbed" to the rising tides and sinking earth. "Yet the occupants had not fled," Crone writes. Abandoned in a kind of limbo, the non-Heir New Orleanians live a life of precariousness where "no one persecuted them exactly, but no one helped them either." Their non-Heir status causes this precarious limbo, but their ambiguous relationship with the larger nation, the United Authority, is a related part of the problem. They had been "let go" by the nation but at the same time were denied true autonomy (29). "This was a place on the edges," Crone writes of New Orleans, in the mind of the nation, "where what was past could be discarded, forgotten, ignored, occasionally visited for the thrill of the exotic. A place with the fortune, or curse, of not mattering" (203).

Outside the city, and except for the Heir neighborhoods on the north shore of the Sea of Pontchartrain and other prosperous enclosures across North America, the continent is falling apart. "The raw landscape was horrible," Crone writes, full of the "empty ruins, the garbage towns, that weren't needed anymore" (95). The Heirs, however, are forever shielded from witnessing this ruined world. They move underground through the continent, in high-speed tunnels with beautiful and convincing landscapes simulated on the walls. In Crone's future, the New Orleanian zone is not the only one that is abandoned by the nation. Other locales susceptible to natural disaster—the entire Pacific Coast of the former United States, for example, as it crumbles westward into the ocean—are subjected to political, economic, and psychosocial disaffiliation. The Heirs' wealth and privileged position in a stratified society allow them to ruin and abandon, damage and disaffiliate, but their financial and social status also allows them to live in ignorance of their own actions. Because they can afford the ticket to move from one paradise to the next in a beautifully orchestrated underground, their eyes are not obliged to see that which they destroy.

Like the environments in which they live, the Heirs' bodies have been profoundly transformed. After their medical procedures, the Heirs have eyes that do not blink, lungs that hardly breath, bodies that retain only uncanny traces of their former selves. Crone describes a bodily movement of Lazarus in this way: "He tried to snap his fingers, but he couldn't, his overskin was too slick for that" (16). Like insects, they "scurry" (45). Their digestive tracts are so fragile that they must eat "brosia," an abbreviation, presumably, of "ambrosia," the mythological food of the gods. They also lose their original voices after treatment. Crone writes of Lazarus's voice: "that voice they all had—full of sizzle, like a rattle" (15). She describes the Heirs as talking with "awful reptile voices" (26).

Unlike other monstrous species that have populated the literary history of New Orleans in the past, the Heirs' bodies of the future register a kind of decadence rather than straightforward horror. In their "elegant emaciation," they do not carry with them the marks of the truly horrible (189). They are, after all, simply aged human bodies slowly aging more. Beneath their elaborately decorated prosthetics, they are becoming barer and barer, being preserved in their decay. Their bodies, unlike the vampiric bodies in the gothic world of Anne Rice, are not undead, supernatural, or otherwise ghostly.[2] They do, however, share some traits with those creatures. Like those abandoned to walk the earth indefinitely, Crone's Heirs produce uneasiness in themselves, in the other characters, and arguably in Crone herself and in her readers, because for the Heirs the end will never come. Stranded within their "timeless time," they cannot achieve satisfaction; they cannot look forward to an easing of tension that comes only with a general foreknowledge of the end (263). Without this sense of an end, as Kermode warns us, their lives, operating as they do perpetually in medias res, will be without meaning. With the final moment of life suspended indefinitely, as Smith warns us, their lives will not achieve closure.

Because of their genesis through scientific progress, albeit a highly suspect scientific progress, they come closer not to the dead and the undead of New Orleans but to another monster, birthed on the other side of the Atlantic: Frankenstein's creature. But because the Heirs come from the preservation of life past its normal range rather than from the reanimation of the dead, they arrive on the scene without all the ugly baggage of the truly monstrous. They instead elicit sympathy and "tenderness" through others' recognition of themselves in the future, whereas Frankenstein sees no kinship with his creation and therefore expels him to live the life of an orphan in an inhospitable world.

Such an ontological status of the Heirs reveals the vulnerability at the heart of their being. They may not be living and aging at the normal human pace, but because they cannot stop the passage of time, they are aging nonetheless. They may be injured and killed; they may fall into depression, dementia, substance abuse and addiction, as well as other forms of madness. They are also at the mercy of the doctors and scientists who sustain them and who all the while do not know for sure where their experiment will end up.

While most of the Heirs are comforted by their unflinching faith in the ability of science and medical technology to solve the known problems of today and the unknown ones of tomorrow, other Heirs are not so lucky. Malcolm's benefactor, Lazarus, in fact, is unable to cope with his existential dilemma. He is particularly troubled by the monotony of his temporal suspension, and he commits suicide. In his suicide note, the character tries to explain his decision to end his own life, writing, "Now, I think it is the greatest gift of all to have a sense of time" (240).

If the signs of decadence reside for Crone in the Heirs' new bodies— as well as in their voices and the environments in which they live—how do these signs also make their appearance in the literary sensibilities of the future? In the year 2121, books themselves have largely become obsolete, active readers extinct, and a new species of passive spectators has emerged. In this new world, the Heirs enjoy dramatic productions called the Sims, a kind of live reality show in which the non-Heirs perform. Because the Heirs "have no sense of time," they cannot be satisfied after the dramatic production has concluded, and they demand encore after encore after encore from the non-Heir actors (35). "The idea of 'once,'" Crone writes, "was beyond them" (73). Here is Crone's description of one of the Sims from the perspective of one of the actors:

> This funny-all was like all the rest, we "mourned" around a coffin, and there were parades, and lots of mock tears—this would go on for days. Then, eventually, the one whose portrait we were all carrying, the one who had "so longed," an Heir, would emerge from hiding at the moment the coffin was found empty, and say, "I'm still here! Ha-Ha! Ha-Ha!" And the music would go up tempo, we'd all dance. A "rough comedy," as Jeremy described it in the publicity "With Old New Orleans touches, and brass." A tragedy with a happy ending. The Heirs devoured these, loved the joke, and the part where they got to cavort with us low types. (72)

One "Sim Verite" is particularly disturbing. Unlike a regular Sim, the "living production" is designed to let Heirs spectate on the most intimate and graphic aspects of non-Heir life: real births, live surgeries, and even the actual process of dying (102). One example of this kind of production involves Ginger, a non-Heir who is dying of cancer and who sells tickets to Heirs who want to watch her illness progress. She agrees to this gruesome act in order to make money for her clan to buy higher ground farther north of the quickly advancing Gulf of Mexico. The Heirs watch Ginger suffer on stage for months. She eventually succumbs to her illness, dying in front of her audience, and her family and friends gather around her on stage, mourning their real loss while the Heirs watch on. At the end of the dramatic production, after the illness and the death and the mourning, the Heirs demand an encore, seemingly unaware that true death happens only once. The Heirs in Crone's novel rule the world, and yet because they have no sense of time, because they exist in a temporal limbo, they have no sense of ethical urgency. Their decadence offers no hope as they sustain their withered and isolated selves.

Where does Crone's world come from? How is she able to envision New Orleans in the twenty-second century and develop the plot of *The Not Yet*? "All plots have something in common with prophecy," Kermode reminds us, "for they must appear to educe from the prime matter of the situation the forms of a future" (83). To make sense of Crone's prophetic plot, then, her readers must make sense of the present in which she prophesies.

For Crone, it is the human fear of aging and dying that generates this new world of the twenty-second century. The desire to escape death creates the total state of the world; everything follows from there. Death is so feared—it is, in fact, so despised—that the Heirs do not even utter its name. Instead, they speak sentences like this one, which oscillates between euphemistic and childish: "The unlucky do the so-long goodbye" (16). The result is a world of haves and have-nots, those with access to the medical science and technology that will allow them to approach immortality and those without such access. The result is a

strict hierarchy of "strats": the Heirs, the Nyets, and the "Nats" (shorthand for "low naturals," individuals barred from surgical intervention
and thus forced to live a life without artificial prolongation). The strats
on the middle and lower rungs of society, furthermore, must demonstrate complete subordination to those on the top.

For Crone, it is not some fundamental cruelty in the human species,
not some destructive base, that makes her characters want to control
and oppress, conquer, and even—in its most extreme form—annihilate
those unlike themselves. Instead, it is a self-preservative drive, an an-
tideath drive, gone berserk. That drive, furthermore, is coupled with a
blinding irresponsibility, an utter disregard for the devastation that is
multiplying in the worlds outside the Heirs' protective shield.

In the literary history of New Orleans, Crone's novel is highly unusual not only for its profound defamiliarization of the ordinary fixtures
of the cityscape but also for the genre in which it is written. For New
Orleans, a city in a seemingly endless love–hate relationship with its
past, many of the city's most accomplished novelists have turned to
historical fiction as a mode of literary invention. George Washington
Cable's *The Grandissimes* (1880), Charles Chesnutt's *Paul Marchand,
F.M.C.* (1921), Nelson Algren's *A Walk on the Wild Side* (1956), Michael
Ondaatje's *Coming Through Slaughter* (1976), Anne Rice's *Feast of All
Saints* (1979), John Biguenet's *Oyster* (2002), Valerie Martin's *Property*
(2003), and Kent Wascom's *Secessia* (2015), to mention only a few of
the most compelling, all set their narratives in the past in order to answer questions about the present.[3] As we move slowly and unsurely into
the twenty-first century, however, New Orleans seems to be even more
uneasy about its future than with its past, even if that past continues
to haunt the minds and bodies and social structures of its inhabitants.

What is it about the future that terrifies in the city of New Orleans?
Environmental risks seem to accumulate rather than dissipate through
time, and every year the Gulf of Mexico grows in circumference, getting closer and closer to the city. The question is only a matter of tim-
ing—when the disaster event, held beforehand in latent form, will
surface and make itself known. The Mississippi River, once an agent

of land building as its waters overflowed its banks seasonally and carried the rich alluvium that settled in the marshlands, is now held in check by a vast levee system. The ancient process in southern Louisiana by which continent and Gulf struggle against each other, one trying always to overtake the other, has largely come to an end. Even if the river were let loose to continue the story, the river is not the same river that it was a century ago. The Mississippi River still drains half a continent, as it has done in the past, but now it brings with it all the refuse of modern agriculture and industry from as far away as Montana and Pennsylvania. Through the river's mouth just below New Orleans now flows the continent's life agents, its fertilizers, and the paradoxical damage they bring in the form of dead zones in the Gulf, as well as its more straightforward death agents, its pesticides, insecticides, and all manner of other -cides.

To complicate matters even further, the petroleum industry's reach along the coastline has radically altered the landscape, the wetlandscape, and the open water surrounding the city. In *American Energy, Imperiled Coast* (2014), Jason P. Theriot measures that reach, the great expanse of the petroleum industry in southern Louisiana. "Approximately 191 major pipeline systems," Theriot writes, "originate from the offshore waters and enter Louisiana's vast coastal zone, an area roughly 220 miles across and reaching as much as seventy-five miles inland from the Gulf, most of it marshlands" (4).

The sheer geographic scale of the pipelines makes monitoring difficult, if not impossible, especially for companies whose bottom line may be negatively impacted by any environmental problem and investigation. One pipeline, owned and operated by Taylor Energy Company, has been leaking continuously since Hurricane Ivan in 2004, and yet that leak has gone underestimated and undermonitored, influenced by the financial incentive simply to ignore it.[4] Many other pipelines, beyond the Taylor Energy fiasco, promise to do the same as they age, as the ground beneath them shifts, as more wetlands go under, as future hurricanes shake their foundations, and as they are left unattended by companies that have long ago cashed in or folded, sold out or simply closed shop.

Such human violence against the environment, against other species, and all the while against humans ourselves, has profound consequences for the imagination. In *The Dominion of the Dead* (2003),
Robert Pogue Harrison poignantly writes about those consequences:
"When history turns against its own memorializing and self-conserving
drive, when it is perceived to have become a force of erasure rather
than of inscription, of assault on the earth rather than humanization
of the earth, then images of an apocalyptic sea inevitably surge up in
the human imagination" (16).

For Valerie Martin, Katie Ford, and Moira Crone, the violent structure of the present seems to be so large, so entrenched and unchanging,
that the days to come can only lead to one thing. For Crone, especially,
in telling the history of the future, political rebellion against strict systems of social classification and stratification, as well as environmental
fallout, lead only to violence and squashed hope. For her, this certain
future is already formed, lying in wait as the "not yet." As such, the
chief target of her critical dystopia is not the future per se but the present, not 2121, when her novel is set, but 2012, when the novel appeared
in public. Crone's quarrel, in other words, is not with the Heirs of the
next century who exert such a "force of erasure" in their future worlds
but with the people of her own time and place.

One cannot help but to wonder, however, to what extent Crone's
apocalyptic vision will become truly actualized in the twenty-second
century. *The Not Yet* takes place long after Crone's contemporary readers will probably be dead, in the year 2121, unless of course the medical
breakthrough the author details in the novel does indeed take place. A
person born in 2012, the year the novel was published, would have to
live to be 109 years old, in fact, to see the chronotope Crone describes.
In this way, the year 2121 in New Orleans is a time and place that is
imaginable without being ultimately verifiable. One hundred years into
the future is more thinkable than two hundred years, and as Crone's
contemporaries live through the twenty-first century, they will be ap-
proaching the temporal marker, but they will probably never get to it

exactly. It sits just out of reach, temporally, just outside the realm of knowability.

New Orleans seems to be caught up in a strange relation with the flow of modern time. It is both a relic of the past and a harbinger of things to come. But predicting the future has always been a risky business. In hurricane forecasting, for example, as in life, the so-called cone of error, also sometimes called the "cone of uncertainty," gets wider and wider as the predictive mark gets further and further into the future. In this way, the future's simple promise—for tomorrow, for next year, for one hundred years from now—may not be so simple after all.

In *The Poverty of Historicism* (1957), the famous philosopher of science Karl Popper presents an important response to those who claim to know the future or who claim, even more simply, that the future is knowable. Presenting his own kind of syllogism, he reaches a very different conclusion than does Katie Ford in her syllogistic poem "Earth." Popper writes his first premise: "The course of human history is strongly influenced by the growth of human knowledge." Popper continues with the second premise: "We cannot predict, by rational or scientific methods, the future growth of our scientific knowledge." If we could predict today what we will know tomorrow, then that knowledge would not be tomorrow's but today's. Popper concludes, "We cannot, therefore, predict the future course of human history" (xi–xii). If the future depends on future knowledge and we cannot ipso facto know future knowledge, we cannot know the future. Using a different argumentative style, Jacques Derrida makes a similar point and writes, in one of his rare moments of precision, "An absolute missile does not abolish chance" (29).[5] For Popper, Derrida, and a host of other philosophers, the future's simple promise may not be so simple after all.

But despite the lack of epistemological simplicity, this cognitive haziness, the current state of the city of New Orleans and of the region cannot help but disappoint advocates of social and environmental justice. The probable projections for the future are not encouraging, either. There is no feasible method to reverse the course of soil subsidence underneath a city, although it can be theoretically slowed, just as there is no way to to keep the global sea level from rising, although that increase can be theoretically slowed as well. Against these challenges, however, there are major plans presently in the works to secure the future of the city and region. These unprecedented efforts include Louisiana's fifty-year, $50 billion coastal master plan to help restore the wetlands, as well as a controversial $48 million grant from the federal government to move a tribal band of Biloxi-Chitimacha-Choctaws from their eroding island to stable land protected by levees, farther north.[6]

One must remember, too, that New Orleans has never been destroyed in its three hundred year history. The fires, the floods, and the outbreaks of disease, the domestic terrorism of slavery and segregation, even the wreckage produced by hurricanes Katrina and Rita—the most recent in a long "series of great mistakes," as Martin might put it—did not destroy the city. In the face of this long history and these best-laid plans, however, the haunting prospect still seems to be anagnorisis sans peripeteia—recognition without change—as the -philias and -phobias of *topos* and *chronos* keep marching along to that number.

NOTES

CHAPTER ONE

1. See Dennis Persica's "N. O. Summer of Discomfort Lies Just Ahead" (2013).

2. Rex Tillerson is quoted in David Koenig's "Exxon: Oil Has No Quick Replacement" (2013). Since making this troubling comment, Tillerson moved on from Exxon to the White House to serve briefly as secretary of state in the Trump administration.

3. The question of the city's exceptionality has generated much scholarly debate. For a critique of the tendency to cast New Orleans as exceptional, see Jennie Lightweis-Goff's "'Peculiar and Characteristic': New Orleans's Exceptionalism from Olmsted to the Deluge" (2014). For a critique of the critique, see C. W. Cannon's "I Want Magic: A Defense of New Orleans Exceptionalism" (2015). My own position is closer to Cannon's than it is to Lightweis-Goff's.

4. See Matei Calinescu's *Five Faces of Modernity: Modernism, Avant-Garde, Decadence, Kitsch, Postmodernism* (1977) and Richard Gilman's *Decadence: The Strange Life of an Epithet* (1979). Other influential studies that figure into my discussion here include John R. Reed's *Decadent Style* (1985) and Ellis Hanson's *Decadence and Catholicism* (1997).

5. This list of names raises an important question about the extent to which decadence in New Orleans is tied specifically to Euro-American men. In chapter five of this book, I address this question by tracing the work of two African American writers—Alice Dunbar-Nelson and Charles Chesnutt—and their approach to decadence in the city.

6. For a deeper analysis of Darwin's scientific innovation and its literary consequences, see my *Queer Environmentality: Ecology, Evolution, and Sexuality in American Literature* (2012).

7. See Joseph Roach's discussion in *Cities of the Dead: Circum-Atlantic Performance* (1996).

8. In "Satellite Planetarity and the Ends of the Earth" (2014), Elizabeth DeLoughrey connects "environmental consciousness of the planetary biosphere to the history of Cold War militarism" (262). She writes, "Our evidence for and understanding of the

Anthropocene has been produced by the very military technologies that brought us the Cold War" (274).

9. See Jeff Adelson's "Water Has Risen 2 Inches at Grand Isle Since 2007, Data Show" (2014).

10. See Anna Shannon Elfenbein's *Women on the Color Line: Evolving Stereotypes and the Writings of George Washington Cable, Grace King, and Kate Chopin* (1989); Violet Harrington Bryan's *The Myth of New Orleans in Literature: Dialogues of Race and Gender* (1993); Barbara Ladd's *Nationalism and the Color Line in George W. Cable, Mark Twain, and William Faulkner* (1996); Richard S. Kennedy's edited volume *Literary New Orleans in the Modern World* (1998); Barbara J. Eckstein's *Sustaining New Orleans: Literature, Local Memory, and the Fate of a City* (2006); and James Nagel's *Race and Culture in New Orleans Stories: Kate Chopin, Grace King, Alice Dunbar-Nelson, and George Washington Cable* (2014). While these books are vital for my own work, they do tend to reflect the preference for the postbellum period, the fiction genre, and the English language.

11. See Joseph Roach's *Cities of the Dead: Circum-Atlantic Performance* (1996); Ruth Salvaggio's *Hearing Sappho in New Orleans: The Call of Poetry from Congo Square to the Ninth Ward* (2012); Catharine Savage Brosman's *Louisiana Creole Literature: A Historical Study* (2013); Keith Cartwright's *Reading Africa into American Literature: Epics, Fables, and Gothic Tales* (2002) and *Sacral Grooves, Limbo Gateways: Travels in Deep Southern Time, Circum-Caribbean Space, Afro-creole Authority* (2013); Rien Fertel's *Imagining the Creole City: The Rise of Literary Culture in Nineteenth-Century New Orleans* (2014); and John Wharton Lowe's *Calypso Magnolia: The Crosscurrents of Caribbean and Southern Literature* (2016). In addition to these studies, see Germain Bienvenu's "The Beginnings of Louisiana Literature: The French Domination of 1682–1763" (2008); Peggy Whitman Prenshaw's "Louisiana and the American Literary Tradition" (2008); and Dianne Guenin-Lelle's *The Story of French New Orleans: History of a Creole City* (2016).

12. James A. Kaser's *The New Orleans of Fiction: A Research Guide* (2014) provides great insight into the sheer vastness of this literary archive. Kaser finds and annotates 514 novels and short story collections published in English between 1828 and 1980 that take up New Orleans as their chief setting. As lengthy as Kaser's bibliographical guide is, it only includes roughly half of the city's three-hundred-year history, only one of its genres, and only one of its languages. It also does not mention the vast number of texts that were written in New Orleans but do not use the city straightforwardly as a setting.

13. The history of language in the social and literary life of the United States is highly complex, of course, and an important body of scholarship has developed to take account of this complexity. My own thinking on the subject has been influenced especially by James Crawford's edited volume *Language Loyalties: A Source Book on the Official English Controversy* (1992); Michael North's *The Dialect of Modernism: Race, Language, and Twentieth-Century Literature* (1994); Rosina Lippi-Green's *English with an Accent: Language, Ideology, and Discrimination in the United States* (1997); Werner Sollors's edited

volume *Multilingual America: Transnationalism, Ethnicity, and the Languages of American Literature* (1998); Evelyn Nien-Ming Ch'ien's *Weird English* (2004); and Wai Chee Dimock's *Through Other Continents: American Literature Across Deep Time* (2006).

CHAPTER TWO

1. See Thomas N. Ingersoll's *Mammon and Manon in Early New Orleans: The First Slave Society in the Deep South, 1718–1819* (1999). Together with Manon, the other figure in Ingersoll's historical interpretation of the colonial period is Mammon, the personification of greed and material wealth, whose origins can be traced back to the New Testament.

2. For a recent scholarly edition of *La relación*, see Rolena Adorno and Patrick Charles Pautz's translation, published as *The Narrative of Cabeza de Vaca* (2003).

3. For historical information regarding the colonial period covered in this chapter, I rely primarily on Fred B. Kniffen, Hiram F. Gregory, and George A. Stokes's *The Historic Tribes of Louisiana, from 1542 to the Present* (1987); Jerah Johnson's "New Orleans's Congo Square: An Urban Setting for Early Afro-American Culture Formation" (1991); Gwendolyn Midlo Hall's *Africans in Colonial Louisiana: The Development of Afro-Creole Culture in the Eighteenth Century* (1992); Caryn Cossé Bell's *Revolution, Romanticism, and the Afro-Creole Protest Tradition in Louisiana, 1718–1868* (1997); Richard Campanella's *Bienville's Dilemma: A Historical Geography of New Orleans* (2008); and Lawrence N. Powell's *The Accidental City: Improvising New Orleans* (2012).

4. In addition to the primary sources referenced in this chapter, other significant travel documents include Pierre Le Moyne Iberville's 1699 writings collected in *Iberville's Gulf Journals* (1981); Marie Madeleine Hachard's letters contained in *Voices from an Early American Convent: Marie Madeleine Hachard and the New Orleans Ursulines, 1727–1760* (2007); and Jean François Benjamin Dumont de Montigny's narrative published as *The Memoir of Lieutenant Dumont, 1715–1747: A Sojourner in the French Atlantic* (2012). For a companion volume to Hachard's writings, see Emily Clark's *Masterless Mistresses: The New Orleans Ursulines and the Development of a New World Society, 1727–1834* (2007). Eighteenth-century poetry written in Louisiana remains elusive, although Dumont also wrote a 4,962-line "Poème en vers touchant l'établissement de la province de la Louisiane [Verse Poem Concerning the Establishment of the Louisiana Province]" that spans the period from 1716 to 1741, and Julian Poydras published "La Prise du morne du Bâton Rouge par Monseigneur de Gálvez [The Capture of the Bluff of Baton Rouge by His Excellency de Gálvez]" in 1779. The problem of literary production during the colonial period, of course, was the paucity of printing technologies and of a widespread reading public. Presses, in fact, did not arrive in New Orleans until 1764, at which time they were controlled by the government and used exclusively for administrative purposes. Only after 1794, with the arrival of the first newspaper, *Moniteur de la Louisiane,* and

especially after the beginning of Americanization, in 1803, did a growing population and economic activity create a demand for what could be considered a modern publishing industry and literary culture. See Samuel J. Marino's "Early French-Language Newspapers in New Orleans" (1966); and Florence M. Jumonville's "'The Art Preservative of All Arts': Early Printing in New Orleans" (2006).

5. Jacques de la Metairie's account is translated and reprinted in Frank de Caro and Rosan Augusta Jordan's *Louisiana Sojourns: Travelers' Tales and Literary Journeys* (1998) as "Vive le Roi: La Salle Reaches the Mississippi's Mouth." On his second voyage, which set sail from France on 24 July 1684, La Salle intended to find the Mississippi River from its mouth along the Gulf Coast. He famously missed the river and ended up in Texas, only to find himself the object of a mutinous crew and shot by Pierre Duhaut, on 19 March 1687. Henri Joutel, La Salle's personal aide, recounts this expedition in *A Journal of La Salle's Last Voyage*, a text written upon Joutel's return to France in 1688, published in Paris in 1713, quickly translated into English, and published in London in 1714.

6. See Keith Cartwright's *Sacral Grooves, Limbo Gateways: Travels in Deep Southern Time, Circum-Caribbean Space, Afro-creole Authority* (2013).

7. Bienville also makes an appearance in LeAnne Howe's novel *Shell Shaker* (2001), in which one of the characters, a woman of Choctaw heritage, "can't imagine living anywhere else but New Orleans, where so much Choctaw history occurred" (41).

8. See Pierre François Xavier de Charlevoix, *Charlevoix's Louisiana: Selections from the* History *and the* Journal (1744).

9. My thinking on these two forms is indebted to Benedict Anderson, who, in *Imagined Communities: Reflections on the Origin and Spread of Nationalism* (1983), famously analyzes the role of the newspaper and the novel in creating "the *kind* of imagined community that is the nation" (25).

10. See André Pénicaut's *Fleur de Lys and Calumet: Being the Pénicaut Narrative of French Adventure in Louisiana* (1723).

11. Marc-Antoine Caillot's memoir is edited and translated by Erin M. Greenwald and published as *A Company Man: The Remarkable French-Atlantic Voyage of a Clerk for the Company of the Indies* (2013). For a companion volume, see Greenwald's *Marc-Antoine Caillot and the Company of the Indies in Louisiana: Trade in the French Atlantic World* (2016).

12. See Craig Colten's "Meaning of Water in the American South: Transatlantic Encounters" (2010). For a deeper analysis, see Anthony Wilson's fascinating *Shadow and Shelter: The Swamp in Southern Culture* (2006).

13. See Gordon Sayre's "Plotting the Natchez Massacre: Le Page du Pratz, Dumont de Montigny, Chateaubriand" (2002).

14. François-René de Chateaubriand is central to Edward Said's work in *Orientalism* (1978), and his name is the first to appear in the book's very first sentence. Said, in fact, goes so far as to claim that orientalism *begins* with Chateaubriand and that many

French nineteenth-century travel writers—"literary pilgrims," as he calls them—follow in Chateaubriand's tropological footsteps (170).

CHAPTER THREE

1. In thinking about Pierre Clément de Laussat's book objects in this chapter, I have been inspired by Shannon Lee Dawdy's *Patina: A Profane Archaeology* (2016).

2. For population changes, I rely on Richard Campanella's helpful time line in *Bienville's Dilemma: A Historical Geography of New Orleans* (2008). See also Nathalie Dessens's *Creole City: A Chronicle of Early American New Orleans* (2015); and Eberhart L. Faber's *Building the Land of Dreams: New Orleans and the Transformation of Early America* (2016).

3. See Florence M. Jumonville's "'The Art Preservative of All Arts': Early Printing in New Orleans" (2006).

4. George Washington Cable devotes a chapter of his *The Creoles of Louisiana* (1884) to the Battle of New Orleans. For an account of the violent conflict written in poetic form, see Thomas Dunn English's "The Battle of New Orleans" (ca. 1885).

5. Arthur Singleton's narrative is excerpted and reprinted as "Parrots, Spider-Monkeys, and Sun Umbrellas" in Frank De Caro and Rosan Augusta Jordan's *Louisiana Sojourns: Travelers' Tales and Literary Journeys* (1998).

6. Frances Trollope's narrative appears as "Entrance of the Mississippi" in Frank De Caro and Rosan Augusta Jordan's *Louisiana Sojourns: Travelers' Tales and Literary Journeys* (1998). For a Francophone complement to Singleton, Trollope, A. Oakey Hall, and other Anglophone travelers examined here, see Elisée Reclus's *A Voyage to New Orleans: Anarchist Impressions of the Old South* (1855).

7. See Paul F. Lachance's "The Foreign French" (1992) for the precise demographic history. For additional work on the subject, see Nathalie Dessens's *From Saint-Domingue to New Orleans: Migration and Influence* (2007). Most recently, John Wharton Lowe provides a detailed account of the impact of the Haitian Revolution on the literary scene in *Calypso Magnolia: The Crosscurrents of Caribbean and Southern Literature* (2016).

8. Scholarship on the Francophone literature of nineteenth-century New Orleans is extensive. Although it would be wrong to equate the city with the whole state of Louisiana, New Orleans served during this time as a hub of people and texts, and the bulk of the state's literary corpus was produced there. Major books and articles on the subject include Alcée Fortier's "French Literature in Louisiana" (1886); Rodolphe Lucien Desdunes's *Our People and Our History* (1911); Ruby Van Allen Caulfeild's *The French Literature of Louisiana* (1929); Charles Barthelemy Rousseve's *The Negro in Louisiana: Aspects of His History and His Literature* (1937); Caryn Cossé Bell's *Revolution, Romanticism, and the Afro-Creole Protest Tradition in Louisiana, 1718–1868* (1997); Michel Fabre's "The New Orleans Press and French-Language Literature by Creoles of Color (1998) and "New Orleans Creole Expatriates in France: Romance and Reality" (2000); Fehintola

NOTES TO PAGES 60–72

Mosadomi's "The Origin of Louisiana Creole" (2000); Sybil Kein's "The Use of Louisiana Creole in Southern Literature" (2000); Caroline Senter's "Creole Poets on the Verge of a Nation" (2000); Clint Bruce's "Caught Between Continents: The Local and the Transatlantic in the French-Language Serial Fiction of New Orleans's *Le Courrier de la Louisiane, 1843–1845*" (2012); Lloyd Pratt's "The Lyric Public of *Les Cenelles*" (2012); Catharine Savage Brosman's *Louisiana Creole Literature: A Historical Study* (2013); Rien Fertel's *Imagining the Creole City: The Rise of Literary Culture in Nineteenth-Century New Orleans* (2014); Juliane Braun's "The Drama of History in Francophone New Orleans" (2015); and Dianne Guenin-Lelle's *The Story of French New Orleans: History of a Creole City* (2016).

9. This chapter and the next deal with a number of French poems that appear in dual-language format in *Creole Echoes: The Francophone Poetry of Nineteenth-Century Louisiana* (2004), edited by M. Lynn Weiss. In that volume, Norman R. Shapiro provides interpretive and, in my opinion, inadequate translations of the poems. I thank Caroline Stas for her help with the literal translations offered here.

10. *Les Cenelles: Choix de poésies indigènes* was edited by the creole poet of color Armand Lanusse.

11. On the Spanish-speaking presence in New Orleans, see Kirsten Silva Gruesz's "The Gulf of Mexico System and the 'Latinness' of New Orleans" (2006); Christopher Dunn's "Black Rome and the Chocolate City: The Race of Place" (2007); and *Hispanic and Latino New Orleans: Immigration and Identity Since the Eighteenth Century* (2015), by Andrew Sluyter, Case Watkins, James P. Chaney, and Annie M. Gibson.

12. *The Mysteries* is one of the first representations of lesbians in modern literature and one that is much more sympathetic than, say, Marcel Proust's or Radclyffe Hall's sixty or seventy years later. One of the most fascinating passages about "lesbian ladies" and their apparent love of water reads, "New Orleans is the Meran [Merano, Italy] of the United States for lesbian ladies, where they hold their mysterious gatherings, unhindered and unseen by the Argus-eyes of morality until now. Strangely enough, as everywhere else, they reside only alongside bodies of water, since their norms hold that they cannot do without the nearness of water. So we find them in clubs of twelve to fifteen on the Hercules Quay, along the Pensacola Landing, and all along the entire left side of the New Basin" (151).

13. The Civil War was a major event in New Orleanian literary history and one that was perhaps rivaled only by Hurricane Katrina in 2005. The period is thus fertile ground for scholarly research, especially the crucial task of recovering and republishing lost texts, many of which were originally written in French. For primary texts, see Richard Grant White's *Poetry Lyrical, Narrative, and Satirical of the Civil War* (1866); and Clint Bruce's *Afro-Creole Poetry in French from Louisiana's Radical Civil War–Era Newspapers* (forthcoming). For background information and an extensive bibliography of primary texts, see Esther Parker Ellinger's *The Southern War Poetry of the Civil War* (1918). The

classic work on the subject is Edmund Wilson's *Patriotic Gore: Studies in the Literature of the American Civil War* (1962), but see Coleman Hutchinson's edited volume *A History of American Civil War Literature* (2016) for a more recent treatment.

CHAPTER FOUR

1. The phrase "shadow of the Ethiopian" comes from George Washington Cable's *The Grandissimes* (1880), 156. I rely especially on John W. Blassingame's *Black New Orleans, 1860–1880* (1973) for historical information about this period.

2. See Anna Brickhouse's "'L'Ouragan de flammes' ('The Hurricane of Flames'): New Orleans and Transamerican Catastrophe, 1866/2005" (2007). See also Brickhouse's work in *Transamerican Literary Relations and the Nineteenth-Century Public Sphere* (2004). For an illuminating eyewitness account of the time period, see *Tribune* editor Jean-Charles Houzeau's *My Passage at the New Orleans Tribune: A Memoir of the Civil War Era* (1872). With the loss of their French language, Brickhouse argues, the creoles of color lost their immediate political connection to the transracial Atlantic and the international solidarity of the *Francophonie*. But with their turn to English, it also is important to note, came a valuable ability to communicate with the Anglophone publics of the larger United States.

3. For histories of this violence, see especially James Hollandsworth Jr.'s *An Absolute Massacre: The New Orleans Race Riot of July 30, 1866* (2001); and James K. Hogue's *Uncivil War: Five New Orleans Street Battles and the Rise and Fall of Racial Reconstruction* (2006). For an account of the extrajudicial murder of immigrants to New Orleans in 1891, see José Martí's "The Lynching of the Italians" (1891); and Georgette Brockman Hall's novelistic adaptation in *The Sicilian* (1975).

4. For more insight into Alfred Mercier's important novel, see Keith Cartwright's *Reading Africa into American Literature: Epics, Fables, and Gothic Tales* (2002); and Benjamin Hoffmann's "Posthumous Louisiana: Louisiana's Literary Reinvention in Alfred Mercier's *The Saint-Ybars Plantation* (1881)" (2016).

5. I explore this novel in the next chapter. For a deeper analysis of the "dialogue" between Cable and Charles Chesnutt, see Violet Harrington Bryan's *The Myth of New Orleans in Literature: Dialogues of Race and Gender* (1993).

6. For a fascinating study of Cable in the context of emerging technologies to record human voice during the 1880s and 1890s, as well as the ethnographic debates surrounding "the inherently unfaithful relationship between the written word and its cultural sound sources," see Brian Hochman's "Hearing Lost, Hearing Found: George Washington Cable and the Phono-Ethnographic Ear" (2010). The quote is on page 521.

7. In addition to Cable and Lafcadio Hearn, Alcée Fortier is another important example of this trend during the postbellum period. See Fortier's "The French Language in Louisiana and the Negro-French Dialect" (1884) and *Louisiana Folktales in French*

Dialect and English Translation (1895). See also Lyle Saxon, Edward Dreyer, and Robert Tallant's *Gumbo Ya-Ya: Folk Tales of Louisiana* (1945). For significant analysis of this turn to folklore, see Simon J. Bronner's "'Gombo' Folkloristics: Lafcadio Hearn's Creolization and Hybridization in the Formative Period of Folklore Studies" (2005); and Nicholas T. Rinehart's "'I Talk More of the French': Creole Folklore and the Federal Writers' Project" (2016). For more recent anthologies, see George E. Lankford's *Native American Legends: Southeastern Legends* (1987); and Carl Lindhahl, Maida Owens, and C. Renée Harvison's edited volume *Swapping Stories: Folktales from Louisiana* (1997).

8. I rely especially on John Wharton Lowe's recent *Calypso Magnolia: The Crosscurrents of Caribbean and Southern Literature* (2016) for my biographical understanding of Lafcadio Hearn.

9. See Edward F. Haas's "John Fitzpatrick and Political Continuity in New Orleans, 1896–1899" (1981).

CHAPTER FIVE

1. For a full account of this fascinating history, see Roger K. Ward's "The French Language in Louisiana Law and Legal Education: A Requiem" (1997).

2. For historical insight into the Toucoutou Affair, I rely on Shirley Elizabeth Thompson's *Exiles at Home: The Struggle to Become American in Creole New Orleans* (2009).

3. The song is reprinted in Rodolphe Lucien Desdunes, *Nos Hommes et Notre Histoire* (1911), 64.

4. See Donald E. DeVore's *Defying Jim Crow: African American Community Development and the Struggle for Racial Equality in New Orleans, 1900–1960* (2015).

5. On Storyville, see especially Alecia P. Long's *The Great Southern Babylon: Sex, Race, and Respectability in New Orleans, 1865–1920* (2004); and Emily Epstein Landau's *Spectacular Wickedness: Sex, Race, and Memory in Storyville, New Orleans* (2013).

CHAPTER SIX

1. Scholarship on the tourism industry in New Orleans is extensive. See especially Anthony J. Stanonis's *Creating the Big Easy: New Orleans and the Emergence of Modern Tourism, 1918–1945* (2006); J. Mark Souther's *New Orleans on Parade: Tourism and the Transformation of the Crescent City* (2006); Kevin Fox Gotham's *Authentic New Orleans: Tourism, Culture, and Race in the Big Easy* (2007); and Lynnell L. Thomas's *Desire and Disaster in New Orleans: Tourism, Race, and Historical Memory* (2014). Although it does not focus exclusively on tourism, see also Richard Campanella's *Bourbon Street: A History* (2014).

2. See Paul de Man's *Allegories of Reading: Figural Language in Rousseau, Nietzsche, Rilke, and Proust* (1979).

3. See Ellen Gilchrist's *In the Land of Dreamy Dreams* (1981) and Moira Crone's *Dream State* (1995) for two particularly compelling examples of this literary trend.

4. See Thomas Bonner Jr.'s "New Orleans and Its Writers: Burdens of Place" (2010).

5. John Kennedy Toole completed *A Confederacy of Dunces* in 1964, and the novel was published posthumously, with the aid of Walker Percy, in 1980. Two other profoundly unsettling novels that deserve note were published during the same period: Walker Percy's *The Moviegoer* (1961) and Shirley Ann Grau's *The House on Coliseum Street* (1961).

6. For a recent study of this horrific trend, and policy recommendations to change it, see Lydia Voigt, Dee Wood Harper, and William E. Thornton Jr.'s edited volume called *Preventing Lethal Violence in New Orleans* (2016).

7. For a particularly stunning example of this complex, see Brenda Marie Osbey's "I Want to Die in New Orleans" (2008). While it does not evince Osbey's exact sentiment, John Pope's *Getting Off at Elysian Fields: Obituaries from the New Orleans* Times-Picayune (2015) seems "naturally N'awlins" in its ability to tell the story of the twentieth century through its deaths.

8. For an excellent overview of this history, see Arnold R. Hirsch's "Simply a Matter of Black and White: The Transformation of Race and Politics in Twentieth-Century New Orleans" (1992). See also Leonard N. Moore's *Black Rage in New Orleans: Police Brutality and African American Activism from World War II to Hurricane Katrina* (2010).

9. Broadmoor is a centrally located neighborhood of New Orleans. For the full story, see Ramon Antonio Vargas's "Broadmoor Man Killed Roommate After Being Told He Had to Move Out, New Orleans Police Allege" (2017).

10. Although Asian Americans had been part of the New Orleanian fabric since the nineteenth century, it was after World War II, especially, that a greater number of immigrants began to come from across the Pacific Ocean. See Marina E. Espina's *Filipinos in Louisiana* (1988); and Edward J. Lazzerini's *The Asian Peoples of Southern Louisiana: An Ethnohistory* (1990). Significant literary texts include Lafcadio Hearn's "Saint Malo: A Lacustrine Village in Louisiana" (1883), in the nineteenth century; and Robert Olen Butler's *A Good Scent from a Strange Mountain* (1992), in the twentieth.

11. Ruby Bridges is immortalized in Norman Rockwell's oil painting *The Problem We All Live With* (1964). Bridges was joined by Leona Tate, Tessie Prevost, and Gail Etienne, who were the first to integrate McDonogh 19 in 1960. For a particularly disturbing description of the kind of horror faced by Bridges and the other black children, see John Steinbeck's account reprinted as "The Cheerleaders" in *Louisiana Sojourns: Travelers' Tales and Literary Journeys* (1998), edited by Frank de Caro and Rosan Augusta Jordan. For the larger view, see Donald E. DeVore and Joseph Logsdon's *Crescent City Schools: Public Education in New Orleans, 1841–1991* (1991). For further insight into the period, see LaKisha Michelle Simmons's *Crescent City Girls: The Lives of Young Black Women in Segregated New Orleans* (2015). For a fictional story about a young black schoolgirl, set in New Orleans in 1965, see Fatima Shaik's "Climbing Monkey Hill" (1987).

12. The rationale appeared as "Students' Rights to Their Own Language" in the journal *College Composition and Communication* in 1974.

13. See Derek R. Wood's "'Art had almost left them': *Les Cenelles* Society of Arts and Letters, the Dillard Project, and the Legacy of Afro-Creole Arts in New Orleans" (2017).

14. For biographical insight, I rely on Sheryl St. Germain's memoir called *Swamp Songs: The Making of an Unruly Woman* (2003).

15. James Baldwin makes his case in "If Black English Isn't a Language, Then Tell Me, What Is?" (1979).

16. Martin Heidegger makes this argument in his "Letter on Humanism" (1947). The longer passage reads as follows: "Language is the house of Being. In its home man dwells. Those who think and those who create with words are the guardians of this home" (217).

CHAPTER SEVEN

1. John Biguenet's three plays are collected in *The Rising Water Trilogy* (2015). Citations for *Rising Water* come from the text's initial publication in *Katrina on Stage: Five Plays* (2011), edited by Suzanne M. Trauth and Lisa S. Brenner. For greater insight into the troubled relationship between coastal Louisiana and hurricanes, see Craig E. Colten's *Perilous Place, Powerful Storms: Hurricane Protection in Coastal Louisiana* (2009); and Stuart B. Schwartz's *Sea of Storms: A History of Hurricanes in the Greater Caribbean from Columbus to Katrina* (2015). The threat of water comes from both the Gulf of Mexico and the Mississippi River. For an understanding of the river's 1927 flood, one of the nation's most devastating, and its consequences for the region, see Lyle Saxon's *Father Mississippi* (1927); John M. Barry's *Rising Tide: The Great Mississippi Flood of 1927 and How It Changed America* (1997); and Susan Scott Parrish's *The Flood Year 1927: A Cultural History* (2017).

2. For particularly compelling accounts of this connection, see Michael P. Bibler's "Always the Tragic Jezebel: New Orleans, Katrina, and the Layered Discourse of a Doomed Southern City" (2008); and Gary Richards's "Queering Katrina: Gay Discourses of the Disaster in New Orleans" (2010).

3. Criminologists Kelly Frailing and Dee Wood Harper, in "Crime and Hurricanes in New Orleans" (2007), offer an important middle ground that both acknowledges crime and seeks to identify its cause. The burglary rate in Orleans Parish was 48.9 per 100,000 people in the month before the hurricane, they claim. In the month after, it was 245.9, or a 402.9 percent increase (63). For the criminologists, the causes for this increase are economic: "Both before Katrina and especially in its wake, the burglary rate was high. In the macrosociological context of New Orleans, with its declining population, high rates of unemployment, and low wages (if working at all), neither of these numbers should be a major revelation. Hurricane Katrina simply intensified and worsened the

story of deprivation and crime, which had for many years plagued New Orleans" (64). Their clincher about the racial disparity is stark: "At no time in New Orleans since 1950 did whites have less than double the household income of African Americans" (58).

4. See John Arena's *Driven from New Orleans: How Nonprofits Betray Public Housing and Promote Privatization* (2012); and Kristen L. Buras's *Charter Schools, Race, and Urban Space: Where the Market Meets Grassroots Resistance* (2015).

5. Abdulrahman Zeitoun, whom Dave Eggers depicts as a supportive family man and victim of Islamophobic sentiment, was arrested in 2012 for attacking his wife and plotting her murder. The domestic violence, according to wife Kathy Zeitoun, was commonplace well before the storm and was ongoing during Eggers's fieldwork and writing. Eggers did not have this knowledge during his investigation, of course, but the controversy does show how one's desire to present one's subject in a certain way may hinder one in seeing the truth of the reality.

6. Although I focus on Martha Serpas and Yusef Komunyakaa in this chapter, many other poets have influenced my thinking about the ways in which poetic language responds to the disaster of Hurricane Katrina. For two especially important compilations, see a special issue of *New Orleans Review* (2006), edited by Christopher Chambers, as well as an anthology called *Hurricane Blues: Poems about Katrina and Rita* (2006), edited by Philip C. Kolin and Susan Swartwout. For single authored books of poetry, see Patricia Smith's *Blood Dazzler* (2008); Raymond McDaniel's *Saltwater Empire* (2008); Gabriel Gomez's *The Outer Bands* (2008); Nicole Cooley's *Breach* (2010); Niyi Osundare's *City Without People* (2011); Alison Pelegrin's *Hurricane Party* (2012); Peter Cooley's *Night Bus to the Afterlife* (2014); and Mona Lisa Saloy's *Second Line Home: New Orleans Poems* (2014). My reading on the subject was greatly aided by Susan Larson's new edition of *The Booklover's Guide to New Orleans* (2013). For the criticism, especially of drama and fiction, see a special issue of *TDR: The Drama Review*, "New Orleans After the Flood" (2013), edited by Jan Gilbert and Kevin McCaffrey, as well as an anthology called *Ten Years After Katrina: Critical Perspectives on the Storm's Effect of American Culture and Identity* (2014), edited by Mary Ruth Marotte and Glenn Jellenik. For an overview and analysis of the representation of the hurricane in film, see Janet Walker's "Moving Home: Documentary Film and Other Remediations of Post-Katrina New Orleans" (2014).

7. See Ruth Salvaggio's *Hearing Sappho in New Orleans: The Call of Poetry from Congo Square to the Ninth Ward* (2012).

8. On the Mardi Gras Indians, see most recently Sascha Just's "Black Indians of New Orleans—'Won't Bow Down, Don't Know How'" (2017). For analysis of the writers listed here, see Keith Cartwright's *Sacral Grooves, Limbo Gateways: Travels in Deep Southern Time, Circum-Caribbean Space, Afro-creole Authority* (2013); Rain P. Cranford Goméz's "Hachotakni Zydeco's Round'a Loop Current: Indigenous, African, and Caribbean Mestizaje in Louisiana Literatures" (2014); and Tracey Watts's "Haunted Memories: Disruptive Ghosts in the Poems of Brenda Marie Osbey and Joy Harjo" (2014).

9. See Jason Theriot's *American Energy, Imperiled Coast: Oil and Gas Development in Louisiana's Wetlands* (2014). For a more personalized account of this devastation, see Mike Tidwell's *Bayou Farewell: The Rich Life and Tragic Death of Louisiana's Cajun Coast* (2003); and Andy Horowitz's "The BP Oil Spill and the End of Empire, Louisiana" (2014). For related work on the significance of the oil and gas industry for the environmental humanities, see Ross Barrett and Daniel Worden's edited volume called *Oil Culture* (2014); and Stephanie LeMenager's *Living Oil: Petroleum Culture in the American Century* (2014). See also Molly Wallace's *Risk Criticism: Precautionary Reading in an Age of Environmental Uncertainty* (2016).

10. See Rob Nixon's *Slow Violence and the Environmentalism of the Poor* (2011).

11. See Maurice Blanchot's *The Writing of the Disaster* (1980).

CHAPTER EIGHT

1. Fredric Jameson is glossing the work of Tom Moylan in *Demand the Impossible: Science Fiction and the Utopian Imagination* (1986). For additional work on the genre, I am indebted to Gerry Canavan and Kim Stanley Robinson's edited volume *Green Planets: Ecology and Science Fiction* (2014); Adam Trexler's *Anthropocene Fictions: The Novel in a Time of Climate Change* (2015); and Rebekah Sheldon's *The Child to Come: Life After the Human Catastrophe* (2016).

2. See especially Anne Rice's famous *Interview with the Vampire* (1976). For a series of haunting tales, see Jeanne deLavigne's *Ghost Stories of Old New Orleans* (1946).

3. Ludwig von Reizenstein's *The Mysteries of New Orleans* (1855) is a notable exception to this general turn to the past. Reizenstein's projective time scale, around two decades into the future, however, is much more abbreviated than Moira Crone's.

4. One of the Taylor Energy Company executives, moreover, attributed the ongoing disaster to an "act of God," a liability claim that would be laughable if it were not so tragic. See Michael Kunzelman's "Taylor Energy Executive Blames Decade-Old Oil Leak in Gulf of Mexico on 'Act of God'" (2016).

5. See Jacques Derrida's "No Apocalypse, Not Now (Full Speed Ahead, Seven Missiles, Seven Missives)" (1984).

6. See Amy Wold's "Isle de Jean Charles Tribe Looks at Moving Entire Community North in First-of-Its-Kind Test Case" (2016). For the larger context, see Carl A. Brasseaux's *French, Cajun, Creole, Houma: A Primer on Francophone Louisiana* (2005). The master plan has been published as *Louisiana's Comprehensive Master Plan for a Sustainable Coast* (2012) by the Coastal Protection and Restoration Authority of Louisiana.

BIBLIOGRAPHY

Adelson, Jeff. "Water Has Risen 2 Inches at Grand Isle Since 2007, Data Show." *New Orleans Advocate*, 10 May 2014, www.theadvocate.com/new_orleans/news/article_f5d1b43b-1d4b-517d-853a-cfe1e63cd040.html.

Algren, Nelson. *A Walk on the Wild Side*. 1956. New York: Farrar, Straus and Giroux, 1989.

Allard, Louis. "Au Moqueur [To the Mockingbird]." 1847. *Creole Echoes: The Francophone Poetry of Nineteenth-Century Louisiana*. Ed. M. Lynn Weiss. Urbana: U of Illinois P, 2004. 4–5.

Allen, William Francis, Charles Pickard Ware, and Lucy McKim Garrison, eds. *Slave Songs of the United States*. New York: A. Simpson, 1867.

Anderson, Benedict. *Imagined Communities: Reflections on the Origin and Spread of Nationalism*. 1983. New York: Verso, 1991.

Anzaldúa, Gloria. "How To Tame a Wild Tongue." *Borderlands / La Frontera: The New Mestiza*. 1987. San Francisco, CA: Aunt Lute, 1999. 75–86.

Arena, John. *Driven from New Orleans: How Nonprofits Betray Public Housing and Promote Privatization*. Minneapolis: U of Minnesota P, 2012.

Azzarello, Robert. *Queer Environmentality: Ecology, Evolution, and Sexuality in American Literature*. Burlington, VT: Ashgate, 2012.

Baldwin, James. "If Black English Isn't a Language, Then Tell Me, What Is?" 1979. *Collected Essays*. Ed. Toni Morrison. New York: Library of America, 1998. 780–783.

Barrett, Ross, and Daniel Worden, eds. *Oil Culture*. Minneapolis: U of Minnesota P, 2014.

Barry, John M. *Rising Tide: The Great Mississippi Flood of 1927 and How It Changed America*. New York: Touchstone, 1997.

Bataille, Georges. "The Big Toe." 1929. *Visions of Excess: Selected Writings, 1927–1939.* Ed. and trans. Allan Stoekl. Minneapolis: U of Minnesota P, 1985. 20–23.

Bell, Caryn Cossé. *Revolution, Romanticism, and the Afro-Creole Protest Tradition in Louisiana, 1718–1868.* Baton Rouge: Louisiana State UP, 1997.

Bernardin de Saint-Pierre, Jacques-Henri. *Paul et Virginie.* 1788. Trans. John Donovan. London: Peter Owen, 2005.

Bibler, Michael P. "Always the Tragic Jezebel: New Orleans, Katrina, and the Layered Discourse of a Doomed Southern City." *Southern Cultures* 14.2 (2008): 6–27.

Bienvenu, Germain. "The Beginnings of Louisiana Literature: The French Domination of 1682–1763." *Louisiana Culture from the Colonial Era to Katrina.* Ed. John Lowe. Baton Rouge: Louisiana State UP, 2008. 25–48.

Biguenet, John. *Oyster.* New York: Ecco, 2002.

———. *Rising Water.* 2006. *Katrina on Stage: Five Plays.* Ed. Suzanne M. Trauth and Lisa S. Brenner. Evanston, IL: Northwestern UP, 2011. 3–52.

———. *The Rising Water Trilogy.* Baton Rouge: Louisiana State UP, 2015.

Blanchot, Maurice. *The Writing of the Disaster.* 1980. Trans. Ann Smock. Lincoln: U of Nebraska P, 1986.

Blassingame, John W. *Black New Orleans, 1860–1880.* Chicago: U of Chicago P, 1973.

Bonner, Thomas, Jr. "New Orleans and Its Writers: Burdens of Place." *Mississippi Quarterly* 63 (2010): 195–209.

Brasseaux, Carl A. *French, Cajun, Creole, Houma: A Primer on Francophone Louisiana.* Baton Rouge: Louisiana State UP, 2005.

Braun, Juliane. "The Drama of History in Francophone New Orleans." *Early American Literature* 50.3 (2015): 763–795.

Brickhouse, Anna. "'L'Ouragan de flammes' ('The Hurricane of Flames'): New Orleans and Transamerican Catastrophe, 1866/2005." *American Quarterly* 59.4 (2007): 1097–1127.

———. *Transamerican Literary Relations and the Nineteenth-Century Public Sphere.* New York: Cambridge UP, 2004.

Bronner, Simon J. "'Gombo' Folkloristics: Lafcadio Hearn's Creolization and Hybridization in the Formative Period of Folklore Studies." *Journal of Folklore Research* 42.2 (2005): 141–184.

Brosman, Catharine Savage. *Louisiana Creole Literature: A Historical Study.* Jackson: U of Mississippi P, 2013.

Bruce, Clint. *Afro-Creole Poetry in French from Louisiana's Radical Civil War–Era Newspapers*. New Orleans: The Historic New Orleans Collection, forthcoming.

———. "Caught Between Continents: The Local and the Transatlantic in the French-Language Serial Fiction of New Orleans's *Le Courrier de la Louisiane*, 1843–1845." *Transnationalism and American Serial Fiction*. Ed. Patricia Okker. New York: Routledge, 2012. 12–35.

Bryan, Violet Harrington. *The Myth of New Orleans in Literature: Dialogues of Race and Gender*. Knoxville: U of Tennessee P, 1993.

Buell, Frederick. *From Apocalypse to Way of Life: Environmental Crisis in the American Century*. New York: Routledge, 2004.

Buell, Lawrence. *The Environmental Imagination: Thoreau, Nature Writing, and the Formation of American Culture*. Cambridge, MA: Harvard UP, 1995.

Buras, Kristen L. *Charter Schools, Race, and Urban Space: Where the Market Meets Grassroots Resistance*. New York: Routledge, 2015.

Butler, Judith. *Precarious Life: The Powers of Mourning and Violence*. New York: Verso, 2004.

Butler, Robert Olen. *A Good Scent from a Strange Mountain*. New York: Grove, 1992.

Cabeza de Vaca, Álvar Núñez. *The Narrative of Cabeza de Vaca*. 1542. Ed. and trans. Rolena Adorno and Patrick Charles Pautz. Lincoln: U of Nebraska P, 2003.

Cable, George Washington. *The Creoles of Louisiana*. 1884. Gretna, LA: Pelican, 2005.

———. "Creole Slave Songs." *The Century Magazine* 31.6 (1886): 807–828.

———. *The Grandissimes*. 1880. New York: Penguin, 2003.

———. "New Orleans Before the Capture." 1885. *Readings in American Literature*. Ed. John Calvin Metcalf and Henry Brantly Handy. Richmond, VA: B. F. Johnson, 1919. 415–421.

———. *Old Creole Days*. 1879. Gretna, LA: Pelican, 1991.

———. "'Tite Poulette." *Old Creole Days*. 1879. Gretna, LA: Pelican, 1991. 213–243.

Caillot, Marc-Antoine. *A Company Man: The Remarkable French-Atlantic Voyage of a Clerk for the Company of the Indies*. 1731. Ed. Erin M. Greenwald. Trans. Teri F. Chalmers. New Orleans, LA: Historic New Orleans Collection, 2013.

Calinescu, Matei. *Five Faces of Modernity: Modernism, Avant-Garde, Decadence, Kitsch, Postmodernism*. 1977. Durham, NC: Duke UP, 1987.

Campanella, Richard. *Bienville's Dilemma: A Historical Geography of New Orleans*. Lafayette: U of Louisiana P, 2008.

———. *Bourbon Street: A History.* Baton Rouge: Louisiana State UP, 2014.

Canavan, Gerry, and Kim Stanley Robinson, eds. *Green Planets: Ecology and Science Fiction.* Middletown, CT: Wesleyan UP, 2014.

Cannon, C. W. "I Want Magic: A Defense of New Orleans Exceptionalism." *Know Louisiana,* 10 Feb. 2015, www.knowlouisiana.org/want-magic-defense-new-orleans-exceptionalism.

Carson, Rachel. *Silent Spring.* 1962. New York: Houghton Mifflin, 2002.

Cartwright, Keith. *Reading Africa into American Literature: Epics, Fables, and Gothic Tales.* Lexington: U of Kentucky P, 2002.

———. *Sacral Grooves, Limbo Gateways: Travels in Deep Southern Time, Circum-Caribbean Space, Afro-creole Authority.* Athens: U of Georgia P, 2013.

Caulfeild, Ruby Van Allen. *The French Literature of Louisiana.* New York: Columbia UP, 1929.

Chambers, Christopher, ed. *New Orleans Review* 31.2 (2006): 1–240.

Charlevoix, Pierre François Xavier de. *Charlevoix's Louisiana: Selections from the History and the* Journal. 1744. Ed. Charles E. O'Neill. Trans. John Gilmary Shea and J. Dodsley. Baton Rouge: Louisiana State UP, 1977.

Chateaubriand, François-René de. *Atala/René.* 1801/1802. Trans. Irving Putter. Berkeley: U of California P, 1952.

Chesnutt, Charles. *Paul Marchand, FMC.* 1921. Princeton, NJ: Princeton UP, 1999.

Ch'ien, Evelyn Nien-Ming. *Weird English.* Cambridge, MA: Harvard UP, 2004.

Chopin, Kate. *The Awakening.* 1899. New York: Penguin, 2003.

Christian, Marcus. *I Am New Orleans.* 1968. New Orleans: Xavier Review, 1999.

Clark, Emily. *Masterless Mistresses: The New Orleans Ursulines and the Development of a New World Society, 1727–1834.* Chapel Hill: U of North Carolina P, 2007.

Crawford, James, ed. *Language Loyalties: A Source Book on the Official English Controversy.* Chicago: U of Chicago P, 1992.

Crone, Moira. *Dream State.* Jackson: UP of Mississippi, 1995.

———. *The Not Yet.* New Orleans: U of New Orleans P, 2012.

Codrescu, Andrei. "My City My Wilderness." 1995. *New Orleans, Mon Amour: Twenty Years of Writings from the City.* Chapel Hill, NC: Algonquin, 2006. 131–171.

Colten, Craig E. "Meaning of Water in the American South: Transatlantic Encounters." *New Orleans in the Atlantic World: Between Land and Sea.* Ed. William Boelhower. New York: Routledge, 2010. 50–70.

———. *Perilous Place, Powerful Storms: Hurricane Protection in Coastal Louisiana.* Jackson: UP of Mississippi, 2009.

Conference on College Composition and Communication. "Students' Rights to Their Own Language." *College Composition and Communication* 25.3 (1974): 1–32.

Cooley, Nicole. *Breach.* Baton Rouge: Louisiana State UP, 2010.

Cooley, Peter. *Night Bus to the Afterlife.* Pittsburgh, PA: Carnegie Mellon UP, 2014.

Crété, Liliane. *Daily Life in Louisiana, 1815–1830.* 1978. Trans. Patrick Gregory. Baton Rouge: Louisiana State UP, 1981.

Darwin, Charles. *The Descent of Man.* 1871. New York: Penguin, 2004.

———. *On the Origin of Species.* 1859. New York: Penguin, 2009.

Dawdy, Shannon Lee. *Patina: A Profane Archaeology.* Chicago: U of Chicago P, 2016.

de la Metairie, Jacques. "Vive le Roi: La Salle Reaches the Mississippi's Mouth." *Louisiana Sojourns: Travelers' Tales and Literary Journeys.* Ed. Frank de Caro and Rosan Augusta Jordan. Baton Rouge: Louisiana State UP, 1998. 16–18.

deLavigne, Jeanne. *Ghost Stories of Old New Orleans.* 1946. Baton Rouge: Louisiana State UP, 2013.

DeLoughrey, Elizabeth. "Satellite Planetarity and the Ends of the Earth." *Public Culture* 26.2 (2014): 257–280.

de Man, Paul. *Allegories of Reading: Figural Language in Rousseau, Nietzsche, Rilke, and Proust.* New Haven, CT: Yale UP, 1979.

Dent, Tom. *Ritual Murder. Callaloo* 2 (1978): 67–81.

Derrida, Jacques. "No Apocalypse, Not Now (Full Speed Ahead, Seven Missiles, Seven Missives)." Trans. Catherine Porter and Philip Lewis. *Diacritics* 14.2 (1984): 20–31.

Desdunes, Rodolphe Lucien. *Nos Hommes et Notre Histoire [Our People and Our History].* 1911. Ed. and trans. Dorothea Olga McCants. 1973. Baton Rouge: Louisiana State UP, 2001.

Dessens, Nathalie. *Creole City: A Chronicle of Early American New Orleans.* Gainesville: UP of Florida, 2015.

———. *From Saint-Domingue to New Orleans: Migration and Influence.* Gainesville: UP of Florida, 2007.

Dessommes, Georges. "Un Soir au Jackson Square [An Evening in Jackson Square]." 1880. *Creole Echoes: The Francophone Poetry of Nineteenth-Century Louisiana.* Ed. M. Lynn Weiss. Urbana: U of Illinois P, 2004. 52–55.

DeVore, Donald E. *Defying Jim Crow: African American Community Development and the Struggle for Racial Equality in New Orleans, 1900–1960.* Baton Rouge: Louisiana State UP, 2015.

DeVore, Donald E., and Joseph Logsdon. *Crescent City Schools: Public Education in New Orleans, 1841–1991.* Lafayette: U of Louisiana P, 1991.

Dimock, Wai Chee. *Through Other Continents: American Literature Across Deep Time.* Princeton, NJ: Princeton UP, 2006.

Dowling, Linda. *Language and Decadence in the Victorian Fin de Siècle.* Princeton, NJ: Princeton UP, 1986.

Dugué, Charles-Oscar. "Souvenirs du désert [Memories of the Desert]." 1847. *Creole Echoes: The Francophone Poetry of Nineteenth-Century Louisiana.* Ed. M. Lynn Weiss. Urbana: U of Illinois P, 2004. 56–59.

Dumont de Montigny, Jean François Benjamin. *The Memoir of Lieutenant Dumont, 1715–1747: A Sojourner in the French Atlantic.* Ed. Gordon M. Sayre and Carla Zecher. Trans. Gordon M. Sayre. Chapel Hill: U of North Carolina P, 2012.

———. "Poème en vers touchant l'établissement de la province de la Louisiane [Verse Poem Concerning the Establishment of the Louisiana Province]." ca. 1741. Trans. Gordon M. Sayre. *Jean François Benjamin Dumont de Montigny (1696–1760).* University of Oregon, 26 Oct. 2015, https://cpb-us-e1 .wpmucdn.com/blogs.uoregon.edu/dist/1/13643/files/2016/12/Dumont-poeme-translation-10dlpdw.pdf

Dunbar-Nelson, Alice. "The Stones of the Village." ca. 1905. *Great Short Stories by American Women.* Ed. Candace Ward. Mineola, NY: Dover, 1996. 130–152.

Dunn, Christopher. "Black Rome and the Chocolate City: The Race of Place." *Callaloo* 30.3 (2007): 847–861.

Eckstein, Barbara. *Sustaining New Orleans: Literature, Local Memory, and the Fate of a City.* New York: Routledge, 2006.

Eggers, Dave. *Zeitoun.* New York: Vintage, 2009.

Elfenbein, Anna Shannon. *Women on the Color Line: Evolving Stereotypes and the Writings of George Washington Cable, Grace King, and Kate Chopin.* Charlottesville: U of Virginia P, 1989.

Ellinger, Esther Parker. *The Southern War Poetry of the Civil War.* Diss. U of Pennsylvania. 1918.

English, Thomas Dunn. "The Battle of New Orleans." ca. 1885. *Poems of American Patriotism.* Ed. Brander Matthews. New York: Scribner, 1922. 58–66.

Espina, Marina E. *Filipinos in Louisiana.* New Orleans: A. F. Laborde and Sons, 1988.

Faber, Eberhart L. *Building the Land of Dreams: New Orleans and the Transformation of Early America.* Princeton, NJ: Princeton UP, 2016.

Fabre, Michel. "New Orleans Creole Expatriates in France: Romance and Reality." *Creole: The History and Legacy of Louisiana's Free People of Color.* Ed. Sybil Kein. Baton Rouge: Louisiana State UP, 2000. 179–195.

———. "The New Orleans Press and French-Language Literature by Creoles of Color." *Multilingual America: Transnationalism, Ethnicity, and the Languages of American Literature.* Ed. Werner Sollors. New York: New York UP, 1998. 29–49.

Faulkner, William. *Mosquitoes.* 1927. *Novels, 1926–1929.* Ed. Joseph Blotner and Noel Polk. New York: Library of America, 2006. 257–540.

Fertel, Rien. *Imagining the Creole City: The Rise of Literary Culture in Nineteenth-Century New Orleans.* Baton Rouge: Louisiana State UP, 2014.

Ford, Katie. *Colosseum.* Minneapolis, MN: Graywolf, 2008.

Fortier, Alcée. "The French Language in Louisiana and the Negro-French Dialect." *Transactions of the Modern Language Association of America* 1 (1884): 96–111.

———. "French Literature in Louisiana." *PMLA* 2 (1886): 31–60.

———., ed. and trans. *Louisiana Folktales in French Dialect and English Translation.* New York: Houghton, Mifflin, 1895.

Frailing, Kelly, and Dee Wood Harper. "Crime and Hurricanes in New Orleans." *The Sociology of Katrina: Perspectives on a Modern Catastrophe.* Ed. David L. Brunsma, David Overfelt, and J. Steven Picou. Lanham, MD: Rowman and Littlefield, 2007. 51–68.

Freud, Sigmund. *The Future of an Illusion.* 1927. Trans. and ed. James Strachey. New York: Norton, 1961.

———. "Mourning and Melancholy." 1917. *The Freud Reader.* Ed. Peter Gay. Trans. James Strachey. New York: Norton, 1989. 584–589.

Gilbert, Jan, and Kevin McCaffrey, eds. "New Orleans After the Flood." *TDR: The Drama Review* 57.1 (2013): 18–101.

Gilchrist, Ellen. *In the Land of Dreamy Dreams.* New York: Little, Brown, 1981.

Gilman, Richard. *Decadence: The Strange Life of an Epithet.* New York: Farrar, Straus and Giroux, 1979.

Gomez, Gabriel. *The Outer Bands.* Notre Dame, IN: U of Notre Dame P, 2008.

Goméz, Rain P. Cranford. "Hachotakni Zydeco's Round'a Loop Current: Indigenous, African, and Caribbean Mestizaje in Louisiana Literatures." *Southern Literary Journal* 46.2 (2014): 88–107.

Gotham, Kevin Fox. *Authentic New Orleans: Tourism, Culture, and Race in the Big Easy.* New York: New York UP, 2007.

Grau, Shirley Ann. *The House on Coliseum Street.* 1961. Baton Rouge: Louisiana State UP, 1996.

Greenwald, Erin M. *Marc-Antoine Caillot and the Company of the Indies in Louisiana: Trade in the French Atlantic World.* Baton Rouge: Louisiana State UP, 2016.

Gruesz, Kirsten Silva. "The Gulf of Mexico System and the 'Latinness' of New Orleans." *American Literary History* 18.3 (2006): 468–496.

Guenin-Lelle, Dianne. *The Story of French New Orleans: History of a Creole City.* Jackson: UP of Mississippi, 2016.

Haas, Edward F. "John Fitzpatrick and Political Continuity in New Orleans, 1896–1899." *Louisiana History* 22.1 (1981): 7–29.

Haas, Mary H., ed. and trans. *Tunica Texts.* Berkeley: U of California P, 1950.

Hachard, Marie Madeleine. *Voices from an Early American Convent: Marie Madeleine Hachard and the New Orleans Ursulines, 1727–1760.* Ed. and trans. Emily Clark. Baton Rouge: Louisiana State UP, 2007.

Hanson, Ellis. *Decadence and Catholicism.* Cambridge, MA: Harvard UP, 1997.

Hall, A. Oakey. *The Manhattaner in New Orleans; Or, Phases of "Crescent City" Life.* New Orleans: J. C. Morgan, 1851.

Hall, Georgette Brockman. *The Sicilian.* Gretna, LA: Pelican, 1975.

Hall, Gwendolyn Midlo. *Africans in Colonial Louisiana: The Development of Afro-Creole Culture in the Eighteenth Century.* Baton Rouge: Louisiana State UP, 1992.

Harjo, Joy. "New Orleans." 1983. *Louisiana Sojourns: Travelers' Tales and Literary Journeys.* Ed. Frank de Caro and Rosan Augusta Jordan. Baton Rouge: Louisiana State UP, 1998. 107–109.

Harrison, Robert Pogue. *The Dominion of the Dead.* Chicago: U of Chicago P, 2003.

Hearn, Lafcadio. "At the Gate of the Tropics." 1877. *American Writings.* Ed. Christopher Benfey. New York: Library of America, 2009. 669–679.

———. *Chita: A Memory of Last Island.* 1889. *American Writings.* Ed. Christopher Benfey. New York: Library of America, 2009. 73–148.

———. "The Creole Patois." 1885. *American Writings.* Ed. Christopher Benfey. New York: Library of America, 2009. 744–748.

———. "New Orleans." 1877. *American Writings.* Ed. Christopher Benfey. New York: Library of America, 2009. 690–699.

———. "New Orleans in Wet Weather." 1877. *American Writings*. Ed. Christopher Benfey. New York: Library of America, 2009. 680–690.

———. "Saint Malo: A Lacustrine Village in Louisiana." 1883. *American Writings*. Ed. Christopher Benfey. New York: Library of America, 2009. 730–743.

Heidegger, Martin. "Letter on Humanism." 1947. Trans. Frank A. Capuzzi. *Basic Writings*. Ed. David Farrell Krell. New York: HarperCollins, 1977. 217–265.

Henry. "La rebellion du sud en permanence [The South's Permanent Revolt]." 1865. *Creole Echoes: The Francophone Poetry of Nineteenth-Century Louisiana*. Ed. M. Lynn Weiss. Urbana: U of Illinois P, 2004. 90–93.

Hirsch, Arnold R. "Simply a Matter of Black and White: The Transformation of Race and Politics in Twentieth-Century New Orleans." *Creole New Orleans: Race and Americanization*. Ed. Arnold R. Hirsch and Joseph Logsdon. Baton Rouge: Louisiana State UP, 1992. 262–319.

Hirsch, Arnold R., and Joseph Logsdon, eds. *Creole New Orleans: Race and Americanization*. Baton Rouge: Louisiana State UP, 1992.

Hochman, Brian. "Hearing Lost, Hearing Found: George Washington Cable and the Phono-Ethnographic Ear." *American Literature* 82.3 (2010): 519–551.

Hoffmann, Benjamin. "Posthumous Louisiana: Louisiana's Literary Reinvention in Alfred Mercier's *The Saint-Ybars Plantation* (1881)." *The Southern Quarterly* 53.2 (2016): 164–181.

Hogue, James K. *Uncivil War: Five New Orleans Street Battles and the Rise and Fall of Racial Reconstruction*. Baton Rouge: Louisiana State UP, 2006.

Hollandsworth, James, Jr. *An Absolute Massacre: The New Orleans Race Riot of July 30, 1866*. Baton Rouge: Louisiana State UP, 2001.

Horowitz, Andy. "The BP Oil Spill and the End of Empire, Louisiana." *Southern Cultures* 20.3 (2014): 6–23.

Houzeau, Jean-Charles. *My Passage at the New Orleans* Tribune*: A Memoir of the Civil War Era*. 1872. Ed. David C. Rankin. Baton Rouge: Louisiana State UP, 2001.

Howe, LeAnne. "The Chaos of Angels." *Callaloo* 17.1 (1994): 108–114.

———. *Shell Shaker*. San Francisco, CA: Aunt Lute, 2001.

Hurston, Zora Neale. "Mother Catherine." 1934. *Folklore, Memoirs, and Other Writings*. Ed. Cheryl A. Wall. New York: Library of America, 1995. 854–860.

Hutchinson, Coleman, ed. *A History of American Civil War Literature*. New York: Cambridge UP, 2016.

Huysmans, J. K. *À rebours*. 1884. Trans. unknown. New York: Dover, 1969.

Iberville, Pierre Le Moyne. *Iberville's Gulf Journals*. Trans. and ed. Richebourg Gaillard McWilliams. Tuscaloosa: U of Alabama P, 1981.

Ingersoll, Thomas N. *Mammon and Manon in Early New Orleans: The First Slave Society in the Deep South, 1718–1819*. Knoxville: U of Tennessee P, 1999.

Jameson, Fredric. *Archaeologies of the Future: The Desire Called Utopia and Other Science Fictions*. New York: Verso, 2005.

Johnson, Jerah. "New Orleans's Congo Square: An Urban Setting for Early Afro-American Culture Formation." *Louisiana History* 32.2 (1991): 117–157.

Joutel, Henri. *A Journal of La Salle's Last Voyage*. 1713. Trans. unknown. New York: Corinth, 1962.

Jumonville, Florence M. "'The Art Preservative of All Arts': Early Printing in New Orleans." *Printmaking in New Orleans*. Ed. Jessie J. Poesch. Jackson: UP of Mississippi, 2006. 87–101.

Just, Sascha. "Black Indians of New Orleans—'Won't Bow Down, Don't Know How.'" *The Southern Quarterly* 55.1 (2017): 72–87.

Kaser, James A. *The New Orleans of Fiction: A Research Guide*. Lanham, MD: Rowman and Littlefield, 2014.

Kein, Sybil. *Gumbo People*. 1981. Donaldsonville, LA: Margaret Media, 1999.

———. "The Use of Louisiana Creole in Southern Literature." *Creole: The History and Legacy of Louisiana's Free People of Color*. Ed. Sybil Kein. Baton Rouge: Louisiana State UP, 2000. 117–154.

Kermode, Frank. *The Sense of an Ending: Studies in the Theory of Fiction*. 1966. New York: Oxford UP, 2000.

Kerouac, Jack. *On the Road*. 1957. New York: Penguin, 1999.

Kennedy, Richard S., ed. *Literary New Orleans in the Modern World*. Baton Rouge: Louisiana State UP, 1998.

King, Grace. "The Little Convent Girl." 1893. *Grace King of New Orleans: A Selection of Her Writings*. Ed. Robert Bush. Baton Rouge: Louisiana State UP, 1973. 150–156.

———. *Memories of a Southern Woman of Letters*. 1932. *Grace King of New Orleans: A Selection of Her Writings*. Ed. Robert Bush. Baton Rouge: Louisiana State UP, 1973. 35–51.

Kniffen, Fred B., Hiram F. Gregory, and George A. Stokes. *The Historic Tribes of Louisiana, from 1542 to the Present*. Baton Rouge: Louisiana State UP, 1987.

Koenig, David. "Exxon: Oil Has No Quick Replacement." *Advocate*, 30 May 2013.

Kolin, Philip C., and Susan Swartwout, eds. *Hurricane Blues: Poems About Katrina and Rita*. Cape Girardeau, MO: Southeast Missouri State UP, 2006.

Komunyakaa, Yusef. "Requiem." *Callaloo* 31.2 (2008): 484–485.

Kunzelman, Michael. "Taylor Energy Executive Blames Decade-Old Oil Leak in Gulf of Mexico on 'Act of God.'" *Advocate*, 21 Jan. 2016, www.theadvocate .com/nation_world/article_1d35c985-bb7d-5682-bcc8-982d7a2d7745.html.

LaChance, Paul F. "The Foreign French." *Creole New Orleans: Race and Americanization.* Ed. Arnold R. Hirsch and Joseph Logsdon. Baton Rouge: Louisiana State UP, 1992. 101–130.

Ladd, Barbara. *Nationalism and the Color Line in George W. Cable, Mark Twain, and William Faulkner.* Baton Rouge: Louisiana State UP, 1996.

Landau, Emily Epstein. *Spectacular Wickedness: Sex, Race, and Memory in Storyville, New Orleans.* Baton Rouge: Louisiana State UP, 2013.

Lankford, George E. *Native American Legends: Southeastern Legends.* Little Rock: AR: August House, 1987.

Lanusse, Armand, ed. *Les Cenelles: Choix de poésies indigènes.* 1845. Shreveport, LA: Tintamarre, 2003.

Larson, Susan. *The Booklover's Guide to New Orleans.* 2nd ed. Baton Rouge: Louisiana State UP, 2013.

Laussat, Pierre Clément de. *Memoirs of My Life.* 1831. Ed. Robert D. Bush. Trans. Agnes-Josephine Pastwa. Baton Rouge: Louisiana State UP, 1978.

Lazzerini, Edward J. *The Asian Peoples of Southern Louisiana: An Ethnohistory.* New Orleans: U of New Orleans P, 1990.

Lightweis-Goff, Jennie. "'Peculiar and Characteristic': New Orleans's Exceptionalism from Olmsted to the Deluge." *American Literature* 86.1 (2014): 147–169.

Lindhahl, Carl, Maida Owens, and C. Renée Harvison, eds. *Swapping Stories: Folktales from Louisiana.* Jackson: UP of Mississippi, 1997.

Lippi-Green, Rosina. *English with an Accent: Language, Ideology, and Discrimination in the United States.* New York: Routledge, 1997.

Long, Alecia P. *The Great Southern Babylon: Sex, Race, and Respectability in New Orleans, 1865–1920.* Baton Rouge: Louisiana State UP, 2004.

Louisiana's Comprehensive Master Plan for a Sustainable Coast. Baton Rouge: Coastal Protection and Restoration Authority of Louisiana, 2012.

Lowe, John Wharton. *Calypso Magnolia: The Crosscurrents of Caribbean and Southern Literature.* Chapel Hill: U of North Carolina P, 2016.

LeMenager, Stephanie. *Living Oil: Petroleum Culture in the American Century.* New York: Oxford UP, 2014.

Le Page Du Pratz, Antoine Simon. *The History of Louisiana.* 1774. Ed. Joseph G. Tregle Jr. Trans. unknown. Baton Rouge: Louisiana State UP, 1975.

Marino, Samuel J. "Early French-Language Newspapers in New Orleans." *Louisiana History* 7.4 (1966): 309–321.

Marotte, Mary Ruth, and Glenn Jellenik, eds. *Ten Years After Katrina: Critical Perspectives on the Storm's Effect of American Culture and Identity.* Lanham, MD: Lexington, 2014.

Martí, José. "The Lynching of the Italians." 1891. *Selected Writings.* Ed. and trans. Esther Allen. New York: Penguin, 2002. 296–303.

Martin, Valerie. *Property.* New York: Vintage, 2003.

———. *A Recent Martyr.* New York: Vintage, 1987.

McDaniel, Raymond. *Saltwater Empire.* Minneapolis, MN: Coffee House, 2008.

Mercier, Alfred. *L'Habitation Saint-Ybars.* 1881. Shreveport, LA: Tintamarre, 2003.

———. "Patrie [Fatherland]." 1842. *Creole Echoes: The Francophone Poetry of Nineteenth-Century Louisiana.* Ed. M. Lynn Weiss. Urbana: U of Illinois P, 2004. 128–133.

Moore, Leonard N. *Black Rage in New Orleans: Police Brutality and African American Activism from World War II to Hurricane Katrina.* Baton Rouge: Louisiana State UP, 2010.

Mortimer-Sandilands, Catriona. "Melancholy Natures, Queer Ecologies." *Queer Ecologies: Sex, Nature, Politics, Desire.* Ed. Catriona Mortimer-Sandilands and Bruce Erickson. Bloomington: Indiana UP, 2010. 331–358.

Mosadomi, Fehintola. "The Origin of Louisiana Creole." *Creole: The History and Legacy of Louisiana's Free People of Color.* Ed. Sybil Kein. Baton Rouge: Louisiana State UP, 2000. 223–243.

Moylan, Tom. *Demand the Impossible: Science Fiction and the Utopian Imagination.* New York: Methuen, 1986.

Nagel, James. *Race and Culture in New Orleans Stories: Kate Chopin, Grace King, Alice Dunbar-Nelson, and George Washington Cable.* Tuscaloosa: U of Alabama P, 2014.

Nixon, Rob. *Slow Violence and the Environmentalism of the Poor.* Cambridge, MA: Harvard UP, 2011.

Nordau, Max. *Degeneration.* 1892. Trans. unknown. Lincoln: U of Nebraska P, 1993.

North, Michael. *The Dialect of Modernism: Race, Language, and Twentieth-Century Literature.* New York: Oxford UP, 1994.

Northup, Solomon. *Twelve Years a Slave.* 1853. Mineola, NY: Dover, 1970.

Ondaatje, Michael. *Coming Through Slaughter.* 1976. New York: Vintage, 1996.

Osbey, Brenda Marie. "I Want to Die in New Orleans." *Louisiana Culture from the Colonial Era to Katrina*. Ed. John Lowe. Baton Rouge: Louisiana State UP, 2008. 245–254.

———. "Peculiar Fascination with the Dead." 1985. *All Saints: New and Selected Poems*. Baton Rouge: Louisiana State UP, 1997. 25–33.

Osundare, Niyi. *City Without People: The Katrina Poems*. Boston, MA: Black Widow, 2011.

Parrish, Susan Scott. *The Flood Year 1927: A Cultural History*. Princeton, NJ: Princeton UP, 2017.

Pelegrin, Alison. *Hurricane Party*. Akron, OH: U of Akron P, 2012.

Pénicaut, André. *Fleur de Lys and Calumet: Being the Pénicaut Narrative of French Adventure in Louisiana*. 1723. Ed. and trans. Richebourg Gaillard McWilliams. Baton Rouge: Louisiana State UP, 1953.

Percy, Walker. *The Moviegoer*. 1961. New York: Vintage, 1998.

———. "New Orleans Mon Amour." 1968. *New Orleans Review* 31.2 (2005): 11–15.

Persica, Dennis. "N. O. Summer of Discomfort Lies Just Ahead." *New Orleans Advocate*. 30 May 2013.

Petronius. *The Satyricon*. Trans. P. G. Walsh. New York: Oxford UP, 1997.

Pfister, Arthur. *My Name Is New Orleans: 40 Years of Poetry and Other Jazz*. Donaldsonville, LA: Margaret Media, 2009.

Piazza, Tom. *Why New Orleans Matters*. New York: HarperCollins, 2005.

Poe, Edgar Allan. "The Masque of the Red Death." 1842. *Poetry, Tales, and Selected Essays*. Ed. Patrick F. Quinn and G. R. Thompson. New York: Library of America, 485–490.

Pope, John. *Getting Off at Elysian Fields: Obituaries from the New Orleans* Times-Picayune. Jackson: UP of Mississippi, 2015.

Popper, Karl. *The Poverty of Historicism*. 1957. New York: Routledge, 2002.

Powell, Lawrence N. *The Accidental City: Improvising New Orleans*. Cambridge, MA: Harvard UP, 2012.

Poydras, Julian. "La Prise du morne du Bâton Rouge par Monseigneur de Gálvez [The Capture of the Bluff of Baton Rouge by His Excellency de Gálvez]." 1779. Ed. and trans. Pearl Mary Segura. *Louisiana History* 17.2 (1976): 203–209.

Pratt, Lloyd. "The Lyric Public of *Les Cenelles*." *Early African American Print Culture in Theory and Practice*. Ed. Lara Cohen and Jordan Stein. Philadelphia: U of Pennsylvania P, 2012. 253–273.

Pratt, Mary Louise. *Imperial Eyes: Travel Writing and Transculturation.* New York: Routledge, 1992.

Prenshaw, Peggy Whitman. "Louisiana and the American Literary Tradition." *Louisiana Culture from the Colonial Era to Katrina.* Ed. John Lowe. Baton Rouge: Louisiana State UP, 2008. 149–158.

Prévost, Antoine-François. *Manon Lescaut.* 1753. Trans. Angela Scholar. New York: Oxford UP, 2004.

Reclus, Elisée. *A Voyage to New Orleans: Anarchist Impressions of the Old South.* 1855. Trans. and ed. John Clark and Camille Martin. Thetford, VT: Glad Day, 2004.

Reed, John R. *Decadent Style.* Athens: Ohio UP, 1985.

Reed, John Shelton. *Dixie Bohemia: A French Quarter Circle in the 1920s.* Baton Rouge: Louisiana State UP, 2012.

Reid-Pharr, Robert F. *Conjugal Union: The Body, the House, and the Black American.* New York: Oxford UP, 1999.

Reizenstein, Ludwig von. *The Mysteries of New Orleans.* 1855. Trans. Steven Rowan. Baltimore, MD: Johns Hopkins UP, 2002.

Rice, Anne. *Feast of All Saints.* New York: Ballantine, 1979.

———. *Interview with the Vampire.* New York: Ballantine, 1976.

Richards, Gary. "Queering Katrina: Gay Discourses of the Disaster in New Orleans." *Journal of American Studies* 44.3 (2010): 519–534.

Rinehart, Nicholas T. "'I Talk More of the French': Creole Folklore and the Federal Writers' Project." *Callaloo* 39.2 (2016): 439–456.

Roach, Joseph. *Cities of the Dead: Circum-Atlantic Performance.* New York: Columbia UP, 1996.

Rouquette, Adrien. *La Nouvelle Atala.* 1879. Shreveport, LA: Tintamarre, 2003.

Rousseve, Charles Bathelemy. *The Negro in Louisiana: Aspects of His History and His Literature.* New Orleans: Xavier UP, 1937.

Rowan, Steven. Introduction. *The Mysteries of New Orleans.* By Ludwig von Reizenstein. 1855. Trans. Steven Rowan. Baltimore, MD: Johns Hopkins UP, 2002. xiii–xxxiii.

Said, Edward W. *Orientalism.* New York: Vintage, 1978.

Saloy, Mona Lisa. *Second Line Home: New Orleans Poems.* Kirksville, MO: Truman State UP, 2014.

Salvaggio, Ruth. *Hearing Sappho in New Orleans: The Call of Poetry from Congo Square to the Ninth Ward.* Baton Rouge: Louisiana State UP, 2012.

Saxon, Lyle. *Father Mississippi.* 1927. Gretna, LA: Pelican, 2000.

Saxon, Lyle, Edward Dreyer, and Robert Tallant. *Gumbo Ya-Ya: Folk Tales of Louisiana*. 1945. Gretna, LA: Pelican, 1987.

Saxon, Lyle, et al. *The WPA Guide to New Orleans*. 1938. New York: Pantheon, 1983.

Sayre, Gordon. "Plotting the Natchez Massacre: Le Page du Pratz, Dumont de Montigny, Chateaubriand." *Early American Literature* 37.3 (2002): 381–413.

Schwartz, Stuart B. *Sea of Storms: A History of Hurricanes in the Greater Caribbean from Columbus to Katrina*. Princeton, NJ: Princeton UP, 2015.

Senter, Caroline. "Creole Poets on the Verge of a Nation." *Creole: The History and Legacy of Louisiana's Free People of Color*. Ed. Sybil Kein. Baton Rouge: Louisiana State UP, 2000. 276–294.

Serpas, Martha. *The Dirty Side of the Storm*. New York: Norton, 2007.

Shaik, Fatima. "Climbing Monkey Hill." 1987. *N. O. Lit: 200 Years of New Orleans Literature*. Ed. Nancy Dixon. New Orleans, LA: Lavender Ink, 2013. 540–560.

Sheldon, Rebekah. *The Child to Come: Life After the Human Catastrophe*. Minneapolis: U of Minnesota P, 2016.

Simmons, LaKisha Michelle. *Crescent City Girls: The Lives of Young Black Women in Segregated New Orleans*. Chapel Hill: U of North Carolina P, 2015.

Singleton, Arthur. "Parrots, Spider-Monkeys, and Sun Umbrellas." 1824. *Louisiana Sojourns: Travelers' Tales and Literary Journeys*. Ed. Frank de Caro and Rosan Augusta Jordan. Baton Rouge: Louisiana State UP, 1998. 80.

Sluyter, Andrew, et al. *Hispanic and Latino New Orleans: Immigration and Identity Since the Eighteenth Century*. Baton Rouge: Louisiana State UP, 2015.

Smith, Barbara Herrnstein. *Poetic Closure: A Study of How Poems End*. Chicago: U of Chicago P, 1968.

Smith, Patricia. *Blood Dazzler*. Minneapolis, MN: Coffee House, 2008.

Sollors, Werner, ed. *Multilingual America: Transnationalism, Ethnicity, and the Languages of American Literature*. New York: New York UP, 1998.

Solnit, Rebecca. *A Paradise Built in Hell: The Extraordinary Communities that Arise in Disaster*. New York: Penguin, 2009.

Somerville, Siobhan B. *Queering the Color Line: Race and the Invention of Homosexuality in American Culture*. Durham, NC: Duke UP, 2000.

Souther, J. Mark. *New Orleans on Parade: Tourism and the Transformation of the Crescent City*. Baton Rouge: Louisiana State UP, 2006.

Stanonis, Anthony J. *Creating the Big Easy: New Orleans and the Emergence of Modern Tourism, 1918–1945*. Athens: U of Georgia P, 2006.

St. Germain, Sheryl. "Getting Rid of the Accent." *Let It Be a Dark Roux: New and Selected Poems*. Pittsburgh, PA: Autumn House, 2007.

———. *Swamp Songs: The Making of an Unruly Woman*. Salt Lake City: U of Utah P, 2003.

Steinbeck, John. "The Cheerleaders." 1961. *Louisiana Sojourns: Travelers' Tales and Literary Journeys*. Ed. Frank de Caro and Rosan Augusta Jordan. Baton Rouge: Louisiana State UP, 1998. 207–217.

Stiegler, Bernard. *The Decadence of Industrial Democracies*. 2004. Trans. Daniel Ross and Suzanne Arnold. Malden, MA: Polity, 2011.

Stowe, Harriet Beecher. *Uncle Tom's Cabin*. 1852. New York: Penguin, 1986.

Talbot, Eugene. *Degeneracy*. London: Walter Scott, 1898.

Theriot, Jason P. *American Energy, Imperiled Coast: Oil and Gas Development in Louisiana's Wetlands*. Baton Rouge: Louisiana State UP, 2014.

Thomas, Lynnell L. *Desire and Disaster in New Orleans: Tourism, Race, and Historical Memory*. Durham, NC: Duke UP, 2014.

Tidwell, Mike. *Bayou Farewell: The Rich Life and Tragic Death of Louisiana's Cajun Coast*. New York: Pantheon, 2003.

Tinker, Edward Larocque. *Toucoutou*. New York: Dodd and Mead, 1928.

Toole, John Kennedy. *A Confederacy of Dunces*. 1964. New York: Grove, 1980.

Trexler, Adam. *Anthropocene Fictions: The Novel in a Time of Climate Change*. Charlottesville: U of Virginia P, 2015.

Trollope, Frances. "Entrance of the Mississippi." 1832. *Louisiana Sojourns: Travelers' Tales and Literary Journeys*. Ed. Frank de Caro and Rosan Augusta Jordan. Baton Rouge: Louisiana State UP, 1998. 21–23.

Twain, Mark. *Life on the Mississippi*. 1883. New York: Library of America, 2009.

Vargas, Ramon Antonio. "Broadmoor Man Killed Roommate After Being Told He Had to Move Out, New Orleans Police Allege." *New Orleans Advocate*, 4 Oct. 2017, www.theadvocate.com/new_orleans/news/crime_police/article_6442cbcc-a893-11e7-a3ee-3ffe748b3880.html.

Virgil. *The Aeneid*. Trans. Robert Fitzgerald. New York: Vintage, 1990.

Voigt, Lydia, Dee Wood Harper, and William E. Thornton Jr., eds. *Preventing Lethal Violence in New Orleans*. Lafayette: U of Louisiana P, 2016.

Walker, Janet. "Moving Home: Documentary Film and Other Remediations of Post-Katrina New Orleans." *Moving Environments: Affect, Emotion, Ecology, and Film*. Ed. Alexa Weik von Mossner. Waterloo, ON: Wilfrid Laurier UP, 2014. 201–223.

Wallace, Molly. *Risk Criticism: Precautionary Reading in an Age of Environmental Uncertainty.* Ann Arbor: U of Michigan P, 2016.

Ward, Jerry W., Jr. *The Katrina Papers: A Journal of Trauma and Recovery.* New Orleans, LA: U of New Orleans P, 2008.

Ward, Roger K. "The French Language in Louisiana Law and Legal Education: A Requiem." *Louisiana Law Review* 57.4 (1997): 1283–1324.

Wascom, Kent. *Secessia.* New York: Grove, 2015.

Watts, Tracey. "Haunted Memories: Disruptive Ghosts in the Poems of Brenda Marie Osbey and Joy Harjo." *Southern Literary Journal* 46.2 (2014): 108–127.

Weiss, M. Lynn, ed. *Creole Echoes: The Francophone Poetry of Nineteenth-Century Louisiana.* Trans. Norman R. Shapiro. Urbana: U of Illinois P, 2004.

Welty, Eudora. "No Place for You, My Love." 1952. *Stories, Essays, and Memoir.* Ed. Richard Ford and Michael Kreyling. New York: Library of America, 1998. 561–580.

White, Richard Grant, ed. *Poetry Lyrical, Narrative, and Satirical of the Civil War.* New York: American News, 1866.

Williams, Tennessee. *A Streetcar Named Desire.* 1947. *Plays 1937–1955.* Ed. Mel Gussow and Kenneth Holditch. New York: Library of America, 2000. 467–564.

———. *Vieux Carré.* 1977. *Plays 1957–1980.* Ed. Mel Gussow and Kenneth Holditch. New York: Library of America, 2000. 825–901.

Wilson, Anthony. *Shadow and Shelter: The Swamp in Southern Culture.* Jackson: UP of Mississippi, 2006.

Wilson, Edmund. *Patriotic Gore: Studies in the Literature of the American Civil War.* New York: Oxford UP, 1962.

Wold, Amy. "Isle de Jean Charles Tribe Looks at Moving Entire Community North in First-of-Its-Kind Test Case." *Advocate,* 12 Apr. 2016, www.theadvocate.com/baton_rouge/news/article_da3cfd6f-7e69-57c9-a040-5262767a3ba2.html.

Wood, Derek R. "'Art had almost left them': *Les Cenelles* Society of Arts and Letters, the Dillard Project, and the Legacy of Afro-Creole Arts in New Orleans." *Southern Quarterly* 55.1 (2017): 55–71.

INDEX